Business Analysis

The British Computer Society

The British Computer Society is the leading professional body for the IT industry. With members in over 100 countries, the BCS is the professional and learned society in the field of computers and information systems.

The BCS is responsible for setting standards for the IT profession. It is also leading the change in public perception and appreciation of the economic and social importance of professionally managed IT projects and programmes. In this capacity, the Society advises, informs and persuades industry and government on successful IT implementation.

IT is affecting every part of our lives and that is why the BCS is determined to promote IT as *the* profession of the 21st century.

Further Information

Further information about BCS can be obtained from: The British Computer Society, First Floor, Block D, North Star House, North Star Avenue, Swindon, SN2 1FA, UK.
Telephone: 0845 300 4417 (UK only) or + 44 (0)1793 417 424 (overseas)
Email: customerservice@hq.bcs.org.uk
Web: www.bcs.org

International Business Systems Development Forum (IBSDF)

The IBSDF is an independent, not-for-profit organization dedicated to the development and promotion of 'best practice' in business analysis and information systems (IS) development. It is wholly owned and run by its international membership.

The objectives of the IBSDF are:

1. to provide a forum for the identification and adoption of international best practice in business analysis and related IS development;
2. to broadcast business analysis and IS development theory and practice within the Business and IS and IT communities;
3. to ensure that business analysis and IS development qualifications meet the requirements of business and IS and IT communities.

To achieve its objectives, the IBSDF:

- organizes conferences and seminars;
- liaises with other standards bodies;
- publishes papers;
- produces books;
- provides consultancy support;
- serves on relevant qualifications committees.

The IBSDF is constantly on the look out for new members who would wish to be active in helping to achieve its objectives.

Further information

Further information about the IBSDF can be obtained from IBSDF, Orchard House, Dingle Lane, Sandbach, Cheshire, CW11 1FY, UK.
Telephone + 44 (0)1270 765363 and fax + 44 (0)1270 750018
Email Jim Stone, Chairman at chairman@ibsdf.net

Business Analysis

EDITED BY

Debra Paul and Donald Yeates

 BCS

Reprinted July 2006, March 2007

The British Computer Society
Publishing and Information Products
First Floor, Block D
North Star House
North Star Avenue
Swindon SN2 1FA
UK
www.bcs.org

ISBN 13 978-1-902505-70-1

British Cataloguing in Publication Data.
A CIP catalogue record for this book is available at the British Library.

Typeset by Tradespools, Chippenham, Wiltshire.
Printed at Antony Rowe Ltd., Chippenham, Wiltshire.

Contents

List of figures and tables

Contributors

James Cadle has been involved in the management services field for 27 years, occupying a variety of roles from consultant to project manager and operations manager. Since 1985, James has specialized in the areas of project management and business/systems analysis, occupying a number of senior management roles within London Regional Transport and then with Sema Group plc. James is currently a director of Assist Knowledge Development and specializes in business analysis and project management training and consultancy.

Malcolm Eva has been working in IT since 1980, first as a programmer and then in systems analysis and business analysis. He has been a senior lecturer in information systems at Thames Polytechnic (now Greenwich University) and University College Northampton. He has also worked for both the Ministry of Defence and BT as a systems analyst and trainer in systems analysis. Malcolm is a founding member of the International Business Systems Development Forum (IBSDF) and a member of the BCS Requirements Engineering and Information Systems Methodologies Specialist Groups.

Keith Hindle has over 30 years of IT and business experience in training and consultancy in the areas of business analysis and system development, in fields ranging from manufacturing to insurance and public education. Keith is currently the business development manager at the international IT solutions company Parity. He is a member of the BCS Business-IT Interface and Requirements Engineering Specialist Groups and a member of the Institute of IT Training. He was the chair of the judging panel for the BCS's Business Analyst of the Year Award.

Tony Jenkins is senior partner in the European consulting group, DOMAINetc, and a chartered member of BCS. He has worked in IT for 37 years, his interests centring on the interfaces between data management, systems development processes, IT service management and business processes. He is a member of the BCS Council, Vice Chair of the BCS Data Management Specialist Group and chair of the founding committee of the IBSDF. He is also a BSD, ITSM, Applications Management and ITILIM examiner for the Information Systems Examinations Board (ISEB).

Debra Paul (co-editor) has worked in IT for over 20 years, in the public and private sectors, occupying a range of roles in both business and systems analysis. Currently she is a director of Assist Knowledge Development and is involved in delivering training and consultancy in her specialist fields of business and systems analysis and consulting skills. Debra was a founding member of the IBSDF and was a judge of the BCS Business Analyst of the Year Award, 2004 and 2005.

Craig Rollason is a senior business analyst with a wide range of experience within the IT industry and extensive experience in the utilities, government and manufacturing sectors. In his current role, Craig has been responsible for business case development, requirements gathering, supplier management and the procurement for multi-million programmes of work covering areas of commercial billing systems, document and drawing management, regulatory changes and management information. Craig is a member of the BCS Business-IT Interface Specialist Group and was a judge of the BCS Business Analyst of the Year Award, 2004 and 2005.

Dot Tudor is a graduate in mathematics, statistics and English. She has worked as a business analyst, systems analyst, programmer, systems implementer and project manager, with a wide variety of projects in both public and private sectors. Dot specializes in facilitation, project management and computer systems development methodologies and supplies facilitation, consultancy and training to companies, nationally and internationally. She is a DSDM Practitioner, and a Prince2 and ISEB Certified Project Manager. She is a founder member of the IBSDF and the BCS Methods and Tools Specialist Group.

Donald Yeates (co-editor) has worked in the IT industry with users and with consulting and computer services organizations in the public and private sectors in the UK and internationally for most of his working life. He is a Visiting Fellow of an international business school in Henley in the UK. He has been a Fellow of BCS since 1984 and was awarded a further Honorary Fellowship in 1994 for his contribution to the work of the ISEB. He was appointed a Fellow of the Royal Society of Arts in 1995.

Foreword

Much has been reported about IT systems that do not satisfy business requirements or that fail to realize the expected benefits to organizations. This has led to extensive efforts in the areas of programme, project and service management, which has undoubtedly produced improvements in recent years. However, without a comprehensive understanding of the business environment in which any IT or information system will need to perform, and of how the resulting business and IT systems are to be aligned, real success is unlikely ever to be achieved. This in conjunction with approaches to solution development and delivery, such as out-sourcing, has increased the importance of roles such as business analyst and requirement analyst.

Such business analysts may come from within the business itself or have a background in IT systems analysis, design or development. In either case, the skills needed and techniques employed are likely to be different to those that the business analysts are accustomed to using. These will include not only the fundamental skills and competencies of business analysis itself, such as identifying business drivers and engineering requirements, but also those of business process modelling, change management, internal consultancy and an ability to understand the information and data needs of a business. All of these are covered in a clear and informative way within this book.

This book, written by some of the best known and respected proponents of business and requirement analysis, provides a thorough grounding in these techniques within a best practice lifecycle, which provides comprehensive coverage of the topic. The guidance included is consistent with and supplies a supporting text for the ISEB examinations within this increasingly important subject area.

The expertise brought together in the development of this book is second to none, and I am convinced that it will inspire those that read it to contribute to the ongoing improvement of the discipline of business analysis and to the full exploitation of its techniques in the successful delivery of IT-enabled change projects. Without this increased professionalism in the area of business and requirements analysis, all the extensive work in the development and implementation of best practice in programme, project and service management in recent years will have been to no avail.

Eur. Ing. Paul Turner FBCS
Business & IS Skills Ltd

Abbreviations

BAM	Business Activity Model
BBS	Balanced Business Scorecard
BCS	British Computer Society
BPEL	Business Process Execution Language
BPM	Business Process Management
BPMI	Business Process Management Initiative
BPML	Business Process Modelling Language
BPMS	Business Process Management System
CARE	Computer-aided Requirements Engineering
CASE	Computer-aided Software Engineering
CATWOE	customer, actor, transformation, Weltanschauung (world view), owner, environment
CEO	Chief Executive Officer
CIA	confidentiality, integrity, availability
CRM	Customer Relationship Management
CSF	Critical Success Factor
DBMS	Database Management System
DCF	Discounted Cash Flow
DMSG	Data Management Specialist Group
DSDM	Dynamic Systems Development Method
DVD	Digital Versatile Disk
EAI	Enterprise Application Integration
ERP	Enterprise Resource Planning
GMC	General Medical Council
HR	Human Resources
IRR	Internal Rate of Return
IS	Information Systems
IT	Information Technology
KPIs	Key Performance Indicator
MoSCoW	must have, should have, could have, want to have but won't have this time
MOST (analysis)	mission, objectives, strategy and tactics (analysis)
NPV	Net Present Value
Ofcom	Office for Communications
Ofsted	Office for Standards in Education
PESTLE (analysis)	political, economic, sociocultural, technological, legal and environmental (analysis)
SBU	Strategic Business Unit

SFIA	Skills Framework for the Information Age
SMART	specific, measurable, achievable, relevant, time-framed
SSADM	Structured Systems Analysis and Design Method
SSM	Soft Systems Methodology
STP	Straight-Through Processing
STROBE	Structured Observation of the Business Environment
SWOT	strengths, weaknesses, opportunities, threats
UML	Unified Modelling Language

Preface

The ideas for this book grew out of research that we carried out for the Information Systems Examinations Board on behalf of the International Business Systems Development Forum. We visited employers in the public and private sectors to collect views about the examinations and qualifications available in the UK in business analysis and systems development. It became clear that demand for business analysts would continue to grow but that there was no readily available text about business analysis.

So, the book was born with the British Computer Society as a willing midwife. All of our contributors are experienced practitioners in the mysterious art of business analysis and have offered their knowledge to illuminate the subject. They share their hard won experiences with you. Notes about each contributor are contained in the acknowledgements.

In addition, there are several people we need to thank. We would like to thank James Cadle for his critiques, suggestions and additional material above and beyond the call of friendship. Thanks Jim! Thanks must also go to Alan Paul who cast his eye over the edited chapters and identified many improvements. We are also grateful for the specialist help we have had from Matthew Flynn, Suzanna Marsh and Florence Leroy of the BCS.

Finally, we hope that you, the reader, enjoy this book and find it useful. Business analysts play a key role in tackling the challenges of today's business world; good luck with meeting these challenges.

Debra Paul – Sonning Common, England
Donald Yeates – Henley, England

1 What is business analysis?

DEBRA PAUL

INTRODUCTION

This is a book about business analysis, a discipline that promises to offer much for the alignment of organizations' business objectives with the possibilities offered by information technology (IT). The reason for producing this book is the perception that this alignment, the holy grail of the information systems world, is somehow out of reach. The term 'business analysis' is often used, but there persists a lack of clarity about what it really means, and this creates more questions than answers. What do business analysts do? What skills do they require? How do they add value to organizations? Also, there is no standard definition of business analysis, and no standard process model exists. There are many reasons for this, but two key issues are as follows:

- Organizations have introduced business analysis to make sure that business needs are paramount when new computer systems are being introduced. However, recognizing the importance of this principle is easier than considering how this might be achieved.

- Many business analysts have a business background and have a limited understanding of IT and how computer systems are developed. This may distance them from the IT developers and result in a failure to ensure that there is an integrated view of the business and computer system.

In this chapter, we examine the discipline known as business analysis and consider how we might define the business analyst role. In Chapter 4, we describe a process model for business analysis, where we provide an overview of how business analysis is carried out and the key techniques to be used at each stage. The aspects of business analysis work that are well defined are, of course, the various techniques that are available for use in business analysis projects. Many of these techniques have been in use for far longer than the business analyst role has been in existence. Much of this book provides guidance on how the various aspects of the business analyst role may be carried out. We describe numerous techniques that we feel should be in any business analyst's toolkit and place them within the overall process model. Our aim is to help business analysts carry out their work, improve the quality of business analysis within organizations and, hence, develop the key ingredient for business success – business/IT alignment.

THE ORIGINS OF BUSINESS ANALYSIS

Developments in IT have enabled organizations to develop information systems that have improved business operations and management decision-making. In the past, this has been the focus of IT departments. However, as business operations have changed, the emphasis has moved on to the development of new services and products. The question we need to ask now is 'What can IT do to exploit business opportunities and enhance the portfolio of products and services?'

Technology has supported the implementation of new business models by providing more flexible communication mechanisms that enable organizations to reach out to the customer, connect their systems with those of their suppliers and support global operation. The use of IT has also created opportunities for organizations to focus on their core processes and competencies without the distraction of the peripheral areas of business. These days, the absence of good information systems would prevent an organization from developing significant competitive advantage. Yet for many years, there has been a growing dissatisfaction in businesses with the support provided by IT. This has been accompanied by recognition by senior management that IT investment often fails to deliver the required business benefit. In short, the technology enables the development of information systems, but these often fail to meet the requirements of the business and to deliver the service that will bring competitive advantage to the organization. This situation applies to all sectors, including the public sector. In 1999, a report from the Select Committee of Public Accounts (1999) reported on over 25 cases from the 1990s 'where the implementation of IT systems has resulted in delay, confusion and inconvenience to the citizen and, in many cases, poor value for money to the taxpayer'. The perception that, all too frequently, information systems do not deliver the predicted benefits appears to be well-founded.

THE DEVELOPMENT OF BUSINESS ANALYSIS

The impact of outsourcing

In a drive to reduce costs, and sometimes in recognition of a lack of IT expertise at senior management level, many organizations have decided in the past decade or so to purchase IT services rather than employ IT staff. Hence, they have moved much of their IT work to specialist service providers. This outsourcing of IT work has been based upon the belief that specialist providers, often working in countries where costs are lower than in the UK, will be able to deliver higher quality at lower cost. So, in organizations that have outsourced their IT functions, the IT systems are designed and constructed using staff employed by an external supplier. This undoubtedly has advantages for both the organization purchasing the services and the specialist supplier. The latter gains an additional customer and the opportunity to increase turnover and make profit from the contractual arrangement; the customer organization is no longer concerned with all staffing, infrastructure and support issues and instead pays a specialist provider for delivery of the required service. In theory this approach has much to recommend it but, as is usually the case, the flaws begin to emerge once the arrangement has been implemented, particularly in the areas of contract management and communication. The issues relating to contract management are not the subject of this book and would require a book in their own right. However, we are concerned with the issue of communication between the business and the outsourced development team. The communication and clarification of requirements are key to ensuring the success of any IT system development, but an outsourcing arrangement often complicates the communication process, particularly where there is geographical distance between the developers and the business. We need to ask ourselves the questions 'How well do our business and technical groups understand each other?' and 'Is the communication sufficiently frequent and open?' Communication failures will usually result in the delivered IT systems failing to provide the required level of support for the business.

Investigation of the outsourcing business model has highlighted that in order to make such arrangements work, new roles are required within the organization. A study by Feeny and Willcocks (1998) listed a number of key skills required within organizations that have outsourced IT. This report specifically identified business systems thinking, a core element of the business analyst role, as a key skill that needs to be retained within organizations operating an outsourcing arrangement. The outsourcing business model has undoubtedly been a catalyst for the development of the business analysis function as more and more organizations recognize the importance of business representation during the development and implementation of IT systems.

Competitive advantage of using IT

A parallel development that has helped to increase the profile of business analysis and define the business analyst role has been the growing recognition that three factors need to be present in order for the IT systems to deliver competitive advantage. First, the needs of the business must drive the development of the IT systems; second, the implementation of an IT system must be accompanied by the necessary business changes; and third, the requirements for IT systems must be defined with rigour and accuracy. The traditional systems analyst role operated primarily in the last area, but today's business challenges require all three areas to be addressed.

The rise of the business analyst

The delivery of predicted business benefits, promised from the implementation of IT, has proved to be extremely difficult, with the outsourcing of IT services serving to add complication to already complex situations. The potential exists for organizations to implement information systems that yield competitive advantage, and yet this often appears to be just out of reach. Organizations also want help in finding potential solutions to business issues and opportunities, sometimes where IT may not prove to be the answer, but it has become apparent that this requires a new set of skills to support business managers in achieving this. These factors have led directly to the development of a new role – the business analyst – where advice and internal consultancy are provided about the use and deployment of IT in order to deliver business benefits.

The use of consultants

It has also been argued that external consultants have played a part in the development of the internal business analysis role. The reasons are clear: external consultants can be employed to deal with a specific issue on an as-needed basis, and they bring a broader business perspective and can provide a dispassionate, objective view of the company. On the other hand, the use of external consultants is often criticized because of their lack of accountability and the absence of any transfer of skills from them to internal staff. Cost is also a key issue. Consultancy firms typically charge upwards of £1500 per day, and although in the main the firms provide consultants with a broad range of expertise, this is not always guaranteed. Consequently, there has been increasing use of internal consultants over the past decade. Reasons for using internal consultants, apart from lower costs, include speed (internal consultants do not have to spend time learning about the organization) and the retention of knowledge within the organization. These factors have been recognized as particularly important for projects where the objectives concern the achievement of business benefit through the use of IT and where IT is a prime enabler of business change. As a result, although external consultants are used for many business purposes, the majority of business analysts are employed by their organizations. These analysts may lack an external viewpoint, but they are knowledgeable about the business domain and crucially will have to live with the impact of the actions they recommend.

THE SCOPE OF BUSINESS ANALYSIS WORK

A major issue for business analysts, based on feedback from a wide range of organizations, is the definition of the business analyst role.

Anecdotal information collected between 2001 and 2005 from several hundred business analysts has highlighted that their job descriptions are unclear and do not always describe accurately their responsibilities. A quick survey of the job advertisements for business analysts also reflects a lack of agreement. For example, in some cases the job description of a business analyst seems, on close inspection, to be similar to that of an analyst/programmer, e.g. 'Candidates must have experience of Java.' In other organizations the business analysts appear to be required to work at the opposite end of the scale and provide strategic analysis for their business units, e.g. 'Candidates must be comfortable working with senior management.' Even though the role of the business analyst emerged over 10 years ago, a formal agreed definition has not been reached. Recently there has been some mention of business analysis in reference texts, but in contrast to the plethora of books on other IT disciplines, this has been brief and has offered only limited guidance. Skidmore and Eva (2004) reflected the wider perspective of the business analysis role by observing that with regard to information systems development, 'business analysts are concerned with exploring business solutions'. A more specific view was taken by Maciaszek (2001), who stated that eliciting and confirming information system requirements is an 'activity conducted by a business analyst'. This view was defined in more detail by Yeates and Wakefield (2004), who clarified that 'the business analyst's responsibility is the production of clearly stated business requirement definitions, which can be passed to a system designer to be turned into specifications that are the input to the development process'.

The range of analysis activities

One way in which we can consider the business analyst role is to examine the possible range of analysis activities. Figure 1.1 shows three areas that we might consider to be within the province of the business analyst. Consultants, both internal and external, who specialize in strategic analysis often have to get involved in business process redesign to make a reality of their strategies, and good systems analysts have always needed to understand the overall business context of the systems that they are developing. However, it is useful to examine them separately in order to consider their relevance to the business analyst role.

Strategic analysis and definition

Strategic analysis and definition are typically the work of senior management, often supported by strategy consultants. Some, albeit a minority, business analysts may be required to undertake strategic analysis and identify business transformation actions, but most will probably have a role to play in supporting this activity. In the main,

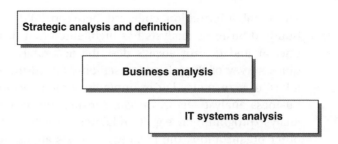

FIGURE 1.1 *Potential range of the business analyst role*

we believe that strategic analysis is mostly outside the remit of business analysis. We would, however, expect business analysts to have access to information about their organization's business strategy and be able to understand it, as their work will need to support the achievement of this strategy. It may also be the case that some business analyst roles will require strategic-level thinking, for example in considering whether technology developments can deliver innovation to the company and open new strategic opportunities. In the light of this, we feel that although strategic analysis work is not core to business analysis, business analysts will need a good understanding of strategy development processes. Therefore, Chapter 3 explores some strategic analysis techniques and provides an overview of the strategic planning process.

IT systems analysis

At the other end of our model, there is the IT discipline of systems analysis. This is concerned with analysing and specifying the IT system requirements in sufficient detail in order to provide a basis for the evaluation of software packages or the development of a bespoke IT system. Typically, systems analysis work involves the use of techniques such as data modelling and process or function modelling. This work is very specific to describing the computer system requirements, and so the products of systems analysis define exactly the data that the computer system will record, the processing that will be applied to that data and the operation of the user interface. Some organizations consider this work to be of such a technical nature that they perceive it to be completely outside the province of the business analyst. They have identified that modelling process and data requirements for the IT system is not part of the role of the business analyst and have separated the business analysis and IT teams into different departments. The expectation here is that the IT department will carry out the detailed IT systems modelling and specification. Nowadays, it is less common for organizations to employ IT staff with the job role 'systems analyst', and the detailed specification of the requirements is often undertaken by systems designers or developers. However, in other organizations the divide between the business analysts and the IT team is less obvious or does not exist. In these cases the business analysts work closely with the IT developers and include the specification of IT system requirements as a key part of their role. In order to do this, the business analysts need a more detailed understanding of IT systems and how they operate and need to be able to use the approaches and modelling techniques that historically fell within the remit of the systems analyst job role.

Business analysis

If the two analysis disciplines described above define the limits of analysis work, then the gap in the middle is straddled by business analysis. Hence, the model highlights the possible extent of business analysis work. Business analysts will usually be required to investigate a business system where improvements are required, but the range and focus of those improvements can vary considerably.

It may be that the analysts are asked to resolve an identified and very localized issue. They would need to recommend actions that would overcome a problem or achieve business benefits. However, it is more likely that the study is broader than this and requires investigation into several issues, or perhaps ideas, regarding increased efficiency or effectiveness. This work would necessitate extensive and detailed analysis. The analysts would need to make recommendations for business changes, and these would need to be supported by a rigorous business case.

Another possibility is that the business analyst is asked to focus specifically on enhancing or replacing an existing IT system in line with business requirements. In this case the analyst would deliver a requirements document defining what the business requires the IT system to provide.

Whichever situation applies, the study usually begins with the analyst gaining an understanding of the business situation in hand. A problem may have been defined in very specific terms, and a possible solution identified, but in practice it is rare that this turns out to be the entire problem, and it is even rarer that any proposed solution addresses all of the issues. More commonly, there may be a more general set of problems that require a broad focus to the study. For any changes to succeed, the business analyst needs to consider all aspects, for example the processes, IT systems and resources that will be needed in order to improve the situation successfully. In such situations, techniques such as stakeholder analysis, business process modelling and requirements engineering may all be required in order to identify the actions required to improve the business system. These three topics are the subjects of later chapters in this book.

Managing business benefits

Analysing business situations and identifying areas for business improvement is only one part of the process. The analyst may also be required to develop a business case in order to justify the required level of investment and consider any risks. One of the key elements of the business case will be the identification and, where relevant, the quantification of the business benefits. In recent years much emphasis has been placed on the delivery or realization of these business benefits. This is largely because there has been a long history of failure to confirm, or dispute, whether this has happened. Supporting the business in order to assess whether the predicted business benefits have been delivered and to take actions that will help deliver those benefits are further key aspects of business analysis.

Supporting business change

At a later stage, the business analyst may be required to support the implementation of the changes. This support may involve advising the business users as they adopt new processes and procedures or assisting, or even directing, the user acceptance testing activity for an IT system. Chapter 13 explores the management of business change and the key elements to be considered here.

Taking an holistic approach

There appears to be universal agreement that business analysis requires the application of an holistic approach. Although the business analyst performs a key role in supporting management to exploit IT in order to obtain business benefit, this has to be within the context of the entire business system. Hence, all aspects of the operational business system need to be analysed if all of the opportunities for business improvement are to be uncovered. Figure 1.2 represents the three viewpoints that it is useful to consider when identifying areas for improving the business system.

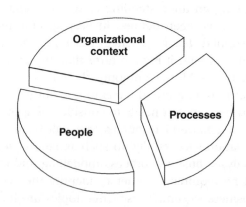

FIGURE 1.2 *The three views of a business system*

This model shows us that business analysts need to consider these three aspects when analysing a business system. For each area, we might consider the following:

- **The processes:** are they well defined and communicated? Is there good IT support, or are several 'workarounds' in existence? Does the process require documents to be passed around the organization unnecessarily?
- **The people:** do they have the required skills for the job? How motivated are they? Do they understand the business objectives that they need to support?
- **The organizational context:** is there a supportive management approach? Are jobs and responsibilities well defined? Is there effective cross-functional working?

We need to examine and understand these three areas if the business system is to be effective. It is often the case that the focus of a business analysis or business change study is on the processes and the IT support. However, even if we have the most efficient processes with high standards of IT support, the system will have problems if the staff members do not have the right skills to carry out their work or the organization structure is unclear.

It is vital that the business analyst is aware of the broader aspects relating to business situations, such as the culture of their organization and its impact on the people and the working practices. The adoption of an holistic approach will to help ensure that these aspects are included in the analysis of the situation.

Business analysis places an emphasis on improving the operation of the entire business system. This means that although technology is viewed as a factor that could enable improvements to the business operations, there are other possibilities. The focus on business improvement rather than the use of automation per se results in recommendations that typically, but not necessarily, include the use of IT. For example, in some situations these recommendations may relate to staff development. It is important that our focus as business analysts is on identifying opportunities for improvement with regard to the needs of the particular situation. If we do this, then we can recommend changes that will help deliver real business improvements.

THE ROLE AND RESPONSIBILITIES OF A BUSINESS ANALYST

So where does this leave us in defining the role and responsibilities of a business analyst? Although there are different role definitions, depending on the organization, there does seem to be an area of common ground where most business analysts work. The responsibilities here seem to be as follows:

- To investigate business systems, taking an holistic view of the situation. This may include examining elements of the organization structures and staff development issues as well as current processes and IT systems.

- To identify actions required to improve the operation of a business system. Again, this may require an examination of organizational structure and staff development needs in order to ensure that they are in line with any proposed process redesign and IT system development.

- To document the business requirements for the IT system support using appropriate documentation standards.

In line with this, we believe that the core business analyst role should be defined as follows:

> **An internal consultancy role that has the responsibility for investigating business systems, identifying options for improving business systems and bridging the needs of the business with the use of IT.**

Beyond this core definition, there are the aspects of business analysis that appear to apply where business analysts are in a more senior role or choose to specialize. These aspects are as follows:

- **Strategy implementation:** here, the business analysts work closely with senior management to help define the most effective business system in order to implement elements of the business strategy.

- **Business process redesign:** here, the emphasis is on both the business process management and operation.

- **Business case production:** more senior business analysts usually do this, typically with assistance from finance specialists.

- **Specification of IT requirements**, typically using standard modelling techniques such as data modelling or case modelling.

Business analysis offers an opportunity for organizations to ensure that technology is deployed effectively in order to support the work of the organization. A new breed of analysts is emerging with both the skills and knowledge about the business domain plus the analytical skills of consultants. The challenge for the analysts is to ensure that they develop the extensive toolkit of skills that will enable them to engage with the business problems and assist in their resolution. The challenge for the business is to support the analysts in their personal development, give them the authority to carry out the business analysis work and listen to their advice. This book has been developed in the light of these challenges; we hope both business users and analysts will find it useful.

REFERENCES

Feeny, D. and Willcocks, L. (1998) Core IS Capabilities for Exploiting Information Technology. *Sloan Management Review*, **39**, 9–21.

Maciaszek, L.A. (2001) *Requirements Analysis and System Design: Developing Information Systems with UML*. Addison-Wesley, Harlow.

Select Committee of Public Accounts (1999) Improving the Delivery of Government IT Projects, First Report. House of Commons, HC 65, 5 January.

Skidmore, S and Eva, M (2004) *Introducing Systems Development*. Palgrave Macmillan, Basingstoke.

Yeates, D and Wakefield, T (2004) *Systems Analysis and Design*. FT Prentice Hall, Harlow.

FURTHER READING

Harmon, P. (2003) *Business Process Change*. Morgan Kaufmann, Boston, MA.

Johnson, G. and Scholes, K. (1999) *Exploring Corporate Strategy*. FT Prentice Hall, Harlow.

Porter, M.E. (1980) *Competitive Strategy: Techniques for Analysing Industries and Competition*. Free Press, New York.

Senge, P.M. (1993) *The Fifth Discipline: The Art and Practice of the Learning Organization*. Century Business, New York.

2 The competencies of a business analyst

CRAIG ROLLASON

INTRODUCTION

Good business analysts can make the difference between a poor and a great investment in IT. They can also help to resolve issues without jumping to premature conclusions. But what exactly is a good business analyst? This chapter aims to address this question by identifying and describing the competencies that business analysts need in order to be effective in the modern business environment. Competence has been described by the Working Group on Vocational Qualifications (1986) as 'the ability to do a particular activity to a prescribed standard'. For the purposes of this chapter, we will define a competency as something that a business analyst needs in order to perform his or her job effectively. The set of business analysis competencies can be divided into three broad groups, as illustrated in Figure 2.1.

Behavioural skills and personal qualities are concerned with how you think and how you interact with the people around you. They are not specific to business analysis but are general skills that are important for developing and progressing in any business environment. Behavioural skills are arguably more important than technical or business skills, as they are a prerequisite for working with other people. It is often said that it is easier to give a person with good behavioural skills the techniques needed for a job than to graft behavioural skills on to a good technician. One of the main reasons for this is that good behavioural skills take many years to develop. We shall have more to say on developing competencies later in this chapter. A business analyst also requires business knowledge, which helps him or her to develop a good understanding of the organization and the business domain or sector within which the organization operates. This knowledge is vital if the business analyst is to offer advice and insights that will help improve the organization's performance. Business knowledge can be developed through reading relevant literature or studying for business qualifications and can be given context by working in a variety of business and project environments. The techniques of business analysis are those specific to the role that differentiate business analysts from other business or IT roles. They are the technical skills required particularly of the business analyst role. Each of the competencies shown in Figure 2.1 is

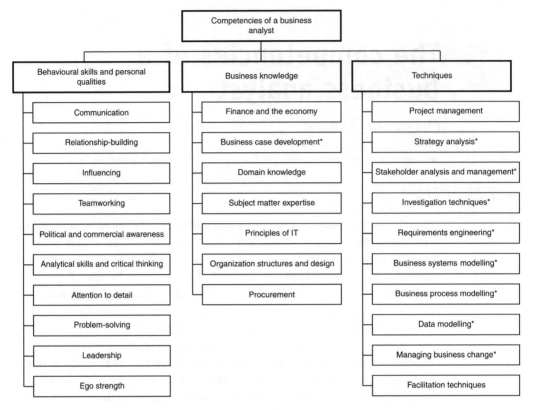

FIGURE 2.1 *Competencies of a business analyst*

discussed in the sections that follow; those marked with asterisks are covered in more detail in specific chapters of this book.

BEHAVIOURAL SKILLS AND PERSONAL QUALITIES

These are the interpersonal skills and characteristics that are useful for a business analyst.

Communication

Communication is perhaps the most important skill that humans possess. It encompasses a wide area of skills, such as building rapport, listening, influencing and creating empathy. Much analysis work involves collecting and analysing data and then presenting back information that brings new perspectives on the project so as to propose a course of action. Poor communication skills are often cited as problematic for IT staff, and this is explained by the fact that communication at the system level is between computer and human. This type of communication is based on logic.

Generally, computers are predictable and do as they are told. When dealing with people, a logical approach does not always apply, and many IT professionals become frustrated with business colleagues when there is a failure to do the 'obvious' thing.

Therefore, you will need to communicate with business colleagues in a language and style that they are comfortable with and avoid what they perceive as 'techno-babble'. Spending time with the intended audience will help you to understand the communication norms and what will be effective.

It is important, too, that business analysts can adjust their communication to align with the people they are talking to. The managing director, for example, will most likely have a different view and different interests, and use different language, compared with shop-floor workers.

Relationship-building

This is an extension of communication skill and concerns the ability to get on well with people at a working if not social level. Some people seem to possess this ability naturally but others have to work at it – either way, it is essential for a business analyst. As a business analyst, you need to get people to impart information and share opinions with you and to listen to your ideas for change. All of these things will be very much easier if the people concerned like and trust you. People who possess this skill naturally seem to have the knack of taking a real interest in the other person and making them feel important and this 'other centredness' seems to be the key to successful relationship-building.

Influencing

Business analysts often conclude their analysis by recommending a course of action. If that conclusion is at odds with preconceived ideas about what is required or calls for radical or unexpected action, then the ability to influence is essential. Successful influencing requires a concerted effort. Emailing the decision-makers with a set of PowerPoint slides is not enough. You need to understand the factors that will influence the decision. Some are obvious, such as the project sponsor, project management, governance committees, project boards and other steering groups. Some are hidden, such as networks of colleagues, personal agendas and hidden information. Identifying each of these stakeholders and understanding the amount of power they exert over the decision-making processes will allow you to target and influence the decision-makers most effectively. Once decision-makers have been identified, you can then define a course of action to take the decision forward. This may involve briefing other colleagues, such as more senior staff or representatives on decision-making groups, or influencing business colleagues directly.

The influencing itself needs careful consideration and prior planning. Business analysts have to develop an understanding of where the other party stands on their proposal, the likely resistance and the influencing style needed to approach the person or group. For example, some managers might defer all decisions to another group, require all information at a very detailed level or ask only for a high-level summary. Some are interested in all the technicalities, others just the 'vision' or the 'big picture'. Tailoring the approach is vital for a successful outcome.

The analysis itself may be questioned, and business analysts are often influenced to take or suggest another course of action. This may involve another round of influencing, facilitating a round-table discussion or seeking support from senior colleagues on the best course of action. This is especially true when the business analyst is caught in the middle of opposing views. It also suggests that another personal quality that business analysts need from time to time is the ability to withstand pressure.

Teamworking

Business analysts often work in teams. The nature of business analysis work requires collecting information from many sources, such as business colleagues, IT suppliers, internal suppliers, project team members and management. Hence, a team approach is often used.

An understanding of your role within the team and of what needs to be done and an appreciation of the working style of others are, therefore, important to ensure that the project objectives are achieved.

Political and commercial awareness

These are a bit like an elephant – hard to describe, but you know it when you see it. One way of defining such awareness is to use the word 'nous', which one dictionary describes as 'common sense; gumption', but that doesn't quite convey what we mean. The term 'streetwise' also captures part of what we are getting at. Essentially, what we are talking about is an ability to work out what is and what is not politically and commercially acceptable in an organization and being able to play a political game to get things done. This means knowing the movers and shakers within the organization, understanding what they like and don't like, and tailoring our approach accordingly. Having political and commercial awareness, by the way, emphatically does not mean accepting the status quo; it does mean using resourcefulness and being astute to get results, even in the face of opposition.

Analytical skills and critical thinking

Since the role we are talking about here is that of a business analyst, it is clear that analytical skills form a major part of the job, but what does this mean in practice? It means not settling for the obvious, not accepting things at face value and not jumping to premature conclusions. It means digging deeper and deeper until the true situation is uncovered and the real problem has been defined. It involves sifting through masses of often conflicting data and determining which is relevant and which is not. And it involves challenging received wisdom at every turn: Why do you do this? What value does it add? Where is it done? How is it done? Who is or should be responsible? When should it happen? Some analysts seem to believe that the job consists simply of amassing more and more data in the hope that the answer will somehow magically reveal itself; but it won't without the active and critical intervention of the analyst.

Attention to detail

Although it is sometimes true that the answer to a business problem is obvious, in most cases this is not so and the real solution is revealed only after painstaking research. In addition, many business cases (described in Chapter 12) fail because there is insufficient detailed evidence for the proposed change. When a project is handed over to the IT specialists, they often find that many important issues of detail have not been addressed. So, it appears that having an eye for detail is also an important attribute of a good business analyst.

Problem-solving

There are many techniques associated with problem-solving, and countless books and training courses address the topic. Chapter 4 describes an approach to creative problem-solving. However, here we are talking about the problem-solving mindset. A business analyst has to approach an issue with the outlook that problems can be solved. A variation on this is that even if the optimal solution cannot be implemented, for financial, technical or political reasons, then the business analyst must be pragmatic and be prepared to find other solutions that will yield at least some business benefit.

Leadership

Leadership is a competency that is often associated with line-management job roles. However, the fundamental characteristics of leadership – developing a vision and undertaking actions to achieve that vision – can be applied to all types of work. Thus, leadership is also applicable to business analysis and in this context may be defined as creating a vision of what needs to be done in order to address a business issue and then driving towards the achievement of that vision.

No two projects are the same. Each project has different objectives, constraints and stakeholders, and hence the required approaches, skills and resources will differ. Unless the approach and processes are predefined for the analysis, you will need to assess each situation on its own merits, decide what is needed and then design the analysis process. The word 'analysis' is used here in a wide sense, not just relating to IT systems. The business analyst should consider all aspects of the environment within which they work, covering business drivers such as people, culture, processes and commercial and technical aspects. Getting the vision and actions right will depend on a lot of consultation to position the project for success with key business stakeholders.

Ego strength

This quality is often overlooked, but it is extremely important. It does not relate to having an enormous ego and wanting to carry all before you. It does mean that you have sufficient self-confidence in yourself, in the quality of your analysis and in the correctness of your solution to be able to withstand pressure and sustain your arguments. Ego strength is also key to successful facilitation of workshops and so on.

BUSINESS KNOWLEDGE

This section considers the range of business knowledge and understanding that is essential as a background and foundation for the business analyst's work.

Finance and the economy

The universal language of business is finance. Even in the public and not-for-profit sectors of the economy, finance plays a key role in deciding what funds are available and what can and cannot be done. A business analyst needs to have a good working knowledge of the economy and of the basics of business finance. This includes a general understanding of financial reports such as the balance sheet and profit-and-loss account, of financial analysis tools such as ratio analysis, and of the principles of costing.

Business case development

Much of the business analyst's work will be to assess the costs and benefits of delivering a project to the organization. Thus, when communicating analysis findings, you will need to ensure that you have a view of the financial impact that the project will have. IT in its own right is only an enabling tool for business benefits to be achieved, and a business analysis project will involve other specialists such as management accountants to understand and model the business activities and determine how IT can deliver financial benefit. To develop the business case, a basic understanding of finance is required along with the financial workings of the business area being considered. Business analysts involved in business case preparation will need to understand basic investment appraisal techniques and work closely with the finance department. These techniques are explained in Chapter 12.

Domain knowledge

This is a good general understanding of the business domain, or sector, in which your organization operates, be it private, public or not-for-profit.

Apart from the general domain, there is more specific domain knowledge, for instance of the supermarket or local government sectors. The reasons why this knowledge is required are threefold:

- It enables you to talk sensibly with the business people involved in the project, in a language that they can understand. The personal qualities of communication and relationship-building also help here.

- It will help you to understand what would and would not be acceptable or useful to this business domain. Issues of profit, for instance, are unlikely to be of interest when working in a social-security department.

- It may enable you to take ideas, particularly those relating to best practice or 'best value' (a UK government term), from part of a sector and apply them elsewhere.

Subject matter expertise

This takes the domain knowledge to a lower level of detail. A good understanding of the business area in which you work is important in order to establish credibility with your customer. The level of expertise required will again depend on the type of work being done; for example, if the project is concerned with strategic matters, then this will require an understanding of industry structures, organization design, business models and business drivers for strategic change. At a more operational level, a discussion on the replacement of existing systems will require an understanding of how the existing systems are configured in order to meet current business needs. Business analysts may be specialists in particular business domains, with a strong and detailed understanding of the subject area, who can pinpoint very quickly areas for improvement and identify what needs to change or be analysed using existing knowledge and contacts. Alternatively, business analysts may be generalists with outline knowledge about individual business areas who rely on others to bring the relevant detailed knowledge. There is no right or wrong answer to being a specialist or generalist. Both types are valuable, depending on the organizational context. The key point is to assess how well your competencies meet the needs of the current situation and to recognize where your competencies need some improvement. You can then take any necessary actions such as developing specialist knowledge, requesting input from specialists or asking for a new perspective from a generalist who can take a broader view.

Principles of IT

Many business analysts do not come from an IT background and say, rightly, that their job is not to be expert in IT-related issues; that, after all, is why there are systems analysts, software engineers and so on. However, as so many business analysis projects result in the use of IT in some way, a general understanding of the field seems necessary so that business analysts can communicate meaningfully with the IT professionals.

The extent to which you will need technical knowledge will depend on the nature of the analysis work being undertaken. Although strong technical knowledge is often useful, this may be better obtained from those with specialist skills, for example systems analysts, developers or external suppliers. The key requirement is that the business analyst can understand the technical terms used by IT specialists and help the business users to appreciate any impacts on the organization. However, as IT solutions are often investigated by business analysts, the latter should also possess an understanding of IT fundamentals, including areas such as:

- how computers work, including operating systems, application software, hardware and networks;
- systems-development lifecycles, for example the 'V' model or the unified process;
- systems-development approaches, for example the dynamic systems development method (DSDM), agile development and the unified modelling language (UML);
- the relative pros and cons of developing systems and buying systems 'off the shelf';
- trends and new opportunities that IT brings, such as ecommerce, grid computing and mobile technologies, and how these impact systems development.

Organization structure and design

As well as involving processes and IT, many business analysis projects involve restructuring organizations to a greater or lesser degree, for example to remove handoffs, to centralize a process or to improve the customer service. Because of this, it is important for business analysts to have a good understanding of the various organization structures that may be encountered – functional, project, matrix and so on – and of their relative strengths and weaknesses.

Procurement

Many organizations use external suppliers to deliver their IT systems, either on an ad-hoc basis or perhaps through a more comprehensive outsourcing arrangement. Selecting an appropriate sourcing strategy involves assessing the work in hand and deciding the most appropriate way to take the project forward on a sound commercial footing. Once the analyst has worked out the type of work that is required, they need to assess the most appropriate supplier – internal or external – to take the work forward and what commercial terms should be employed. In some cases business analysts may recognize that they themselves lack the necessary skills for this work, for example if there are detailed contractual arrangements to be organized, and may wish to bring in specialist help. Even so, as with other aspects of the business work, a business analyst needs at least a broad understanding of the different contractual arrangements that are available, for example:

- **Time and materials:** where the contracted party is paid on the basis of the time worked.
- **Fixed-price delivery:** where the contracted party is paid the price that they originally agreed for the delivery of a piece of work according to the precise specification.
- **Risk and reward:** where the contracted party has agreed to bear some or all of the risk of the project, for example by investing resources such as staff time, materials or office space, but where the potential rewards are greater than under other contractual arrangements.

TECHNIQUES

Finally, we consider the techniques that, eventually, the business analyst will wish to master.

Project management

The Association for Project Management's Body of Knowledge has seven sections that describe the work of a project manager. The Project Management Institute's equivalent publication lists the project management context and processes: scope management, integration management, time management, cost management, quality management, human resource management, communications management, risk management and procurement management. It is unlikely that a business analyst will be called upon to display skills in all of these areas, but if the project team is small the business analyst may be required to undertake the role of project manager. Larger projects often employ a specialist project manager. However, there are some project skills that an analyst should have. For example, understanding project initiation is vital as it allows the analyst to understand, or even define, the terms of reference for the project. It is also important that the analyst understands project management planning approaches – he or she will have to work within a plan – and is aware of particularly relevant aspects, such as quality and risk management.

Strategy analysis

This covers a range of techniques that can be used to understand the business direction and the strengths and weaknesses of an organization, or part of an organization. Strategy analysis is explored in more detail in Chapter 3.

Stakeholder analysis and management

This includes understanding who are the stakeholders in a business analysis project and working out how their interests are best managed. Stakeholder analysis and management is the subject of Chapter 6.

Investigation techniques

Clearly, to get to the root of a business issue the analyst will have to undertake detailed analysis of the area. Investigation techniques are reviewed in Chapter 5.

Requirements engineering

This is the set of practices and processes that lead to the development of a set of well-formed business and system requirements, from which IT and other solutions can be developed. The topic is examined in Chapter 9.

Business systems modelling

Business systems modelling is an approach to understanding business systems through the creation of conceptual models of those systems. The techniques concerned are described in Chapter 7.

Business process modelling

Whereas a business systems model looks at the entire business system in overview, more detailed process models are used to map and analyse how the business processes actually work and to help identify opportunities for process improvement. Business process modelling is the subject of Chapter 8.

Data modelling

Analysing the data held and used within a business system affords valuable insights into how a business system operates. For example, what are the data items that are held about our customers? What is the relationship between customers, products and suppliers? Some data modelling techniques are discussed in Chapter 10, and the wider topic of data management is covered in Chapter 11.

Managing business change

This covers the techniques needed to implement changes within an organization and to make them 'stick'. Managing business change is the subject of Chapter 13.

Facilitation skills

The interpersonal skills required for effective facilitation, usually exhibited within the context of a workshop, are those described in the section 'Behavioural skills and personal qualities' on page 14. But there is another aspect to facilitation – having a range of techniques available. These techniques include such approaches as brainstorming, mind-mapping, the use of Post-it notes, Edward de Bono's 'six thinking hats' (de Bono 1990) and so on. There is not the space to cover these topics in depth here, but an introduction is provided in Chapter 5. In addition, the 'Further reading' section at the end of this chapter identifies some useful publications. Effective facilitation usually results from a combination of the right qualities in the facilitator and the choice of the right techniques to match the task and the cultural context of the organization in which it is being used.

HOW CAN I DEVELOP MY COMPETENCIES?

The sections on pages 14–23 have identified a wide range of competencies that a business analyst will want to master eventually. To someone new to the role, the list may appear to be rather daunting. Also, of course, the question 'Do I have to have all of these competencies in order to be a useful analyst?' is raised. The answer to this question is clearly 'no', and business analysts usually start out in the role with well-developed competencies in some areas and less ability in others.

The first step in developing as a business analyst is to understand the competencies required of a business analyst in your organization. This should include an assessment of both the current and the future competencies required. Your human resources (HR) department or line management may be able to provide an outline definition of the competencies required of business analysts in your organization. Future competencies are more difficult to assess and depend on factors such as projects that may develop in the future, business issues and technological developments. Your organization may already have a framework in place, or you could use an existing framework such as the Skills Framework for the Information Age (SFIA), which has been developed by e-skills UK and the SFIA Foundation. This framework is described more fully in the section 'The skills framework for the information age' on page 24.

There are, essentially, three ways in which business analysts can develop their competencies: training, self-study and work experience.

Training

This is particularly useful for the concrete techniques and, to some extent, for the behavioural skills and personal qualities. Classroom-based training allows skills to be learned and practised in a relatively safe environment, with a tutor on hand to offer support, guidance and encouragement. Computer-based training is also good if the skills to be practised are primarily technical in nature.

Self-study

Self-study is an excellent way for analysts to grow their business knowledge. Apart from reading textbooks, browsing publications such as the *Financial Times, The Economist,* the *Harvard Business Review* and other technical and professional journals will broaden and deepen the analyst's understanding of the business world.

Work experience

This provides an opportunity to use and improve techniques and to deepen business knowledge. It is also the best arena in which business analysts can develop their behavioural skills and personal qualities. The performance of most analysts improves over time as their experience grows, but this can be heightened and accelerated if your organization operates a proper coaching or mentoring programme. Even if it does not, there is a lot to be said for finding more experienced business analysts whose work you admire and studying how they go about it. But remember to adapt their approach to your personality: what works for one person does not necessarily work for another.

THE SKILLS FRAMEWORK FOR THE INFORMATION AGE

SFIA and SFIAplus, the British Computer Society's (BCS) model, are the two major standard frameworks for the definition of skills and competencies in the information systems field. Both frameworks include definitions for the skill set of business analysis. Both define various levels of competency for each skill, and these can be used as building blocks for any job role that requires these skills. In both SFIA and SFIAplus, these definitions are provided for different levels, numbered 3 to 6: 3, apply; 4, enable; 5, ensure, advise; and 6, initiate, influence.

The categories of information provided within each of the two standards are shown below.

SFIA

A description of the overall skill set provided in the SFIA framework for business analysis is as follows:

> The methodical investigation, analysis, review and documentation of all or part of a business in terms of business functions and processes, and the information they use. The definition of requirements for improving any aspect of the processes and systems. The creation of viable specifications in preparation for the construction of information and communication systems.

For each level defined for business analysis, SFIA provides a more detailed definition of the skills required. For example, for level 4 it states:

> • The analysis, design, creation, testing and documentation of new and amended programs from supplied specifications in accordance with agreed standards.
> • Creates requirements specification and business case for development of ICT solutions by investigating business processes and business needs.

SFIAplus

SFIAplus provides the same description for the business analysis skill set as SFIA, but it also provides details on the following:

- related skill sets (in this case, data analysis, business process improvement and systems design);
- technical overview, including typical tools and techniques;
- overview of training, development and qualifications;
- careers and jobs;
- professional bodies;
- standards and codes of practice;
- communities and events;
- publications and resources.

For each applicable level within this skills set (3–6 in the case of business analysis), details are also provided under the following headings:

- background;
- work activities;
- knowledge/skills;
- training activities;
- professional development activities;
- qualifications.

Although SFIAplus provides more detail than SFIA, it is important to realize that the two frameworks should be implemented in different ways. SFIAplus should be treated as a standard and is not designed to be customized, whereas SFIA is intended to be used as a basis for tailoring to an organization's needs. As a result, care should be taken when deciding which of the two is most appropriate within a specific organization.

SFIAplus enables organizations to classify and benchmark their IT skills and to train and develop their teams to meet the defined skill requirements. As a business analyst, this provides a basis for you to gauge where you are against the skills and corresponding level of competence defined in the framework. You could obtain an objective assessment of your competencies from your line manager and peers. This can be used to look ahead to assess how you, and your employing organization, want your skill set and career to develop. The final step is to identify a set of actions that will help you with your development. You could try some or all of the following:

- Seek out assignments that give you opportunities to develop.
- Identify a role model who demonstrates your desired competencies. Ask them what is required or ask them to mentor your development or arrange to work for them direct.
- Use training providers to target specifically those areas that need development.
- Consider a secondment to an organization that excels in the required competencies.
- Do your own research into specific competencies. There are many more detailed books covering the competencies identified in this chapter.
- Ask for regular feedback from your boss or peers.
- Join an industry specialist group, for example one of the BCS specialist groups that focus specifically on the competencies, such as project management.
- Develop as you go and gain from experience. Record what you've learned so that you don't forget it.

SUMMARY

Competence development is the most important aspect of career development for any professional. This chapter has sought to categorize and describe the most common competencies for being a successful business analyst. Every organization will have a different interpretation of what a business analyst does, and we have seen the importance of matching the competencies to the role that an individual is expected to perform. If you wish to develop and improve your performance, you need to understand your levels of competence in the various skill areas and then take the necessary steps to improve.

Historically, business analyst jobs and qualifications have focused on the construction of systems that meet business requirements. This has meant that the focus is on collecting requirements in an organized and logical fashion, which are then used to select or build systems that meet those needs. The need for people who can do this is now much wider, and there is far more emphasis on the importance of this task, often as a result of the sourcing options available to organizations. Where external suppliers are used, defining IT requirements is even more important, particularly if they are located in other countries – offshore sourcing, as this is known. Critically, the stakes are being raised higher for IT projects. IT departments that cannot show or communicate how they add value are becoming an endangered species. Business analysts can survive and evolve only if they offer a much broader set of competencies that allows them to demonstrate how they can identify, analyse and develop options for adding value to their organization.

It is in the area of behavioural skills and personal qualities where perhaps the biggest challenge for business analysts lies. Staff members involved in IT projects have been characterized in the past as showing far more aptitude for communicating with machines rather than human beings. In addition, anyone working in business change is only too aware of the apprehension and even resentment that change projects engender. So, business analysts face a major challenge. They need to use all of their behavioural skills to invalidate the stereotypes and overcome the opposition in order that they can work with their business colleagues to deliver the business improvements that their organizations demand.

REFERENCES

de Bono, E. (1990) *Six Thinking Hats*. Penguin, London.

FURTHER READING

Laborde, G.Z. (1987) *Influencing with Integrity*. Anglo American Book Company, Bancyfelin, Wales.

Patching, K. and Chatham, R. (2000) *Corporate Politics for IT Managers: How to get streetwise*. Butterworth-Heinemann, Oxford.

Stanton, N. (2003) *Mastering Communication*, 4th edn. Macmillan, Basingstoke.

Townsend, J. and Donovan, P. (1999) *The Facilitator's Pocketbook*. Management Pocketbooks, Alresford.

Whiddett, S. and Hollyforde, S. (2003) *A Practical Guide to Competencies*, 2nd edn. Chartered Institute of Personnel and Development, London.

Zuker, E. *The Seven Secrets of Influence*. (1991) McGraw-Hill, New York.

USEFUL WEBSITES

British Computer Society: www.bcs.org
Management Standards Centre: www.management-standards.org
SFIA Foundation: www.sfia.org

3 Strategy analysis

DONALD YEATES

INTRODUCTION

This chapter is about four aspects of strategy analysis:

- understanding what strategy is and why it is important, the assumption being that strategy is important;
- exploring some ideas about how strategy is developed;
- implementing strategy;
- working out what all of this means for business analysts.

We intend here not to try to turn you into a strategic planner but instead to enable you to understand the process of strategy development, be comfortable with the tools that managers use and be able to use them yourself as you explore how new or different information systems could push forward the activities of the organization that employs you.

THE CONTEXT FOR STRATEGY

Why do organizations bother about strategy? What advantage do they hope to get? Let us look at what is happening in the world. Most of us would probably support the idea that business is becoming increasingly unpredictable and changes are more turbulent. The information revolution and the digital economy have caused much of this dramatic change, and barriers between previously separate businesses are falling like dominoes. For example, who will be the big financial players in the future? It could be the global banks, or retail outlets like Tesco and Sainsbury's, or strong brands like Amazon and Virgin. If you are working in the finance sector, how do you know where to move next?

There are some big changes that organizations face and that strategy development tries to moderate. There are the changes to the ways that we are employed. There is much more use of part-time and contract employees, who may have little long-term loyalty to their employer and who have their own individual career and work/life balance plans. The growth of knowledge-based industries and the continuous change experienced by organizations means that individual employees, consultants and contractors – permanent, full-time or part-time – have become valuable assets. This is more than ever the case, as organizations everywhere, in both the public and private sectors, flatten their organization structures, decentralize decision-making and give more freedom to individuals to make business, deal with customers and resolve problems. There are no longer jobs for life, and attitudes to work have changed. We all now want great job satisfaction, higher rewards, more personal recognition and flexible working environments.

Society has changed. There is greater freedom of expression and of thought. Freedom of information legislation means that individuals have access to evidence and decisions taken by government that previously were hidden. There is less respect for authority and office unless it has been earned. Our attitudes to change, direction, reorganization and other people knowing better than we do have shifted, and the development and implementation of new strategies need to take this into account.

Organizations are responding to these changes by doing everything they can to increase their flexibility and responsiveness. This means that they seek to reduce employment costs. Without trade unions to apply a brake, we see central government and European institutions taking this role.

The world is full of contradictions, for example:

- **Global versus local:** globalization creates the largest markets ever known, and until we have intergalactic businesses this will remain the case. But it also means that the players in a global market can be small. Having a global reach does not mean being the biggest. The scarcity of the product, its brand reputation and its distribution channels make the difference. The paparazzi know this: one paparazzo, a camera, the right moment and the internet sell his or her product across the world in less than a day.

- **Centralized versus decentralized organization structures:** finance may be a central process, but prices and discounts are set locally.

- **Hard and soft management:** developing strategy is seen as a 'hard' discipline like finance and technology, but the creativity and change skills that make strategy work are the 'soft' skills.

Finally, there are two questions. How can anyone create, formulate or build a strategy if the future is inherently unknowable and unpredictable? And how can it be implemented in a coherent way in decentralized structures with delegated authorities and an ever changing environment? This makes it appear very difficult for a business analyst to understand the nature and permanence – or impermanence – of the business strategies against which information systems (IS) strategies are to be built. However, as we shall see, through an examination of the nature of strategy and the use of some well-tried tools, effective steps can be taken to deal with this difficulty.

WHAT IS STRATEGY?

The concept of strategy begins in a military context. The word 'strategy' is derived from the Greek word *strategia*, meaning 'generalship'. The term has a getting-ready-for-battle sense to it, and the deployment of troops, weapons, aircraft and ships before engagement with the enemy begins. Once the enemy is engaged, then battlefield tactics determine the success of the strategy. The transfer of these ideas into business is easy to make, therefore, and we expect to deal with the following:

- The goal or mission of the business: in strategy terms, this is often referred to as the 'direction'.
- The timeframe: strategy is about the long term. The problem here is that it differs widely across industries, with petrochemicals and pharmaceuticals at the really long end and domestic financial services products at the short end.
- The organization of resources such as finance, skills, assets and technical competence so that the organization can compete.
- The environment within which the organization will operate, and its markets.

A popular definition appears in Johnson and Scholes (2001):

> **Strategy is the direction and scope of an organisation over the long term, which achieves advantage for the organisation through its configuration of resources within a changing environment and to fulfil stakeholder expectations.**

However, writers and gurus have offered their own definitions for at least the past 30 years, including Steiner (1979), who did not so much define it as paint a picture of it by saying that strategy:

- is what top management does;
- is about direction;
- sets in motion the important actions necessary to achieve these directions;
- is what the organization should be doing.

Finally, another definition from Johnson and Scholes (2001) is more helpful to us when considering strategy analysis. They wrote that strategic decisions are concerned with:

- the direction of an organization's activities;
- matching these activities to the environment;
- the capability of the organization to support the chosen direction;
- the values and expectations of stakeholders;

- the implementation and management of change.

Strategies exist at different levels in an organization, ranging from corporate strategies at the top level affecting the complete organization, down to the operational strategies for product/services offerings. Typical levels of strategy could be as follows:

- Corporate strategy concerned with the overall purpose and scope of the business: strategies at this level are influenced by investors, governments, global competition and the context set out earlier in this chapter. It is the basis of all other strategies and strategic decisions.

- Business unit strategy: below the corporate level are the strategic business units (SBUs), organizational units for which there are distinct external markets that are different from those of other SBUs. SBU strategies address choice of products, pricing, customer satisfaction and competitive advantage.

- Operational strategy focusing on the delivery of the corporate and SBU strategies through the effective organization and development of resources, processes and people.

STRATEGY DEVELOPMENT

This section begins with some fundamental questions: How do we start to develop a strategy? Where does strategy development come from? How do we know what kinds of strategy to develop? We can identify several starting points:

- Strategy associated with an individual, often the founder of a business: UK examples include Stelios Haji-Ioannou of easyJet, Sir Ken Morrison of Morrisons supermarkets, Sir Richard Branson and Sir Alan Sugar. In already established businesses, we might suggest Allan Leighton of Asda and the Royal Mail and Stuart Rose of Marks & Spencer, both introduced into these businesses to turn them around and to change their strategy. So strategy sometimes starts and is associated strongly with an individual leader. This can work all the way down an organization, where new leaders bring new ideas – strategies – to operating units, divisions and departments.

- Decentralized and empowered organizations, where all managers are encouraged to use the techniques of strategy analysis and be 'intrapreneurial' – internally entrepreneurial – and actively create and champion new initiatives.

- However, it does not always need strong individual strategy champions to create new strategies. Groups of managers may meet regularly and review trends in the market and their own business progress. They plan new actions and try them out. Strategy thus evolves in an incremental way.

- Strategies resulting from a formal planning process: some organizations find this to be essential, especially those for which strategy is truly long term.

We could, therefore, see the origins of strategy development as in Figure 3.1.

The sizes of the triangles shown in Figure 3.1 are not necessarily the same and, indeed, change over time. Formal planning or intrapreneurial strategies may follow entrepreneurially driven strategy as an organization grows, a crisis may call for new entrepreneurial strategies – perhaps associated with a new chief executive – and the cycle begins again.

The three different ways in which strategies come about are described by Johnson and Scholes (2001) by seeing strategy development through three different lenses. These lenses are the design lens, the experience lens and the ideas lens.

The design lens sees strategy resulting from 'the deliberate positioning of the organisation' through a detailed and comprehensive analysis and a subsequent directive strategy that is formulated by top management and pushed down through the organization. A key factor here is that the structure of the organization and all of the central systems can be aligned to report on the performance of the strategy. It is unlikely that any organization could withstand frequent major revisions of strategy of this kind. Also, it is unlikely that strategy by design always gets it right and certainly not in every detail. It is likely that adaptations and incremental changes will be made to the strategy.

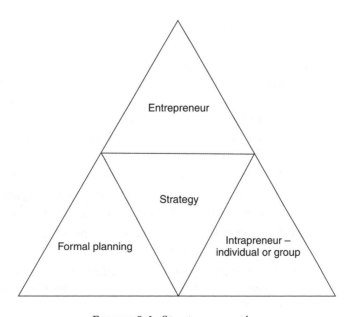

FIGURE 3.1 *Strategy creation*

This brings us to the experience lens view of strategy development, where the collective experience of the organization and its organizational culture operate on the existing strategy to give it a new form. In other words, the strategy is modified to a continually evolving environment, and each modification may form the basis for the next, and so on. Although this seems a sensible approach, these small slow steps taken as they are rooted in a collective experience and a past strategy are unlikely to be innovative and may produce responses that are just 'more of the same' and inadequate in responding to bigger than normal external changes.

Entrepreneurial strategies come through the ideas lens and are the result of an innovative climate or the introduction of new thinkers, very often new chief executive officers (CEOs). These ideas can also come from environmental scanning – looking at what is happening outside the organization and identifying new opportunities or stronger competitor pressure, new customer demands or imminent technological change.

We also have to recognize another force in the making of strategy: its politics. So far the development of strategy has been considered as a rational, logical and organized process. It often is developed like this, and in this chapter we will consider many of the tools that are used to inform the strategy process. However strategy is developed, it cannot always be done by flashes of inspiration and no hard work. There are views now that show organizations as political systems that manipulate the formation of strategy through the exercise of power. Different interest groups form around different strategic ideas or issues and compete for resources and the support of stakeholders to achieve the dominance of their ideas. On this basis, strategic direction is achieved not through a universally accepted rational analysis but through the promotion of specific ideas of the most powerful groups. This power comes from five main sources:

- **Dependency:** departments are dependent on those departments that have control over the organization's resources. The power of the HR department increases if all new staff requisitions have to be authorized by HR.
- **Financial resources:** where are the funds to invest in the development of new ideas, products or services? Who has these funds? What financial frameworks constrain or give freedom to different groups?
- **Position:** where do the actors live in the organization structure, and how does their work affect the organization's performance?
- **Uniqueness:** no other part of the organization can do what the powerful group does.
- **Uncertainty:** power resides with people, and groups can cope with the unpredictable effects of the environment and protect others from its impact.

It is interesting, therefore, when considering strategic direction and the implementation of strategy to assess the extent to which politics influences the outcome.

Finally, there is the garbage-can model for strategy formulation. This is the process that is furthest away from cool, calm and scientific deliberation. It is said to be most appropriate when there is collective and great uncertainty about what to do, where the technology or technological change is unclear or unknown, and where strategy-makers' preferences and ideas are unclear and their choices about what to do inconsistent. The garbage can stores many different processes and solutions that are thrown into it independently of each other. Indeed, the problems, solutions and decision-makers are not necessarily connected, and it seems to be a chance alignment of components that generates the required action when the garbage can is inspected. So when there is a need to do something – a choice opportunity, as it is called – we look in the garbage can and find a collection of solutions and ideas that we can use but that were not intended for us or to be used in this way when they were thrown into the bin.

So we know that there are many different drivers for strategy development. Even though strategy appears to be formulated in different ways, they will all incorporate some external analysis – 'What's happening out there?' – some internal analysis – 'Where do we fit in to what's happening out there?' – and some consideration of how new strategies could be implemented.

We do all of this to provide a written statement of our strategy. This written statement is needed for many reasons:

- It provides a focus for the organization and enables all parts of it to understand the reasons behind top-level decisions and how each part can contribute to its achievement.

- It provides a framework for a practical allocation of investment and other resources.

- It provides a guide to innovation, where new products, services, systems etc are needed.

- It enables appropriate performance measures to be put in place that measure the key indicators of our success in achieving the strategy.

- It tells the outside world, and especially our outside stakeholders, about us and enforces the expectations that they develop about us.

EXTERNAL ENVIRONMENT ANALYSIS

Most organizations face a complex and changing external environment of increasing unpredictability. Let us take as an example a retail electrical and electronics store that faces some or all of the following external changes:

- The state of the national and local economies: product demand is influenced by local employment and incomes and the cost of credit.
- Product cost: price competition is high, and there is a continuing shift to move manufacturing to lower-cost economies, with the possible impact on supply and after-sales support.
- Changes in consumer lifestyles and tastes: the high cost of housing leads to a greater incidence of smaller houses and a growth in the supply of flats calling for small televisions and kitchen equipment. DVDs (digital versatile disks) replace videocassette technology.
- Changes in technology: there is a greater demand for smaller devices, flatter screens and multipurpose devices.
- New marketing approaches, with consumers buying over the internet or from catalogue retailers.

With a little thought it would have been possible to identify these kinds of environmental trend, but many of the more dramatic changes have come from surprising places. When the deregulation of the UK financial services sector stimulated supermarket banks and insurance companies, existing banks sought to obtain critical mass by takeover, while mutual societies such as building societies became public companies, rewarded their members and were themselves predators or victims in takeovers. More dramatic and unexpected are the activities of environmental or animal rights campaigners or a sudden change in technology that changes generally accepted business models.

There is a framework to help organizations assess its broad environment – the PESTLE (sometimes called the PESTEL or PEST) analysis. This is an examination of the political, economic, sociocultural, technological, legal and environmental issues in the external business environment.

Political influences include:

- trade regulations and tariffs;
- social welfare policies.

Economic influences include:

- business cycles;
- interest rates;
- money supply;
- inflation;
- unemployment;
- disposable income;
- availability and cost of energy;
- internationalization of business.

Taken together, these economic factors determine how easy – or not – it is to be profitable, because they affect demand.

Sociocultural influences include demand and taste issues and how tastes and preferences change over time. Specific influences include the following:

- Demographics: for example, an ageing population in Europe.
- Social mobility: will people move in order to work, or stay where they are, but unemployed, and rely on state support? To some extent this is now a political issue, with an enlarged Europe enabling a freer movement of labour across the community.
- Lifestyle changes: for example, the desire to retire earlier and general changes in people's views about work/life balance.
- Concern for the environment, including waste disposal, recycling and energy consumption.

Technological issues include:

- government spending on research, the quality of academic research and the 'brain drain';
- the focus on technology, and support for invention and innovation;
- the pace of technological change and the creation of technology-enabled industries.

Legal issues include:

- legislation about trade practices and competition;
- environmental-protection legislation, such as new laws on recycling and waste-disposal industries;
- employment law, such as employment protection and discrimination.

Environmental issues include:

- global warming and climate change;
- animal welfare;
- waste, such as unnecessary packaging.

It is important that we do not view PESTLE analysis as a set of checklists, as these are not of themselves useful in making a strategic assessment. The key tasks are to identify those few factors that will really affect the organization and to develop a real understanding of how they might evolve in the future. How can this be done? In some cases a few issues may be so important that they provide a natural focus. It may also be helpful to get some outside expert opinions.

Having examined the external environment, we should now consider the competition that our organization faces. Few businesses have no competition, and most seek to develop and keep a competitive advantage over their rivals. They aim to be different or better in ways that appeal to their customers. An analysis tool that helps to evaluate an industry's profitability and hence its attractiveness is Michael Porter's five forces model (Porter 1979) (Figure 3.2). In the centre is the competitive battleground, where rivals compete and competitive strategies are developed. Organizations seek to understand the nature of their competitive environment. Additionally, organizations will be in a stronger position if they understand the interplay of the five forces and can develop defences against the threats they pose.

New entrants may want to move into the market if it looks attractive and if the barriers to entry are low. Globalization and deregulation both give new entrants this opportunity, but there are barriers to entry that organizations build, including the following:

- Economies of scale: if substantial investment is necessary before a new entrant can compete, then this may be a deterrent.
- Product differentiation: if existing products and services are seen to have strong identities that are supported by high expenditure or branding, then new entrants may be deterred from entry.
- Substantial capital investment by a new entrant.
- Access to distribution channels: existing distribution channels may be committed to existing suppliers, thus requiring new entrants to find new and different distribution channels.
- Technologies and the use of patented processes.

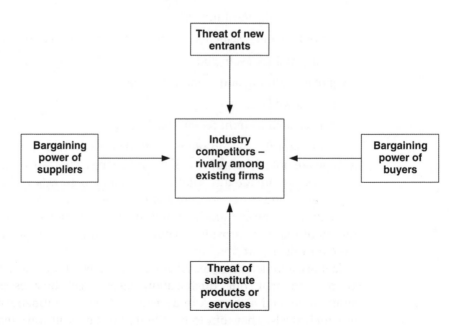

FIGURE 3.2 *Porter's five forces model*

Supplier power limits the opportunity for cost reductions when:

- there is a concentration of suppliers and when supplying businesses are bigger than the many customers they supply;
- the costs of switching from one supplier to another are high because of supply contracts, interlinking systems with suppliers, supply logistics or the inability of other suppliers to deliver;
- the supplier brand is powerful, e.g. the power of Intel Inside;
- customers are fragmented.

Customer power – or the 'bargaining power of buyers', as Porter called it – is high when:

- there is a small concentration of buyers and many small organizations in the supplying industry, for example in the supply of food to supermarkets;
- alternative sources of supply are available and easy to find;
- the cost of the product or service is high, thus encouraging the buyer to search out alternatives;
- switching costs are low.

The threat from substitute products – for example, budget air travel for cross-channel ferries – is high when:

- product substitution from new technologies is more convenient, for example DVDs for videos;
- the need for the product is replaced by a different need;
- we decide to 'do without it'.

Other examples that affect us all are the impact of high-speed trains on airlines, particularly between London, Paris and Brussels, and the impact of low-cost airlines on ferry operators.

All of these forces impact on the competitive battleground in some way. On the battleground itself, there is competitive rivalry. This is high when:

- there are many competing firms;
- buyers can switch easily from one firm to another;
- the market is growing only slowly or not at all;
- the industry has high fixed costs, and responding to price pressure is difficult;
- products are not well differentiated, and so there is little brand loyalty;
- the costs of leaving the industry are high.

Porter's framework is simple to use and understand, and it helps to identify the key competitive forces affecting a business. The framework is used widely in the development of strategies. There are, however, some weaknesses, of which the most often mentioned is that government is not treated as the sixth force. Porter's response is that the role of government is played through each of the five forces – legislation affects entry and rivalry, for example – and so it has not been ignored. There are also views that it is difficult to apply the model to not-for-profit organizations and that since the 1980s the increasing development of international businesses has led to a more complex set of competitive and collaborative relationships. Nonetheless, Porter's framework is accepted widely as a useful analytical tool.

Having worked hard on our PESTLE and Porter analyses, we will have much useful data about the attractiveness of the business we have and the external conditions it may face. How can this data be used? Generally, even with this data, the world springs surprises on organizations from time to time. There is a high level of uncertainty, and some different approaches are needed in order to understand potential future impacts. Scenarios may be used to do this. They look at the medium- and long-term future and by evaluating possible different futures prepare the organization to deal with them and prepare managers to deal with future shocks. Scenarios begin by identifying the potential high-impact and high-uncertainty factors in the environment. It is tempting to choose just two scenarios – good and bad – when doing this, but really four or more are needed, and they should be plausible and detailed. Next, what futures could these factors construct, and what combination of these factors could build a plausible scenario? In doing this, we are concerned with predetermined events such as demographic changes, key uncertainties – often political and economic, including regulation and world trade – and driving forces such as technology and education. This information comes from the PESTLE analysis.

INTERNAL ENVIRONMENT ANALYSIS

The external environment creates opportunities and threats and can give an 'outside-in' stimulus to the development of strategy. Successful strategies depend on something else as well – the capability of the organization to perform. Can an organization continue to change its capability so that it constantly fits the environment in which it operates? Can an organization always be innovative in the way it exploits this capability? We will look at two techniques in this section to address these issues – the resource audit and portfolio analysis using the Boston Matrix. All of this begins, however, with an understanding of the current business positioning. For this, we will use the MOST analysis technique, which examines the current mission, objectives, strategy and tactics and considers whether these are clearly defined and supported within the organization. We can define the MOST terms as follows:

- **Mission:** a statement declaring what business the organization is in and what it is intending to achieve.
- **Objectives:** the goals against which the organization's achievements can be measured.
- **Strategy:** the approach that is going to be taken by the organization in order to achieve the objectives and mission.
- **Tactics:** the detailed means by which the strategy will be implemented.

A clear mission driving the organization forward, a set of measurable objectives and a coherent strategy will enhance the capability of the organization and be a source of strength. On the other hand, if there are a lack of direction, unclear objectives and an ill-defined strategy, then the internal capability is less effective and we have a source of weakness.

Reflecting on core competences starts the strategy process from inside the organization and so this is an 'inside-out' approach based on the belief that competitiveness comes from an ability to create new and unexpected products and services from a set of core competences. The resource audit can help us to identify core competences or may highlight where there is a lack of competence that could undermine any competitive moves. There are five key areas to examine. First, there are three sets of tangible resource:

- the **physical** resources that the organization owns or has access to, including features such as buildings, plant, equipment and land;
- the **financial** resources that determine the organization's financial stability, capacity to invest in new resources and ability to weather fluctuations in the market;
- the **human** resources and their expertise, adaptability, commitment etc.

Second, there are the intangible resources such as the **know-how** of the organization, which may include patents and trademarks but may also be derived from the use of technology that is specific to the business, for example manufacturing technology. Another intangible resource is the **reputation** of the organization, for example the brand recognition and the belief that is held about the quality of the brand, and the goodwill – or antipathy – that this produces. An analysis of the organization's resources will identify where these provide a source of competence – strengths – or where there is a lack of capability – weaknesses.

Some organizations have a single or limited range of products and can focus their efforts on delivering these products in such a way that they delight their customers. However, many businesses have a diversified range of products and services; they might all be computer software but different products are produced for different markets and for different users. Each will have developed its own strategic direction, perhaps using the tools described in this chapter, and decisions have to be taken now about the resources to be put into each product or service. Portfolio analysis was developed to address this problem. The underlying idea is that the portfolio of businesses is managed to achieve balance with a mixture of high-growth, profit-maximizing, investment-needing and declining businesses making up a balanced overall organization.

The original portfolio matrix – the Boston Box – was developed by the Boston Consulting Group. This analysis concentrates on immediate financial gain and does not connect with any long-term strategic direction or core competences. A company's SBUs – parts of an organization for which there is a distinct and separate external market – are identified, and the relationship between each SBU's current or future revenue potential is modelled against the appropriate management of it. Put simply, as in Figure 3.3, the cows are milked, the dogs are buried, the stars get the gold and the wild cats are examined carefully until they behave themselves or join the dogs and die.

A successful product or SBU starts as a wild cat and goes clockwise round the model until it dies or is revitalized as a new product or service or SBU. The wild cats or problem children are unprofitable but are investments for the future; the stars strengthen their position in a growth industry until they become the big profit earners. They are mature products or services and often market leaders. They provide the funding for the other segments of the matrix. The dogs are businesses that have low market share in markets with low growth. The cash cows are mature products in well-established markets where they are the market leaders; they are the most profitable products in the portfolio.

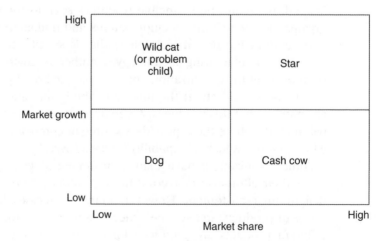

FIGURE 3.3 *The Boston Box*

SWOT ANALYSIS

SWOT (strengths, weaknesses, opportunities, threats) analysis is often used to pull together the results of an analysis of the external and internal environments. Too often one sees it used as the first analytical tool before enough preparatory analysis has been done. When this approach is adopted, the results are usually weak, inconclusive and insufficiently robust to be of much use. If we use the techniques described earlier, they help identify the major factors both internal and external to the organization that the business strategy needs to take account of. Hence, the SWOT analysis is where we summarize the key strengths, weaknesses, opportunities and threats in order to carry out an overall audit of the strategic position of a business and its environment. A SWOT analysis is often represented as a two-by-two matrix, as shown in the Figure 3.4.

The language of a SWOT analysis is important. It needs to be brief, with strengths and weaknesses related to critical success factors. Strengths and weaknesses should also be measured against the competition. All statements should be specific, realistic and supported by evidence. Some examples – not for the same organization – could be as follows:

- **Strengths:** strong product branding – market research shows a high awareness of our brands compared with the competition. We secure 'best space' in all branches of the top five supermarkets.

- **Weaknesses:** we have poor cash flow. Against industry benchmarks we are in the bottom quartile. We exceed our overdraft limits on 19 days every quarter.

- **Opportunities:** demographic change in Europe will provide a greater market for our products.

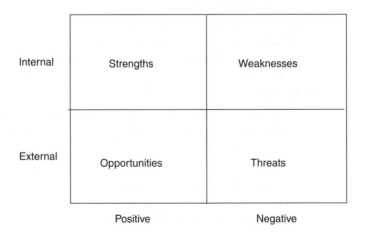

FIGURE 3.4 *Format of a SWOT matrix*

- **Threats:** low market growth will see increased concentration of business through acquisition. The poorest-performing businesses will fail.

It is important to get right the balance between the external and the internal analysis. Completely changing the nature of the organization because of what the external analysis says leads to radical change; basing everything on an internal analysis may lead to little or no change. Either case could be right of course, but both analyses are likely to contribute towards the creation of a new strategic direction.

IMPLEMENTING STRATEGY

Implementing new strategies implies risk because it involves change. In Chapter 13 we discuss how business change should be managed to maximize the benefits and minimize the risks of implementing change. In this section we consider three particular aspects of implementing strategy: the context for the strategy, the role of the leader and two tools – the balanced business scorecard and the McKinsey 7-S model. We will deal first with the five contextual issues:

- **Time:** how quickly does the new strategy need to be implemented? What pace of change is needed?

- **Scope:** how big is the change? Is the new strategic direction transformational or incremental?

- **Capability:** is the organization used to change? Are the experiences of change positive or negative? Are the change implementers skilled?

- **Readiness:** is the whole organization, or the part of it to be affected, ready to make the change?

- **Strategic leadership:** is there a strategic leader?

In this context, the strategic leader will have the key role. The strategic leaders we read about are usually the top managers, but strategic leadership does not have to be delivered from the top – there are many successful strategic changes that have been driven from other parts of the organization. The key characteristics seem to be that the leader does the following:

- Challenges the status quo all the time and sets new and demanding targets, never being prepared to tolerate unsatisfactory behaviour or performance.

- Establishes and communicates a clear vision of the direction to be taken, why it has to be taken and how the journey will be achieved. This means establishing the new mission, setting out objectives, identifying the strategies for achieving those objectives and defining the specific tactics to deliver them. The leader will also communicate clearly the values that underpin the new ways of doing business.

- 'Models the way', demonstrating through their behaviour how everyone else should behave and act in order to deliver the strategy.
- Empowers people to deliver their part of the strategic change within the vision, values and mission that have been set out, because the leader cannot be everywhere at once.
- Celebrates success with those who achieve it.

Two tools that help in the implementation of strategy are the McKinsey 7-S model (Figure 3.5) and the balanced business scorecard (BBS) (Figure 3.6).

The McKinsey 7-S model supposes that all organizations are made up of seven components. Three are often described as 'hard' components – strategy, structure, systems – and four as 'soft' – shared values, style, staff, skills.

These are the seven levers that can be used in the implementation of strategic change. All seven components need attention if the implementation is to be successful, because if there is a change in one, then others will be affected. Changing the strategy means that all of the other components have to change as well:

- The structure, which is the basis for building the organization, will change to reflect new needs for specialization and coordination resulting from the new strategic direction.
- Formal and informal systems that supported the old system must change.

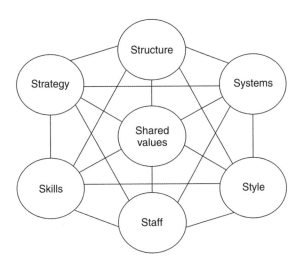

FIGURE 3.5 *The McKinsey 7-S model*

- The style or culture of the organization will be affected by a new strategic direction. Values, beliefs and norms, which developed over time, may be swept away.

- The way in which staff are recruited, developed and rewarded may change. New strategies may mean relocating people or making them redundant.

- Skills and competences acquired in the past may be of less use now. The new strategy may call for new skills.

- Shared values are the guiding concepts of the organization, the fundamental ideas that are the basis of the organization. Moving from an 'engineering first' company to a 'customer service first' company would change the shared values.

The BBS can be thought of as the strategic balance sheet for an organization as it captures both the financial and the non-financial components of a strategy. The BBS shows, therefore, how the implementation process is working and the effectiveness with which the levers for change are being used. The BBS supplements financial measures with three other perspectives of organizational performance – customers, learning and growth, and internal business processes. Vision and strategy connect with each of these, as shown in Figure 3.6.

Although the emphasis of the BBS is to measure all aspects of performance, many people pay more attention to the non-financial measures, since these have not been measured previously, but financial measures retain their importance. The customer perspective measures those critical success factors that provide a customer focus. It forces a detailed examination to be made of statements like 'superior customer service' so that everyone can agree what it means and measures can be established in order to show the progress being made. But perhaps little

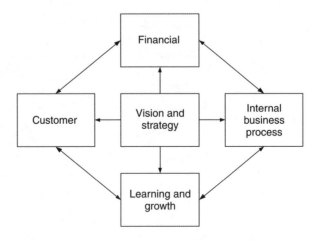

FIGURE 3.6 *The balanced business scorecard*

progress is possible without new skills and different attitudes – a link to the learning and growth perspective, which in turn could generate a need for new internal processes to give the newly skilled people the tools to use. Each perspective then answers questions like the following:

- Financial: to succeed financially and have the resources to deliver our strategy, how must we be seen by our stakeholders?
- Customer: to achieve our vision, what do we want customers to say about us?
- Learning and growth: how will we sustain our ability to change and improve so that we constantly keep ahead of the competition?
- Internal business processes: what are the business processes that we must excel at in order to deliver customer value?

Having a strategy is not enough by itself, but the task of implementing it is difficult. Apart from the issues associated with change, the environment gives a shifting context within which to work. But without effective implementation, the work in developing the strategy will be of doubtful value.

SUMMARY

In this chapter we have looked at the reasons why organizations develop strategies and how they might do this. We have explored the complexity of this process and offered ideas about how strategies are developed, taking account of entrepreneurial approaches and formal planning. The chapter also described the external factors influencing strategy – the outside-in approach – and an internal analysis approach – the inside-out approach. Finally we looked at the implementation of strategy and IS strategy considerations.

REFERENCES

Johnson, G. and Scholes, K. (2001) *Exploring Corporate Strategy*, 6th edn. FT Prentice Hall, Harlow.

Porter, M. (1979) How competitive forces shape strategy. *Harvard Business Review*, March/April.

Steiner, G. (1979) *Strategic Planning*. Free Press, New York.

FURTHER READING

Bannock, G., Davis, E., Trott, P. and Uncles, M. (2003) *Dictionary of Business*. Economist Books, London.

Grant, R.M. (2001) *Contemporary Strategy Analysis*, 4th edn. Blackwell, Malden, MA.

Kaplan, R.S. and Norton, D.P. (1996) Using the balance scorecard as a strategic management system. *Harvard Business Review*, January/February.

Owen, A.A. (1982) How to implement strategy. *Management Today*, July.

Quinn, J. and Mintzberg, H. (2002) *The Strategy Process*. Prentice Hall, Englewood Cliffs, NJ.

Thompson, J.L. (2002) *Strategic Management*, 4th edn. Thomson Learning, London.

Whipp, R. (2002) The politics of strategy making. In Warner, M. (ed), *The International Encyclopaedia of Business and Management*. Thomson Learning, London.

4 The business analysis process model

DEBRA PAUL

INTRODUCTION

There are many tools and techniques available for the business analyst to use but, because of the nature of business analysis work, an overview framework is useful to place these in context and help determine the most appropriate technique for each individual situation. In this chapter we have set out a business analysis process model as a framework within which both standard modelling techniques and organizational templates can be used. This approach also incorporates the principles of requirements engineering to highlight best practice when defining system requirements.

AN APPROACH TO PROBLEM-SOLVING

One of the requirements of business managers is that business analysts examine the entire business area and take a thoughtful or even creative approach to developing ideas for solutions. Creative problem-solving is vital in the current business world as, increasingly, organizations need to develop innovative ideas in order to respond to changes in the business environment, including actions from competitors. However, many people find this difficult, often because they feel under pressure to produce ideas very quickly. In this context, Isaksen and Treffinger's (1985) creative problem-solving model (Figure 4.1) provides a useful framework for understanding problems and developing creative solutions, particularly as the model emphasizes the need to investigate and analyse rather than leap to quick, possibly premature, solutions.

This model proposes an approach that may be applied usefully to business analysis. In this section, we describe the implications and suggestions that the model has for business analysts. The first stage, **mess-finding**, is where we often begin when undertaking a problem investigation. In business analysis, this stage is concerned with finding out about the complexity of the problem situation. Many problems are defined poorly, and each problem situation is likely to be complex and contain various issues and concerns. In other words, there is likely to be a 'mess' and different situations will have different components to that mess.

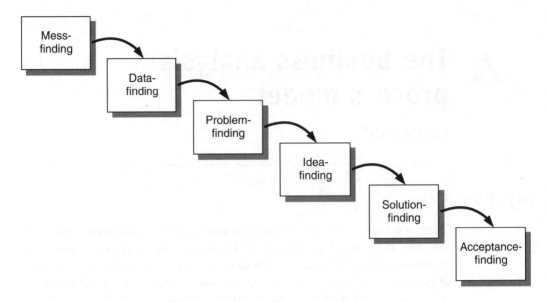

FIGURE 4.1 *Problem-solving model*

Identifying this as the starting point in this model helps to emphasize that we need to gain some understanding about the complete situation before diving into options and solutions. The rich-picture approach, described in Chapter 7, is particularly useful to help document and analyse the 'mess' in problematic business situations. Mind maps are also described in Chapter 7 and are similarly helpful.

Data-finding, the second stage of the model, is concerned with analysing the opinions, concerns, knowledge and ideas uncovered in the previous stage in order to identify where this information can be quantified and supporting data obtained. It is often useful to examine the rich picture or mind map to clarify your thinking about the situation. It is particularly important to consider which information is factual and which is based on opinion. This can help lead us to the aspects that we can, and should, verify and also emphasizes the need to divorce opinion from fact. Chapter 5 explains some techniques that will help you to obtain quantitative data, such as questionnaires and activity sampling.

Problem-finding then uses the work of the previous two stages to help uncover the heart of the problem. We now know the complexity of the situation facing us and have been able to quantify some elements, whilst appreciating that other elements are personal views or opinions. You may have been presented with a statement of the problem at the outset, but at this point, having carried out the previous two stages, it is important to revisit this statement in order to really understand where the problems lie. Finding the right problem to solve is often a necessary part of business analysis, as analysts are often pointed at symptoms and have to dig deeper in order to find out where the real problems lie.

So these first three stages are concerned with understanding the problem and provide a structure for doing this. The next two stages focus on developing solutions.

First, there is **idea-finding**, during which business analysts try to generate a wide range of ideas. Analysts often use brainstorming approaches to uncover ideas, but this can be difficult as it requires a group to generate ideas 'cold'. Sometimes this works, but often different approaches need to be used with brainstorming in order to stimulate ideas, so during this stage it may be useful to use some creative thinking techniques. Two examples of techniques that can provide stimuli for creative ideas are assumption reversal, where assumptions about a situation are listed and reversed, and random words or pictures, where unrelated words or pictures are used to generate different ideas about a situation. More information about these techniques can be found in the creative thinking texts mentioned in the 'Further reading' section of this chapter.

When some ideas have been identified, they can be evaluated. We can focus on the ideas that could provide solutions to the problem(s). This is the **solution-finding** stage, and it is significant that this stage appears so late in the model. Business analysts are often expected to deliver solutions quickly, and yet here we can see that it is important to resist the pressure to develop solutions at too early a stage – there are other aspects that need to be considered first. Also, Isaksen and Treffinger (1985) stress the importance of identifying criteria in order to help evaluate solutions, and this would not be possible without the earlier work. Therefore, it is important to work through the earlier stages as they will help you to develop better, more appropriate solutions that will be more beneficial to the business situation.

The final stage in the model is **acceptance-finding**, which is concerned with managing the implementation of the solution, an aspect that is critical to the success of any change project but often fraught with difficulty. Chapter 12 considers how a robust business case may be made in order to obtain approval from the business for the recommendations. Chapter 13 examines the area of managing the implementation of change and hence the acceptance by the organization of the new working practices.

THE PROCESS MODEL

One of the aspects that make business analysis work so interesting is the range and nature of business analysis projects. The business systems under consideration can be very varied. For a particular project, business analysts may need to apply several techniques and analyse a number of different views. Sometimes the project may be to investigate a problematic part of the organization and produce outline recommendations for ways

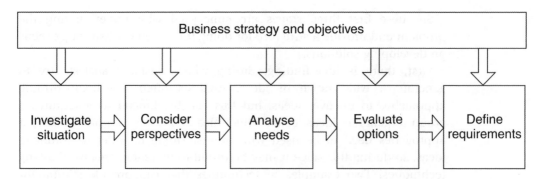

FIGURE 4.2 *The business analysis process model*

forward. Other projects may require the business analyst to analyse and document specific system requirements. So the challenge faced in developing a process model is to offer something that is sufficiently flexible while providing a framework that will help people to carry out their work. Our process model (Figure 4.2) is intended to provide this help.

The process model sets out the key stages for a business analysis project, with each stage representing the areas that need to be considered. However, it should be noted that although some projects may require a detailed exploration of all of the stages, other projects may focus on a subset of the model and possibly only one stage. One of the most important aspects of a business analysis project is to decide what the focus is and which areas need to be investigated. For example, on some projects the focus may be to explore possible improvements to how part of the organization works. In this case, we might begin by examining all of the current working practices, including the staffing and job roles, and the work may focus on analysing and evaluating the options for the future business system. Another project may focus on the IT system needs, and although understanding the situation and all of the stakeholder perspectives is important, the potential for the use of IT to improve the business system will dominate the analysis. The rest of this chapter describes the stages of this process model.

INVESTIGATING THE SITUATION

This stage is concerned with uncovering issues and problems. The terms of reference for the project, or possibly a more detailed project initiation document, are needed in order to set out the context within which the business analysis work will take place. A key area for the analyst is to clarify the objective of the study and tailor the approach accordingly, often a task that requires a good deal of skill. During the initial period of business analysis work, the analyst may be presented with a statement of 'the problem'; it is important to investigate further in order to determine exactly where the problems lie and not to confuse symptoms of problems with the real issues. It is also vital that the analyst does not make false assumptions or accept all of the information provided without question. Business analysis always requires an appreciation of the business context, particularly the overall business objectives and strategy for the organization or business unit. It is important that these should be available during the investigation stage so that the analysts can understand the business context for the work they have been asked to carry out. Once the analyst has begun to understand the situation, some form of description will be required, first so that there is a record of the results of the investigation so far and second to help other members of the team understand the situation.

Investigation techniques

There are many investigative approaches that business analysts can use, and these are explored in detail in Chapter 5. It is important that you consider the range of possible investigative approaches and choose those that are most appropriate to the work in hand.

The level of detail required during this stage may vary considerably depending on the focus of the business analysis work. If the analyst is trying to gain an overall appreciation of the business area, for example to identify the key stakeholders and acquire an understanding of their views and opinions, and to appreciate the nature of the work and the range of people and skills, then often the techniques used will be those that provide an overall perspective and generalized view; thus, interviewing, observation and workshops would be particularly useful. However, if the work is concerned with eliciting more detailed information such as data requirements or the flow of a business process, then the most appropriate fact-finding techniques are those that focus on the detail such as scenario analysis or prototyping. Much of the information gained here may be subjective and may require more detailed analysis; in this case, techniques such as record-searching or questionnaires may be very useful in order to quantify some of the information put forward.

Documenting business situations

There are a number of useful techniques for documenting the initial investigation of a business system. It is typical that a high-level overview of the situation will be required during the initial investigation, particularly where the issues are complex and originate from different causes. As we mentioned earlier, a rich picture can be very useful in capturing the essence of a situation. An alternative, but similar, approach is the mind map, which also allows for a degree of structuring of the information. These techniques are described in further detail in Chapter 7.

Stage summary

Procedure

(i)   Study background material: project initiation document, terms of reference.

(ii) Carry out initial investigation with key stakeholders.

(iii) Document the results of the investigation using meeting reports plus a diagram such as a rich picture or a mind map.

Inputs

- Terms of reference or project initiation document.
- Business objectives and strategy.

Outputs

- View of the existing business situation, including meeting reports and diagrams such as rich pictures and mind maps.
- List of issues/problems.

Techniques

- Investigation techniques, such as interviewing, observation and workshops.
- Rich pictures from Soft Systems Methodology, developed by Checkland (1981).
- Mind maps (Buzan and Buzan 2000).

CONSIDERING THE PERSPECTIVES

This stage is concerned with analysing stakeholders and their perspectives on the situation. Many stakeholders hold very strong views about why problems exist and what needs to be done to improve the situation. Where some of the issues arise from differences in stakeholders' view, it is vital that they are explored and, where possible, taken into account when making recommendations for the way forward.

Stakeholder identification and analysis

Every business situation will affect a range of individuals. In this group there will be varying levels and types of impact. Some stakeholders may be affected directly by any recommendations and may hold strong views on how the systems and working practices should be changed. Other stakeholders may be affected only indirectly and, whilst having opinions, may be less concerned about the nature of the new system. The range of possible stakeholders and mechanisms for stakeholder analysis and management are discussed in detail in Chapter 6.

Stakeholder perspectives

Stakeholders often have different views on what is important about a business system and the improvements that are needed. These views are often contradictory and can lead to hidden agendas, conflicts and inconsistent priorities. As business analysts, it is important that we are aware of the potential for such conflicts and are alert to situations where these might arise. We can often detect where the different stakeholder conflicts might originate by considering the underlying set of values and beliefs of the stakeholders. For example, we might reflect on what an individual stakeholder considers to be the main focus of the business system and, critically, why this is the case. Understanding these values and beliefs allows the analyst to approach issues and problems from an informed position and, hence, to have an improved chance of resolving the situation. These different perspectives can be analysed using the CATWOE (customer, actor, transformation, Weltanschauung, owner, environment) approach advocated by Checkland (1981), as discussed fully in Chapter 7.

Business activity modelling

The stakeholder perspectives can be analysed further by considering the business activities that would be required in order to fulfil a particular perspective. This approach, originally developed by Checkland (1981) and extended by Wilson (1992), allows analysts to build a conceptual model of a business system envisaged by a particular stakeholder. For example, where a manager believes a training organization should focus on quality, then there would be an emphasis on activities such as:

- the development of highly skilled staff;
- the introduction of customer-focused processes;
- monitoring of customer satisfaction levels.

An alternative view could be that the focus should be on 'no-frills' training. In this system, the emphasis would be on the following activities:

- keeping costs low;
- monitoring the number of attendees at events.

This approach allows business analysts to consider where the priorities lie and what the focus of the new, improved business system should be. One stakeholder's view may take precedence over the others, or several models may be synthesized in order to provide an agreed business activity model. The business activity modelling technique is explained further in Chapter 7.

Stage summary

Objectives

The objective of this stage is to take stock of the range of stakeholder perspectives about the business system under investigation. These perspectives may then be analysed in order to uncover stakeholder values and beliefs and developed into business activity models. However, where there is a narrow remit for the business analysis work, for example if you are concerned primarily with improving a particular process, then although it will be important to identify and manage the stakeholders, consideration of the entire business system may be beyond the scope of the work.

Procedure

(i)   Identify key stakeholders whose perspectives are important to the business analysis project.

(ii) Investigate the values, beliefs and priorities of the key stakeholders.

(iii) Develop and analyse the stakeholder perspectives.

(iv) Build conceptual models of activities in order to fulfil the stakeholder perspectives.

(v)   Synthesize conceptual models into one view of the desired business system.

Inputs

- Terms of reference or project initiation document.
- Business objectives and strategy.
- View of the existing business system.

Outputs

- Stakeholder perspectives.
- Business activity models of desired systems.
- Agreed business activity model.

Techniques

- Investigation techniques.
- Analysis of stakeholder perspectives (possibly CATWOE from Soft Systems Methodology) (Checkland 1981).
- Business activity modelling (after Checkland 1981 and Wilson 1992).

ANALYSING THE NEEDS

The focus of this stage is to identify where improvements can be made to the business system. The approach used is known as 'gap analysis', whereby a current or 'as-is' view is compared with a desired future or 'to-be' system. This method contrasts with the traditional more systematic approach to business or systems improvement, where new features are added to an existing set of procedures or an IT system. With gap analysis, the emphasis is on understanding where we want to be and, by looking at where we are now, identifying what needs to change in order to take us there.

Analysing activities

If we have developed a business activity model from a stakeholder perspective, this can be used to carry out a detailed analysis of the desired business system by examining each activity in turn. This analysis will allow us to identify where there are issues that need to be addressed in any solution that we recommend. As the model provides a conceptual picture of the desired business activities, it allows the business analyst to see where the current business system is lacking. When examining the model, the range and extent of the gaps found will vary from activity to activity. Some activities may be in place and operating satisfactorily, but others may be inadequate in the current business system and some may not exist at all. There may be good support for the activity from the organization's information systems, or support may be poor and in need of improvement. Identifying the gaps at this level will help us to determine the potential for change to the business system and the degree to which this is required.

Analysing business processes

Another approach to identifying opportunities for improvement is to consider the business processes carried out within the business system. Whereas the activities modelled on the business activity model show what needs to be included within the desired business system, the business process models allow us to consider how the work is carried out. A business process begins with a trigger, which is sometimes called a business event, and concludes when the goal of the process has been achieved. This view of the business situation cuts across departments and job roles in order to show a more results-oriented view that is focused on meeting customer needs. In overview, the approach is to model the current business process and then to consider possible changes to the process before designing the desired process. Hence, we develop a current or 'as-is' model that provides a basis for developing the required or 'to-be' model. When redesigning a process, we can look for small changes that affect one or two process steps or we might decide to design a completely new process. The business process modelling technique is explored in further detail in Chapter 8.

Stage summary

Objectives

To explore the differences between the current and desired situation, and to identify opportunities for business change by analysing these differences or gaps.

Procedure

(i)   Examine the activities on the business activity model.

(ii) Consider how well each activity is carried out in the current business system and how well it is supported by the organization's information systems.

(iii) Identify the key business events to be handled within the business system and develop 'as-is' process models for the key business events.

(iv) Develop 'to-be' process models for the key business events.

(v)   Analyse the gaps between the existing and the desired situation. Use these as a basis for identifying potential business system improvements.

Inputs

- Agreed business activity model.
- View of the existing business system.
- Business objectives and strategy.

Outputs

- Analysis of activities.
- 'As-is' and 'to-be' process models.
- List of potential improvements to the business system.

Techniques

- Business process modelling.
- Activity analysis.

EVALUATING THE OPTIONS

This stage is concerned with examining the potential improvements identified so far, developing some business options, and evaluating those for acceptability and feasibility. The analysis of the gaps between the existing and desired systems will have produced some ideas for improvements; the work now is to develop these ideas into business potential. These options may include options for changes in a number of areas; for example, they may change the business processes, the job roles, the management structure or the IT systems. At this point, the changes are likely to be defined in outline only but in sufficient detail so that a business case may be developed to support the recommendations and provide a basis for decision-making. Once the work to define the changed areas begins in earnest, there may be a need for further consideration of options. For example, where changes are required to an IT system, this may be agreed in principle at this stage but it is likely that the detailed requirements will need to be evaluated and the business case revisited at a later date.

Identifying potential options

The first step is to identify possible options by considering where improvements might be made and which would result in the greatest potential benefits. Once a number of options have been identified, these can be reduced to a shortlist of options to be developed further. The business objectives and strategy are considered as part of the development and evaluation of options as they must be supported by any changes.

Assessing feasibility

All of the options that are to be considered in detail need to be evaluated for business, technical and financial feasibility. In addition, aspects such as the impact of options on the organization and the risks that may be associated with an option need to be considered, as they will affect the acceptability of the option. Impacts and risks may give rise to additional costs that need to be fed into the cost/benefit analysis for the option. Chapter 12 explores these aspects of evaluation in further detail. Consideration of the business objectives and strategy should also form part of this work, because any new business system will need to be aligned with the strategy and support delivery of the business objectives.

Stage summary

Objectives

The objective of this stage is to collect together the range of potential changes into packages of improvement actions. These packages form the basis for developing a set of options, which are then developed and documented in further detail. They are then presented to business managers for consideration.

Procedure

(i)   Identify range of business options.

(ii) Explore acceptability of options and reduce to a shortlist.

(iii) Develop and document each option in detail. In particular, consider the business, technical and financial feasibility of each option.

(iv) Develop the business case, including presenting options and recommendations to business managers.

Inputs

- Project initiation document/terms of reference.
- Business objectives and strategy.
- List of potential improvements to the business system.

Outputs

- Shortlist of business options.
- Business case, including options, feasibility assessment and recommendations.

Techniques

- Business options identification.
- Cost/benefit analysis.
- Impact analysis.
- Risk analysis.

DEFINING THE REQUIREMENTS

This stage is concerned with gathering and documenting the requirements for changes to the business system. These changes may be to any or all of the three aspects of a business system described in Chapter 1: the processes and supporting IT systems, the people or the organization. Where the changes are to the business processes, the process modelling technique described in Chapter 8 should be used in order to define how the new processes should look. If the recommendations include the implementation of redesigned processes, then this is likely to require changes to the structure of the organization and the job roles, plus development of staff skills. It is sometimes the case that the improvements to the business system can be made simply through changes such as improved job definitions or additional training for the staff. However, more extensive change is usually required, for example to the business processes, and it is likely that this will require enhancements to existing IT systems or even the introduction of a new IT system. Business analysts have a responsibility to define the requirements comprehensively and accurately, as their documentation will form the basis for the development of the system. If the requirements are not documented clearly, then this is likely to cause problems not only during the development of the system but also once the system has been implemented. Business analysts should ensure that requirements are related directly to business needs and will support business objectives.

Requirements engineering

The requirements engineering approach has been developed as a response to the lack of rigour often found in requirements documentation. Requirements engineering proposes a framework to help analysts improve their requirements work by highlighting the need for proactive analysis, organization, documentation and management of stated requirements. Chapter 9 provides an overview of requirements engineering.

Modelling IT systems

There are many modelling techniques available to business analysts. These techniques originated mainly from systems analysis and design approaches such as UML. Each modelling technique provides insight into a particular aspect of the IT system. For example, techniques such as object class modelling and entity relationship modelling provide a clear and unambiguous means of documenting the system data. You will find such techniques extremely useful when exploring requirements, as they help to generate additional questions. Building models and comparing different models of a system will also uncover omissions, errors and inconsistencies. Chapter 10 provides an overview of some of the more popular modelling techniques for business analysts. There are many books devoted to explaining systems modelling techniques in detail, some of which are included in the list of further reading in Chapter 10.

Stage summary

Objectives

The objective of this stage is to produce definitions for the changes to the business system. This is likely to include models of new processes and a documented set of requirements for the IT system. New job definitions and organizational structures may also be required. The IT requirements should be documented in a standard format, which should include a means of tracing the requirement from its origin through to resolution. Modelling techniques may be used to represent the requirements diagrammatically and hence improve the rigour of the requirements definition.

Procedure

(i) Document the required changes to the business system, including, as appropriate:
– business process models for the new processes;
– changes to the organizational structure necessitated by the new processes;
– new job roles and training needs in line with the requirements of the new processes;
– requirements documentation for the new or enhanced IT system.

(ii) Where the IT requirements are to be documented:
– elicit and analyse business requirements for the IT system;
– document and manage the IT requirements;
– validate the documented requirements.

Inputs

- Selected option for revised business system.
- Business objectives and strategy.
- Terms of reference/project initiation document.

Outputs

- 'To-be' process models.
- Job definitions.
- Training specifications.
- Revised organizational structure.
- Validated requirements document including:
  – requirements catalogue;
  – models of system requirements.

Techniques

- Business process modelling.
- Investigation techniques.
- Requirements elicitation, analysis and validation.
- Requirements documentation and management.
- IT systems modelling techniques.

SUMMARY

Business analysis projects are usually concerned with improving the working practices within business systems. This may involve changes to a range of aspects that form the business system, including staff capability, business processes or the supporting information technology systems. The process model for business analysis is intended to assist you in deciding how to begin and structure your business analysis work. The model also includes references to some of the techniques in popular use and identifies when these techniques may be particularly useful.

The implementation of business changes poses major challenges for organizations. The business analyst often plays a key role in business change projects and has to be aware of, and deal with, a range and variety of issues that may arise. The final chapter in this book, Chapter 13 'Managing business change', provides some techniques and insights to help you with this work.

REFERENCES

Buzan, T. and Buzan, B. (2000) *The Mind Map Book*. BBC Books, London.

Checkland, P. (1981) *Systems Thinking, Systems Practice*. John Wiley & Sons, Chichester.

Isaksen, S.G. and Treffinger, D.J. (1985) *Creative Problem Solving: The Basic Course*. Bearly, Buffalo, NY.

Wilson, B. (1992) *Systems, Concepts, Methodologies and Applications*. John Wiley & Sons, Chichester.

FURTHER READING

Arlow, J. and Neustadt, I. (2002) *UML and the Unified Process*. Addison-Wesley, Boston, MA.

de Bono, E. (1990) *Six Thinking Hats*. Penguin Books, London.

Burlton, R. (2001) *Business Process Management: Profiting from Process*. Sams Publishing, Indianapolis, IN.

Harmon, P. (2003) *Business Process Change*. Morgan Kaufmann, Boston, MA.

Holt, J. (2005) *Business Process Modelling*. British Computer Society, Swindon.

Kotonya, G. and Sommerville, I. (1998) *Requirements Engineering*. John Wiley & Sons, Chichester.

McFadzean, E.S. (1998) *Creativity Tool Box: A Practical Guide for Facilitating Creative Problem Solving Sessions*. Henley Management College, Henley-on-Thames.

Rummler, G.A. and Brache, A.P. (1990) *Improving Performance: How to Manage the White Space on the Organization Chart*. Jossey Bass Wiley, San Francisco, CA.

Skidmore, S. and Eva, M. (2004) *Introducing Systems Development*. Palgrave Macmillan, Basingstoke.

Yeates, D. and Wakefield, T. (2004) *Systems Analysis and Design*. FT Prentice Hall, Harlow.

5 Investigation techniques

DEBRA PAUL AND MALCOLM EVA

INTRODUCTION

There is a range of techniques that may be used by business analysts to investigate business situations and elicit requirements. The two most commonly used techniques are interviewing and workshops, but these are usually supplemented by other techniques, such as observation and scenarios. This is particularly the case when detailed investigations or quantitative data are required.

INTERVIEWS

The interview is a key tool in the business analyst's toolkit. A well-run interview can be vital in achieving a number of objectives, including:

- making an initial contact with key stakeholders and establishing a basis for the business analysis work;
- building and developing rapport with different business users and managers;
- acquiring a range of information about the business situation, including any personal issues and problems.

Interviews often take place on a one-to-one basis, which is one reason why they can be invaluable in obtaining personal concerns. They tend to focus on the views of an individual and provide an environment in which the interviewee has the opportunity to discuss his or her concerns and feels that he or she is given individual attention. As a result, interviewing can be rather time-consuming. The interviewer has a responsibility to ensure that the interviewee's time is not wasted, the required information is acquired and a good degree of understanding is achieved.

The following three areas are considered during interviews:

- current functions that need to be fulfilled in any new business system;
- problems with the current operations that need to be addressed;
- new features required from the new business system.

The last point can be the hardest part of an interview, as we are asking business users to think beyond their experience. They may offer vaguely worded suggestions, and the skill of the interviewer is needed in order to draw out more detailed information.

Advantages and disadvantages of interviewing

The first benefit of conducting an interview is that it gives an opportunity to build a relationship with the users or clients. Whether we are helping the business to improve operations or replace a legacy of IT systems, it is critical that we understand the perspectives of the people involved with the business system. This means that we need to appreciate what they do, their concerns and what they want from any new processes or systems. For their part, the users need to have confidence in the analysts, and to know that we are aware of their concerns, are professional, and are not leaping to a design that overlooks the user's own needs and worries. Spending time to form good relationships early on in the project will increase the opportunities to understand the context and details of the business users' concerns and needs.

The second major benefit is that the interview can yield important information. The focus of the information will vary depending on the needs of the project, but usually it will include details about the current operations, including difficulties in carrying out the work, and will help with the identification of requirements for the new business system.

Additional advantages of interviews include the following:

- opportunity to understand different viewpoints and attitudes across the user group;
- opportunity to investigate new areas that arise;
- collection of examples of documents, forms and reports that the clients use;
- appreciation of political factors that may occur;
- study of the environment in which the new system will operate.

Although interviewing is an effective technique, there are some disadvantages. Interviews take time and can be an expensive approach, particularly if the business users are dispersed around the country. Interviews take up the interviewees' time, and they may try to hurry the interview or resent the time that it takes. It is also important to realize that the information provided during interviews may be only the opinion from an interviewee's perspective and may need to be confirmed by quantitative data before any firm conclusions are drawn.

Preparation for interviewing

The interviewing process is improved greatly when the interviewer has prepared thoroughly, as this saves a lot of time by avoiding unnecessary explanations and demonstrates interest and professionalism.

The classic structure of Who?, Why?, What?, When? and Where? provides an excellent framework for preparing for interviews.

- **Who?** This involves identifying the stakeholders you will interview and considering the order in which they will be interviewed. We usually begin with the more senior stakeholders, as this helps us to understand the context for the problem before moving to the details, so it is useful to interview someone who can provide an overview. A senior person is also able to identify the key people to interview and make any necessary introductions.

- **Why?** This involves considering why a particular interviewee is to be interviewed and the place of the interviewee in the organization.
- **What?** This involves considering the information that could be provided by this interviewee and the areas you might explore during the interview.
- **When and where?** These involve considering the venue, timing and duration of the interview. Typically, the interviewee will dictate the exact timing and duration, as this will depend upon availability. Limiting each interview to a maximum length of one hour is a good idea for the following reasons:
    - Almost certainly, interviewees will be busy and will have trouble finding slots of more than an hour in their diaries.
    - It is difficult to concentrate for more than an hour, and thus very long interviews are often unproductive.
    - You have to write up your notes afterwards – the longer the interview, the harder this is and the more likely you are to forget some vital point.

Conducting the interview

It is important to structure interviews if the maximum amount of information is to be elicited. The basic structure comprises introduction, body of interview and close (Figure 5.1).

The introduction

In addition to making personal introductions, it is also important that the analyst makes sure that the interviewee understands the purpose of the project in general and the interview in particular. Ideally the interviewee should know this purpose, but we cannot assume this – explaining the context helps to put the interviewee at ease and will help them to provide

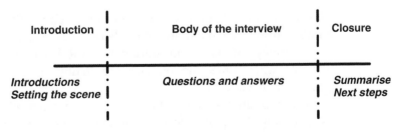

FIGURE 5.1 *Structure of an interview*

the relevant information. It is also useful to make sure that the interviewee has received the agenda and to clarify any points that they wish to raise.

Body of the interview

The main part of the interview is where the facts and issues are uncovered. It is useful to think about how you are going to structure this part. A good approach is to begin by obtaining a context for the information that this interviewee can provide. Once you have a context, you can structure the interview by examining each area separately and in detail. This will enable you to consider the issues, and the impact of those issues, in each area and to uncover any specific problems and requirements.

It is essential to take notes during the interview. Even if you have an excellent memory, you will not remember everything discussed during the interview. A good way of taking notes can be to draw a diagram, such as simple flowchart or mind map.

Closure

It is equally important to formally close the interview. The analyst should:

- summarize the points covered and the actions agreed;
- explain what happens next, both following the interview and beyond that in the project. You will usually want to advise the interviewee that you will send them a copy of the written-up notes so that they can check for any errors;
- ask the interviewee how any further contact should be made, as this will help if any additional information or clarifications are required.

Following up the interview

It is always a good idea to write up the notes of the interview as soon as possible, ideally straight away and if not then, the next day. If it is not possible to write up the notes immediately, you will find the task easier if you read through the notes after the interview and extend them where they are unclear.

WORKSHOPS

Workshops provide an excellent forum in which issues can be discussed, conflicts resolved and requirements elicited. As a result, workshops may be used at many different points during the project. Workshops are especially valuable when time and budgets are tightly constrained and several viewpoints need to be canvassed.

Workshops are also a useful forum for carrying out other activities, such as analysing the quality of a requirements set before it is documented formally. This aspect is explored further in Chapter 9.

Advantages and disadvantages of workshops

Many advantages are claimed for using workshops including the ability to:

- gain a broad view of the area under investigation: having a group of stakeholders in one room will allow the analyst to gain a more complete understanding of the issues and problems;

- increase speed and productivity: it is much quicker to have one meeting with a group of people than to interview them one by one;

- obtain buy-in and acceptance for the project;

- gain a consensus view or group agreement: if all the stakeholders are involved in the decision-making process, then the chance of them taking ownership of the results is improved.

However, these advantages are possible only if a workshop is well organized and run. The means of achieving this are discussed in the rest of this section.

Although workshops are extremely valuable, there are some disadvantages to using them, including the following:

- Workshops can be time-consuming to organize, for example it is not always easy to get all the necessary people together at the same time.

- It can be difficult to get all of the participants with the required level of authority, which may mean that decisions are reversed after the workshop.

Preparing for the workshop

The success or failure of a workshop session depends in large part upon the preparatory work done by the facilitator and the business sponsor for the workshop. They should spend time before the event planning the following areas:

- **Objective of the workshop:** this has to be an objective that can be achieved within the time constraints of the workshop. If this is a sizeable objective, then the duration of the workshop will need to reflect this, possibly running to several days. In this case, the objective should be broken down into sub-objectives, each of which is the subject of an individual workshop session. For example, a two-day workshop may be broken into four sessions, each of which is focused upon a particular sub-objective.

- **Stakeholders to be invited to participate in the workshop:** it is important that all stakeholders interested in the objective should be invited to attend or be represented. It is the facilitator's responsibility to ensure that all stakeholders are able to contribute, which may mean using breakout groups or other techniques in order to help this happen.

- **Interests of each participant:** the facilitator should carry out research in order to appreciate each participant's concerns and viewpoints.
- **Structure of the workshop and techniques to be used:** these need to be geared towards achieving the defined objective and should take into account the needs of the participants. For example, a standard brainstorming session may not work very well with a group of people who have never met before.
- **Arranging a suitable venue:** this may be within the organization's building, but it is sometimes useful to use a neutral venue, particularly if the issues to be discussed are contentious.

Facilitating the workshop

The workshop should start with a discussion of the objective and endeavouring to secure the participants' buy-in. It is often helpful here to get the business sponsor to open the workshop and hence show their commitment to the process. During the workshop, the facilitator needs to ensure that the issues are discussed, views are aired and progress is made towards achieving the stated objective. The discussion may range widely, but the facilitator needs to ensure that it does not go completely off the track and that everyone has an opportunity to express his or her concerns and opinions. A record needs to be kept of the key points emerging from the discussion. This is often done by the facilitator keeping a record on the flipchart, but sometimes someone else takes the role of scribe during the workshop. At the end of the workshop, the facilitator needs to summarize the key points and actions. Each action should be assigned to an owner and allocated a timescale for completion.

Techniques

There are two main categories of technique required for a workshop, techniques for discovery and techniques for documentation (Figure 5.2).

Discovery techniques are those that help the facilitator to elicit information and views from the participants. It is vital that the facilitator considers which technique would be most suitable for a particular situation and group of participants. Examples of useful techniques are:

- brainstorming (also known as idea-storming), where the participants are asked to call out ideas, all of which are listed, and the evaluation of the ideas is suspended until everyone has finished;
- round-robin discussions, where the workshop participants are asked for their ideas in turn;
- brainwriting or exercises using Post-it notes, where participants write down ideas, which are then collated and grouped;

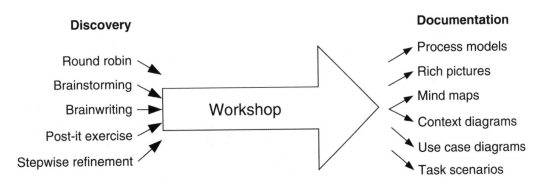

FIGURE 5.2 *Workshop techniques*

- stepwise refinement, where we take a statement or idea and keep asking 'Why?' to every answer given until we think we have got to the heart of a problem, idea or situation.

A wide variety of documentation techniques are suitable for use in a workshop. Several useful diagrammatic techniques are explored during the course of this book, including process models, use case diagrams, rich pictures and mind maps. These techniques help the business users to visualize the area under discussion. Text-based documentation may also be required to keep records of agreed action points or issues for further discussion. Another approach is to structure the discussion using recognized organizational analysis techniques. For example, if the workshop is concerned with the implementation of the business strategy, then a higher-level approach, such as critical success factor (CSF) analysis can be employed. This will begin by agreeing the CSFs for the part of the organization under discussion and cascade down to consider the information requirements needed to measure how each CSF is achieved. This can then lead to the definition of more detailed requirements in areas such as data capture and management reporting.

Following the workshop

After the workshop, any key points and actions are written up and sent to the relevant participants and stakeholders. This should be done as quickly as possible, because this will help to keep up the momentum and highlight the need for quick action.

OBSERVATION

Observing the workplace and the staff members carrying out their work is very useful in obtaining information about the business environment and the work practices. There are several different approaches to observation, depending on the level and focus of interest. If you want to observe a unionized worksite, you must ensure that approval is gained from the trade union representatives and that the various protocols are observed.

Advantages and disadvantages of observation

The views of the stakeholders involved in a project may have been sought during interviews, but in order to really obtain a feel for the situation there is no substitute for seeing the workplace and practices. Apart from collecting actual facts, it is also possible to clarify areas of tacit information and hence increase your understanding. This has two advantages:

- You will have a much better understanding of the problems and difficulties faced by the business users.
- It will help you to devise workable solutions that are more likely to be acceptable to the business.

Conversely, being observed can be rather unnerving and the old saying 'you change what you observe' needs to be factored into your approach and findings.

Formal observation

Formal observation involves watching specific tasks being performed. There is a danger here of being shown just the 'front story' without any of the everyday variances, but it is still a useful tool in understanding the environment. It is important that the staff members being observed are prepared beforehand and that they understand that you are watching them in order to understand the tasks, not, as many will fear, that you are assessing their own competence and performance. Self-consciousness can influence how staff members perform, and a lack of preparation will serve to accentuate this problem. If staff members perceive you as having been sent by management, then they are more likely to perform tasks according to the rulebook, rather than how, perhaps, they have evolved over time.

Protocol analysis

Protocol analysis is simply getting the users to perform a task and describe each step as they perform it. Protocol analysis is a way of eliciting skills that cannot be expressed in words alone. This is similar to how student drivers are taught on a first lesson: rather than being lectured in a classroom on how to begin moving a car into traffic and then trying it for real, the instructor will perform the task for them, talking them through each gear change, check of the mirrors and so on.

Shadowing

Shadowing involves following a user for a period such as one or two days in order to find out what a particular job entails. This is a powerful way of understanding a particular user role. Asking for explanations of the workflow, and how the work is performed, is a good way of clarifying some of the taken-for-granted aspects. The longer the analyst spends shadowing a user, the better the rapport they can build over the time and the better chance there is of capturing the 'back story' aspects that may not be uncovered on a single 45 minute interview. Shadowing key staff members is a useful precursor to a more structured requirements exercise because it provides a visual context for processes described in subsequent interviews or workshops. (See Chapter 9 for explanations of 'front story', 'back story' and 'taken for granted'.)

Office decor						
Cool colour walls Fluorescent lights No decoration	1	2	3	4	5	Warm colour walls Incandescent lights Framed graphics
Signs of brought-in information						
No signs of outside information	1	2	3	4	5	Four or more journals/ newspapers
Visible information-processing aids						
No calculators or PCs visible	1	2	3	4	5	Calculator/PCs accessible without leaving the chair
No storage cabinet in office or sub-office	1	2	3	4	5	Four or more file cabinets or shelves
Decision-maker's space versus visitor's space						
Desk placed against wall	1	2	3	4	5	Desk used as barrier, with little visitor space
Decision-maker's clothing style						
Casual or sports-style clothes	1	2	3	4	5	Conservative business dress
Accessibility of decision-maker						
Office located on separate floor from subordinates	1	2	3	4	5	Office within 50 feet of subordinates

Adapted from Kendall and Kendall (2002), p.188.

FIGURE 5.3 *STROBE*

STROBE

STROBE stands for STRuctured Observation of the Business Environment. It comes from the work of two US systems analysts, Kenneth and Julie Kendall. STROBE represents a checklist approach to observation and is used to appraise a working environment. It is intended to be quick and fairly informal and is probably carried out as you enter a new building to meet an interviewee for the first time. As the acronym implies, it involves moving your eyes back and forth to spot those elements you have decided on before, so that as you write your interview notes later you can also incorporate the STROBE findings. Its focus is on the cultural and political climate in the workplace. The scale in Figure 5.3 is taken from Kendall and Kendall's (2002) work and shows the typical elements in the workplace that you might wish to note. The five-point scale in the answers gives semi-objective guidance on how to rate your observations. You can, of course, apply this approach to any observation exercise, such as an area that does not yield easily to a one-to-one interview.

Ethnographic studies

Ethnographic study is, sadly, beyond the budget of most developments, but it would yield high returns if it could be achieved. It comes from the discipline of anthropology and involves simply spending an extended period of time – six months, say – in the target environment so that the user community sees the analyst as a fly on the wall rather than the agent of change and behaves more naturally and authentically. The only time when an ethnographic study is likely to be approved is when trying to capture rules for an expert system. This cannot be done in one or two sessions but needs extended interaction with the experts as they perform their decision-making.

SCENARIOS

Scenario analysis is essentially telling the story of a task or transaction. Its value is that it helps a user who is uncertain about what is needed from a new system to visualize it more clearly. Scenarios are also useful when analysing or redesigning business processes. A scenario will trace the course of a transaction from an initial business trigger through each of the steps needed to achieve a successful outcome. Pre-conditions for the scenario are defined. These are characteristics of the business or IT system that must be true in order for the scenario to begin. Post-conditions, the characteristics that must be true following the conclusion of the scenario, are also defined. One of the key strengths of scenarios is that they provide a framework for discovering alternative paths that may be followed to complete the transaction. Scenarios are extremely useful in requirements elicitation and analysis because they help you to discuss real-life situations, including the exceptional circumstances, with the users. They are also used to help with risk analysis; this is done through the use of what Alexander (Alexander and Maiden 2004) calls 'misuse cases'.

Advantages and disadvantages of scenarios

Scenarios offer significant advantages to the analyst:

- They force the user to include every step, so that no elements are taken for granted and the problem of tacit knowledge is addressed.
- By helping the user to visualize all contingencies, beginning at an overview level, and refining this into further detail, they help to cope with the uncertainty about future systems.
- A workshop group refining a scenario will identify those paths that do not suit the corporate culture or that are not congruent with any community of practice involved.
- Requirements that mitigate risk can be identified through 'misuse' cases.
- They provide a tool for preparing test scripts.

The disadvantages of scenarios are that they can be time-consuming to develop and some scenarios can become very complex, particularly where there are several alternative paths. Where this is the case, you will find it easier to analyse the scenarios if each of the alternative paths is considered as a separate scenario.

Figure 5.4 shows an overview approach to developing scenarios. It includes the following steps:

- Identify the task or interaction to be modelled as a scenario, and the trigger or event that causes that interaction to take place.
- Identify the steps that will be carried out during the usual progress of the interaction, and the flow of these steps.

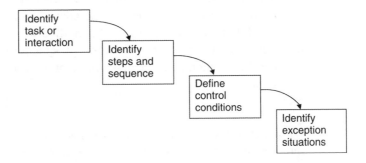

FIGURE 5.4 *Process for developing scenarios*

- Define the control conditions, i.e. the conditions that must be met in order to follow the typical sequence of steps.
- Identify the alternative paths that would be required in order to handle the situations where the control conditions are not met.

This approach establishes a default path for the scenario that assumes no complications and everything running as expected. This path is sometimes known as the 'happy day scenario'. The power of the use of scenarios in elicitation is in breaking down each of the default steps to ask the questions 'What needs to be true in order to continue with this path?' and 'At this point, what might happen instead?' Once the range of possibilities has been uncovered, we should ask the question 'What should we do if this is true?'

If we consider an example scenario where a customer wishes to place an order, then the default steps could be:

(i)   Enter customer reference number.

(ii)   Confirm customer details.

(iii) Record order items.

(iv)   Accept payment.

(v)   Advise customer of delivery date.

For this scenario to flow in the order shown, the control conditions to go from step (i) to step (ii), from step (ii) to step (iii), and so on must be true. For example, the order items recorded in step (iii) must be available for step (iv) to take place. However, if there is insufficient stock, then the next step to be followed would be not step (iv) but an alternative step. For each deviation, there may be several possibilities, such as:

- pending the order until stock arrives;
- allocating a substitute item;
- putting an order straight through to the supplier, with the customer's delivery address on, so the customer will still be satisfied.

All of the possibilities should be explored and documented as alternative paths. These are termed 'extensions' to the default scenario. The example scenario above is described in a generalist abstract manner that some users find difficult to apply to the reality of their work. Another approach is known as a 'concrete scenario', where a specific narrative or story is developed that is then tested against the requirements already identified to find the gaps.

Here is an example of a concrete scenario for a vehicle parts system:

Turpin Coaches calls with an urgent request for 800 type 2 gaskets. They are a highly valued – and valuable – customer. Turpin Coaches tells the clerk that if we cannot satisfy them, they must go elsewhere. The stock records show that there are 150 type 2 gaskets available; 400 were allocated to ZED just 30 minutes previously. The ZED order will not be processed for another two hours. The clerk wishes to amend the ZED order.

After walking through this concrete scenario, we may record additional requirements to those reflected in the 'happy day', such as the ability to prioritize orders and to amend orders already accepted. It can be useful to get the participants of a workshop to create concrete stories like this in order to uncover where all of the possible extensions lie. The analyst may set the ball rolling with a prepared 'happy day' scenario that is then used as the basis for a discussion. All extensions and resultant requirements that are uncovered are then added to the analysis documentation.

Documenting scenarios

A popular approach to documenting scenario descriptions is to develop use case descriptions to support use case diagrams. This technique is part of the UML method and is a textual approach. However, there are a number of graphical methods of documenting a scenario, such as storyboards, activity diagrams, task models and decision tree diagrams.

PROTOTYPING

Prototyping is an important technique for eliciting, analysing, demonstrating and validating requirements. Analysts often complain that the users do not know what they want, often because it is difficult for users to envisage the new system before it is actually built. Prototypes offer a way of showing the user how the new system might work and the ways in which it can be used. If a user is unclear about what they need the system to do for them, then utilizing a prototype often releases the blocks to thinking and can produce a new wave of requirements. Incremental and iterative approaches to systems development, such as the DSDM, use evolutionary prototyping as an integral part of their development lifecycle.

Prototyping involves building simulations of a system in order to review them with the users to increase understanding about the system requirements. Working with prototypes can help the user to visualize the new system and hence give them greater insight into possible requirements. There is a range of approaches to building prototypes. Prototypes may be built using the system development environment so that they exactly mirror the system; alternatively images of the screens and navigations may be built using presentation software packages such as Microsoft PowerPoint, or they may be mock-ups on paper. A quick but effective form of prototyping is to use flipchart sheets, pens and packs of Post-it notes to work with the users to develop paper prototypes. This will enable the users to develop screens, identify navigation paths, define the data they must input or reference, and prepare lists of specified values that they know will apply.

There is a strong link between scenarios and prototyping because scenarios can be used as the basis for developing prototypes that will demonstrate to users how the system will handle the requirements identified in the scenario. In addition to confirming the users' requirements, prototyping can often help the users to identify requirements that they had not considered previously.

Advantages and disadvantages of prototyping

Prototypes are useful for a variety of reasons, including:

- to clarify any uncertainty on the part of the analysts and to confirm to the user that we have understood what they asked for;
- to open the user to new requirements as they understand what the system will be able to do to support their jobs;
- to show users the look and feel of the proposed system and to elicit usability requirements;
- to validate the system requirements and identify any errors;
- to provide the users with a means of assessing the navigation paths and system performance.

Prototyping has a number of hazards, most of which can be avoided by setting clear objectives for the prototyping exercise and managing the users' expectations:

- The prototyping cycle can spin out of control, with endless iterations taking place.
- If the purpose of the exercise has not been explained clearly, then the users may think that when they are happy with the mock-up the system is now complete and ready for use.
- User expectations can be raised unnecessarily by failing to mimic the final appearance of the system or its performance. A system that is on a standalone machine with six dummy data records to search through will be more responsive than a machine that is sharing resources with 1000 other machines on a national network and has over 10,000 records to access. If there is likely to be a delay in the real response time, then it is important that you build that into the prototype.

QUANTITATIVE APPROACHES

Questionnaires

Questionnaires can be useful if we need to get a limited amount of information from a lot of people but interviewing them all would not be practical or cost-effective. However, questionnaires are difficult to use successfully and have to be designed carefully in order to have any chance of success.

The exact design of a questionnaire depends upon its purpose, but there are three main areas to consider:

Heading section

This is where the purpose of the questionnaire is explained and instructions for returning the questionnaire are given.

Classification section

This is where the details about the respondent are held that allow the information to be categorized by predefined analysis criteria, such as age, gender or length of service. If it is decided that the questionnaire should be completed anonymously, perhaps because it asks some controversial questions, then you must make sure that the respondents cannot be identified by other means, otherwise confidence in the process will be lost and you will be unlikely to get a truthful response, if you get one at all.

Data section

This is where the main body of questions is posed. It is vital to think carefully about the phrasing of the questions. They must be unambiguous and, ideally, allow for straightforward answers such as 'yes/no', 'agree/neutral/disagree' or 'excellent/satisfactory/inadequate'. The answer must provide a clear response to the question so that the data can be analysed properly. For example, if we asked 'Have you stopped smoking recently?' and someone answered 'No', then would that tell us that the person:

- is a smoker and has no intention of stopping? or
- has never smoked at all and so has nothing to stop? or
- stopped smoking a year ago but the respondent does not consider that to be 'recently'?

We will need to analyse the results once the questionnaires have been returned. If we are sending out a lot of questionnaires, then we want to be able to build a summary of the answers and draw conclusions without having to do too much interpretation.

Advantages and disadvantages of questionnaires

Questionnaires provide a cost-effective means of acquiring quantitative data from a large, often dispersed, group of people.

The key drawback with using questionnaires is that people will find many good reasons for not replying, such as:

- they accidentally threw it in the bin;
- they were on holiday when it arrived;
- they were very busy when it arrived;

- they didn't realize it was double-sided and so completed only half of it.

A concise, well designed questionnaire will help improve the response rate to a questionnaire survey.

Special-purpose records

This technique involves the business users in keeping a record about a specific issue or task. For example, they could keep a simple five-bar-gate record about how often they need to transfer telephone calls; this could provide the analyst with information about the problems with the business process. There are difficulties with getting people to carry out this type of survey, chief of which is that they forget to record the occurrence at the time and then make up the numbers later. Notwithstanding these problems, it can still be useful sometimes to get people to keep such records, for example to show what happens during their working day or how they spend their time. The main advantages of this approach are that it avoids the problems associated with observation and it is a more effective use of the analyst's time.

If getting people to keep special-purpose records is to be useful, then two important criteria have to be satisfied:

- The people undertaking the recording must be induced to buy in to the exercise. This may be by persuading them of the need or benefits, but another possibility is that they are instructed to do this by their manager.

- The survey must be realistic about what people can reasonably be expected to record.

Activity sampling

This is a rather more quantitative form of observation and can be used when it is necessary to know how people spend their time, for example how much time is spent on invoicing? How much on reconciling payments? How much on sorting out queries?

One way to find out how people spend their time would be to get them to complete a special-purpose record, but sometimes the results need to have a guaranteed level of accuracy, for example if they are to be used to build a business case. An activity-sampling exercise is carried out in five steps:

(i) Identify the activities to be recorded. This list should include a 'not working' activity.

(ii) Decide on the frequency and timings, i.e. when and how often you will record the activities being undertaken.

(iii) Visit the study group at the times agreed upon and record what each group member is doing.

(iv)   Record the results.

(v)   After a set period, analyse the results.

The results from an activity-sampling exercise provide you with quantifiable data about the number of times an activity is carried out per day by the group studied. By analysing that figure against other data, such as the total amount of time available, you are able to calculate the total length of time spent on that activity and the average time one occurrence of the activity will take. This information can be useful when developing business cases and evaluating proposed solutions. Also, it will raise other questions, such as 'Is the average time reasonable for this task, or does it indicate a problem somewhere else in the process?'

Document analysis

Document analysis involves reviewing samples of documents in order to uncover information about an organization, process or system. For each document, we should analyse:

- how the document is completed;
- who uses it;
- when it is used;
- how many are used or produced;
- how long the document is retained by the organization, and in what form;
- details of the information shown on the document.

Document analysis is useful to supplement other techniques such as interviewing, workshops and observation. Samples of the completed documents or system printouts help to provide a clearer picture of how the organization works in that area and the key items of information used to carry out the work.

SUMMARY

Any business analysis project will inevitably include investigating business situations or system requirements. To do this well, the business analyst has to acquire a toolkit consisting of a range of investigative techniques. A key element of this toolkit is the ability to appreciate when particular techniques will be appropriate and the skill to apply them effectively.

REFERENCES

Alexander, I. and Maiden, N. (2004) *Scenarios, Stories and Use Cases.* John Wiley & Sons, Chichester.

Kendall, J.E. and Kendall, K.E. (2002) *Systems Analysis and Design*, 5th edn. Prentice Hall, Upper Saddle River, NJ.

FURTHER READING

Kotonya, G. and Sommerville, I. (1998) *Requirements Engineering*. John Wiley & Sons, Chichester.

Skidmore, S. and Eva, M. (2004) *Introducing Systems Development*. Palgrave Macmillan, Basingstoke.

Stapleton, J. (2003) *DSDM: The Method in Practice*. Addison-Wesley, Harlow.

Tudor, D.J. and Tudor, I.J. (2002) *The DSDM Student Workbook*. Galatea Training Services, Knutsford.

Yeates, D. and Wakefield, T. (2004) *Systems Analysis and Design*. FT Prentice Hall, Harlow.

6 Stakeholder analysis and management

JAMES CADLE

INTRODUCTION

Effective stakeholder management is absolutely crucial to the success of any business analysis project. It is vital to know who the stakeholders are and what they expect from the project and delivered solution if they are to remain involved and supportive of the undertaking. One of the major reasons why business analysis projects do not succeed – or do not succeed fully – is poor stakeholder management: the project team does not recognize the importance, or even the existence, of a key stakeholder and the team then finds that its plans are constantly frustrated. On the other hand, if the right stakeholders are identified and managed properly, most obstacles can be cleared from the path. In fact, much of the groundwork for stakeholder management takes place before the business analysis project proper begins – during project inception and initiation – and that work must be revisited constantly during the project itself. The basic steps involved are illustrated in Figure 6.1.

The main responsibility for stakeholder management rests, of course, with the project manager, although in a business analysis project this role may actually be assumed by one of the analysts. However, all team members have important roles to play, in identifying stakeholders, in helping to understand their needs and in helping to manage their expectations from the project.

STAKEHOLDER CATEGORIES AND IDENTIFICATION

As Figure 6.1 illustrates, the first step in stakeholder management involves finding out who the stakeholders are. A good working definition of a stakeholder is 'anyone who has an interest in, or may be affected by, the issue under consideration'. This means, more or less, anyone affected by the project or who may be in a position to influence it.

Of course, each project will have its own distinctive set of stakeholders, determined by the nature of the project and the environment in which it is taking place. However, we can identify some generic stakeholder categories that may apply to many projects, as illustrated in Figure 6.2.

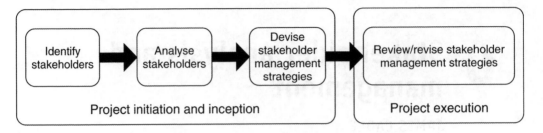

FIGURE 6.1 *Stakeholder management in the project lifecycle*

Customers

These are the people or organizations for whom the organization provides products or services. They are stakeholders because anything the organization does in the way of change has a potential effect on them. The organization must consider how to manage that change most effectively so as not to lose customers that it wishes to retain. It may be useful to subdivide this general category to reveal more detail about the stakeholders, for example:

- large or small;
- regular or occasional;
- wholesale or retail;
- corporate or private;
- commercial or public-sector;
- civilian or military;
- domestic or export.

FIGURE 6.2 *Generic stakeholder categories*

We may even have different categories that we simply label 'good customers' and 'bad customers', however we define these.

Partners

These are the organizations that work with our organization, for example to provide specialist services on our behalf. An example of a partner organization may be an outsourcing company that provides call-centre services.

Suppliers

These provide our organization with the goods and services that we use. Again, we may wish to subdivide them, perhaps as follows:

- major or minor;
- regular or occasional;
- domestic or overseas.

Suppliers are stakeholders because they are interested in the way we do business with them, what we wish to buy, how we want to pay and so on. Many change initiatives have the effect of altering the relationships of organizations with their suppliers; as with the customers, such changes need to be managed carefully in order to make sure that they achieve positive and mutually beneficial results.

Competitors

Competitors vie with us for the business of our customers. Competitors therefore have a keen interest in changes made by our organization. We have to consider what their reactions might be and whether they might try, for instance, to block our initiative or to produce some sort of counter-proposal.

Regulators

Many organizations are now subject to regulation or inspection, either by statutory bodies such as the Office for Communications (Ofcom) and the Office for Standards in Education (Ofsted) or by professional bodies such as the General Medical Council (GMC) and the Law Society. These regulators will be very interested in making sure that changes proposed by an organization are within the letter and spirit of the rules they enforce.

Owners

For a commercial business, the owners are just that – the people who own it directly. The business may be, in legal terms, a sole trader or partnership, or it could be a limited company, in which case the owners are the shareholders. For public limited companies, the majority of shares are held by institutions such as investment companies and pension funds, and so the managers of these share portfolios become proxy owners.

Employees

The people who work in an organization clearly have an interest in the way it is run and in changes that it makes. In a small firm the employees may be regarded as individual stakeholders in their own right, but in larger concerns the employees are probably best considered as groups. Sometimes, employees belong to trade unions, whose officials therefore become stakeholders too.

Managers

Finally, we have the professional managers of the organization, i.e. those to whom its direction is entrusted. In a large organization, there may be many layers of management, each forming a distinctive stakeholder grouping, for example:

- board-level senior managers;
- middle managers;
- junior managers;
- front-line supervisors.

As with many aspects of stakeholder management, it is an error to assume that a group such as 'managers' is homogeneous in its views and concerns. Junior managers may well have a very different perspective, and a different set of hopes and fears, compared with those on the board who make the major strategic decisions.

Other stakeholders

Of course, the groups shown in Figure 6.2 are generic and in particular cases there may well be other stakeholders. For example, the insurers of an organization may be interested in any areas that could affect the pattern of risk that is covered. Or perhaps the police force might be interested in the law-and-order implications of some actions. In some organizations, the views of trade unions or staff associations are also significant.

It is important for each project that the identification of stakeholders is as complete as possible, as it will otherwise be impossible to develop and implement effective management strategies for them. It may be useful to conduct some sort of workshop with people knowledgeable about the organization and the proposed project in order to make sure that the coverage of stakeholders is comprehensive.

ANALYSING STAKEHOLDERS

Having identified the stakeholders, the next step is to make an assessment of the weight that should be attached to each. No stakeholder should be ignored completely, but the approach to each will be different depending

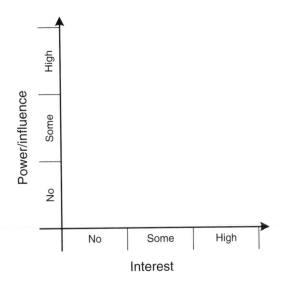

FIGURE 6.3 *Stakeholder power/interest analysis*

on (i) their level of interest in the project and (ii) the amount of power or influence they wield in order to further or obstruct it.

A simple way of analysing stakeholders is to use the power/interest grid illustrated in Figure 6.3. In using this grid, it is important to plot stakeholders where they actually are, not where they should be or perhaps where we would like them to be. We can then explore strategies for managing them in their positions or perhaps for moving them to other positions that might be more advantageous for the success of our project.

STAKEHOLDER MANAGEMENT STRATEGIES

There are, of course, an infinite number of positions that could be taken on the power/interest grid, but it is probably sufficient here to consider the nine basic situations illustrated in Figure 6.4.

No interest and no power/influence

These are stakeholders who have neither a direct interest in the project nor any real power to affect it. For practical purposes, they can be ignored with regard to day-to-day issues on a project, and no special effort needs to be made to 'sell' them its benefits. However, as stakeholders do change positions on the map (see the section on 'Managing Stakeholders' on page 91), it is probably wise to inform them occasionally about what is going on, perhaps through vehicles such as organization newsletters.

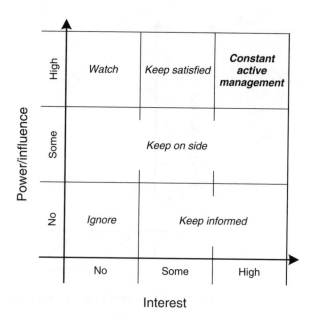

FIGURE 6.4 *Basic stakeholder management strategies*

Some or high interest but no power/influence

These groups can be very difficult to manage effectively because, although they may be affected directly by a change project, they feel powerless to shape its direction in any way. This can result in frustration and a sort of passive resistance to change, which, although overcome by positional power, can lead to delay and less-than-optimal results.

The basic management strategy here is to keep such stakeholders informed of what is going on and, in particular, of the reasons for the proposed change. However, this is a rather passive approach, and in most circumstances more effort has to be devoted to 'selling' the project. This can best be done by being as honest as possible about the need for change, by highlighting the positive aspects of the change or the negative consequences of not making it and by frequent and focused communication of progress.

No to high interest but some power/influence

This is a rather varied group. It includes some stakeholders such as middle or senior managers who do have some power or influence but who, because their interests are not affected directly, are not very concerned about the direction that a project is taking. Regulators may also fall into this category; they will start to get involved only if some breach of the rules is suspected, at which point they could, in effect, squash an initiative. The group can also include people with more interest in the project but only some power or influence over it.

The best approach with these people is to keep them supportive of the project, possibly by frequent positive communication with them but perhaps also by involving them more with the project. As the old saying has it, it is better to have them inside the glasshouse throwing stones out than outside throwing them in.

No interest but high power/influence

These are probably very senior managers who, for one reason or another, have no direct interest in the project. This may be because it is too small or unimportant for them to bother with or because it is in an area that does not interest them; the group marketing director, for instance, probably will not be concerned about a project to streamline the stationery-purchasing procedures. For many purposes, it might be thought that people in this group can be ignored, but this is a rather risky approach. The marketing director, for instance, may suddenly become very interested in the stationery system if she keeps getting pens that do not work or cannot obtain any adhesive notes for a conference. So, if a situation arises that might cause this group to take a greater interest in the project, we might want to address their needs directly, perhaps via one-to-one meetings, in order to ensure that they do not start to raise concerns or even decide to exert their influence. In some situations we may wish to encourage the increased interest of influential stakeholders, for example if we felt that their support would help achieve the project objectives. Where this is the case, we may need to highlight any aspects of the project that will have a direct impact on the stakeholders' business area; some form of discussion will be required, which, with very influential stakeholders, typically would involve a meeting.

Some interest and high power/influence

These people have some interest in the project – probably an indirect interest, as the project is happening within or affecting their empire – and they have real power. The usual stakeholder management strategy here is to keep them satisfied and, perhaps, to prevent them from taking a more direct (and possibly more obstructive) interest in the project. In other circumstances, the strategy may be precisely the opposite – to get the stakeholder involved more actively in a project. For example, if the finance director of an organization can be persuaded to get positively involved in a project, then he will often be a powerful force for success, since he can make resources available that would otherwise be hard to come by.

High interest and high power/influence

These are the key players, the people who are interested in the project and have the power to make it work – or not. Often, the key players are the managers of the functions involved in a project. Initially, it is important to determine whether individual key stakeholders are positive or negative in their approach to a project. If positive, then their enthusiasm must be sustained, especially during times of difficulty. It is also important to appreciate the concerns and opinions of key stakeholders, and you will need to take these into account when making any recommendations. For example, if one of the key stakeholders has a particular solution in mind, then it is important to know about this as early as possible in order to ensure that, at the very least, the solution is evaluated as one of the options. It is also vital that the key stakeholders understand the progress of the project and why certain decisions have been made. These are the people to whom any final recommendations will be presented and who will have the final say on any decisions. They need to be kept informed at all stages of the project so that none of the recommendations comes as a shock to them.

Those key players who are negatively inclined towards a project can be managed in various ways, depending on the circumstances. By far the best approach is to find some personal benefits for them in the proposed course of action. Or, a more powerful counter-force must be found to outweigh their negative influence. This may mean engaging the interest of someone in one of the high-power areas of the grid.

Individuals and groups of stakeholders

An individual customer may not be of much concern to, say, a big supermarket chain. However, if that customer writes to newspapers, organizes petitions and, perhaps, makes a lot of complaints to trading standards officers, then they can increase their apparent power considerably. A lot of 'people power' can damage even large concerns considerably and force them into major reversals of course. The classic example of this is the mighty Coca-Cola being forced to reintroduce its traditional Coke in the face of a massive worldwide customer revolt against a new formula. Individual employees can be marginalized by an organization, but if those employees are members of a trade union their power is greater. A single civil servant who objects to a policy may be relatively powerless, but if he or she 'blows the whistle' to national newspapers it can cause considerable difficulty.

All of these examples illustrate the dangers of mistaking individual weakness for collective weakness. Stakeholders must be considered not only as individuals but also as potential groups.

Summary of stakeholder management strategies

The basic strategies for stakeholder management are summarized in Figure 6.4. However, individual stakeholders will not fit neatly into one of the nine types, and management approaches must be tailored for each. Also, as we discuss in the next section, stakeholders do not stay in the same place over time, and so the ways in which they are managed must be adapted accordingly.

MANAGING STAKEHOLDERS

Stakeholders' positions on the framework in Figure 6.4 do not remain static during the life of a project. At the most obvious level, a manager may get promoted from being in the high-interest/low-power situation to being both interested and powerful. Alternatively, a manager may lose interest in a project if he or she is promoted into a job with a wider remit. The circumstances of an organization may change, so that, for example, senior managers begin to focus more on IT projects. Or a scandal within a competitor may cause a regulator to take a closer interest in all companies in a sector. This means that stakeholder analysis must be a continuing activity throughout the project and afterwards in order to find out what the stakeholders thought of the final outcome. The project team and project manager should be constantly on the lookout for changes in stakeholders' positions and should be re-evaluating their management strategies accordingly. Once stakeholders' initial positions have been plotted, a plan should be drawn up for what to do with each stakeholder and how to approach it. A one-page assessment can be made for each stakeholder. Alternatively, to be able to see all stakeholders at a glance, set up a spreadsheet with columns with the following headings:

Name of stakeholder

It may also be useful to record the stakeholder's current job title.

Current power/influence

Based on the information in the grid.

Current interest

Based on the information in the grid.

Issues and interests

This is a brief summary of what interests each stakeholder and what we believe each stakeholder's main issues with the project are likely to be.

Current attitude

Here, we need to devise a classification scheme, perhaps using the following descriptions:

- **Champion:** will actively work for the success of the project.
- **Supporter:** in favour of the project but probably will not be very active in promoting it.
- **Neutral:** has expressed no opinion in favour of or against the project.
- **Critic:** not in favour of the project but probably not actively opposed to it.

- **Opponent:** will work actively to disrupt, impede or derail the project.
- **Blocker:** will obstruct progress, maybe for reasons outside of the project itself.

Desired support

This lists what we would ideally like from this stakeholder, perhaps using a simple scale of high, medium or low.

Desired role

We may wish to get this stakeholder actively involved in the project, perhaps as the project sponsor or as part of a steering committee.

Desired actions

This states what we would like the stakeholder to do, if at all possible, in order to advance the project.

Messages to convey

This is where we define the slant that should be put on any communications to this stakeholder, for example we might need to identify any issues that are of particular interest to the stakeholder. The 'messages' are likely to be tailored to each stakeholder. Therefore, the more we know about each stakeholder and their concerns, the more effective our communications will be.

Actions and communications

This is the most important part of the plan, where we define exactly what actions we will take with regard to this stakeholder. It may be just to keep the stakeholder informed in a positive way about the project and progress to date. Alternatively, it may be a more active approach, for example meeting the stakeholder to engage their interest in the project. Where a strategy has been devised to change a stakeholder's position – perhaps to encourage the stakeholder to take a closer interest – then its success must also be evaluated and other approaches developed if the desired results are not being achieved. We mentioned earlier that the high-interest/low-power stakeholders – the key players – require positive management, such as frequent meetings, in order to ensure that they are kept informed about a project and are happy with the approach that we are taking.

SUMMARY

Effective stakeholder management is key to the success of any business analysis project. It should begin before the project starts, at the inception stage, and be continued throughout the project and afterwards to ensure that the changes are implemented effectively. Although the project manager has the key responsibility in this area, all team members have roles to play. Stakeholders can be assessed in terms of their interest in the project and their power or influence over it, and strategies must be defined in order to actively manage them in accordance with this assessment.

FURTHER READING

Johnson, G. and Scholes, K. (2004) *Exploring Corporate Strategy*. FT Prentice Hall, Harlow.

Laborde, G.Z. (1998) *Influencing with Integrity*. Anglo American Book Company, Bancyfelin, Wales.

Pinto, J.K. (1998) *The PMI Project Management Handbook*. Jossey-Bass, San Francisco, CA.

Stanton, N. (2003) *Mastering Communication*, 4th edn. Macmillan, Basingstoke.

Turner, J.R. (1998) *The Handbook of Project-Based Management*, 2nd edn. McGraw-Hill, London.

Turner, J.R. and Simister, S.J. (2000) *Handbook of Project Management*, 3rd edn. Gower, Aldershot.

Zuker, E. (1991) *The Seven Secrets of Influence*. McGraw-Hill, New York.

7 Modelling the business system

DOT TUDOR

INTRODUCTION

Business analysts are usually trying to improve situations that are in some way seen as problematic. One of the frequent issues is that any business situation can be viewed from several perspectives, and stakeholders may have different needs and priorities. Earlier chapters have discussed investigation techniques and stakeholder analysis, and Chapter 8 presents techniques for modelling business processes. Process modelling essentially explores how an organization operates and is concerned with finding more efficient ways of operating. However, before defining the new processes, business analysts often have to have a broader view. First, they need to make sure that they have a good understanding of the situation under investigation, including any issues raised by stakeholders. Second, they need to consider why an organization – or part of an organization – operates as it does and what it is trying to achieve. Techniques for modelling business situations and understanding the 'why' and 'what' of a business system are the subject of this chapter.

To illustrate why we need to explore the 'why' and 'what' of an organization, let us consider a business that makes and sells pens. Obviously the products are used by their purchasers to write with, but beyond that the pen manufacturer could be aiming at different markets:

- The manufacturer may be offering well-engineered, reliable but cheap ballpoint pens for sale in bulk to commercial customers.

- The manufacturer may be creating desirable luxury goods that appeal to well-off and design-conscious buyers.

In the first case, the emphasis of the company will be on efficient and effective production and wholesale processes. In the second case, there will be an emphasis on stylish design, brand marketing and sales through specialist retailers and good department stores. But which approach should the company adopt?

Of course, the overall direction of the company will – or should be – the subject of the business strategy, as discussed in Chapter 3. But a business strategy, whilst taking business environment considerations into account, is also influenced by the vision that senior management have of the business. Any business analysis project must operate in the light of the core values and beliefs of the organization in which it is being undertaken.

At an organizational level these beliefs are often expressed using the MOST (mission, objectives, strategy, tactics) structure explored in Chapter 3. It is important that business analysts are familiar with the MOST structure for their organization, because any change must be in support of, or at least not counter to, this expression of organizational intent. However, the MOST structure reflects the core values of the organization as a whole, and even assuming that everyone in the organization shares these values, which is by no means always the case, there is usually plenty of room for divergences in interpretation and implementation by stakeholders within different departments or business units. We call these divergent stakeholder views 'business perspectives'.

Understanding different stakeholder beliefs is extremely relevant to business analysts and will influence the types of business change recommended and, ultimately, the nature of the business processes that are required. Before going on to process modelling, therefore, we need to be clear about the values and beliefs of stakeholders concerned with implementing the organization's business strategy. We can use this understanding to develop models of desired future business systems, which we can then assess against the current real-world situation.

SOFT SYSTEMS METHODOLOGY

This whole issue of why an organization does what it does was the subject of much study by Peter Checkland and his team at Lancaster University. This work led to the development of the Soft Systems Methodology (SSM). Checkland followed the tradition of systems thinking developed through the work of writers such as Stafford Beer and proposed that business situations should be considered as systems. Checkland also showed that much previous work on systems had taken a 'hard' approach and had assumed that the goals and objectives of such systems were clear, the role of the analyst being simply to follow a systematic approach in order to correct problems and thereby make the system more efficient. This contrasted with the reality of business situations, where problems are rarely clear-cut and there is usually plenty of room for differences of opinion about the nature of the business problem, let alone where suitable solutions might be found.

As an alternative to the hard systems thinking approach, Checkland proposed the soft systems model, the main features of which are shown in Figure 7.1.

As shown in Figure 7.1, SSM begins with an investigation into a real-world situation of concern. Checkland proposed a technique known as a 'rich picture' to document such situations; we shall look at these later in this chapter. The investigation of the situation is followed by speculation about different 'world views', each of which would give rise to a conceptual system that could shape the future for the business situation. These

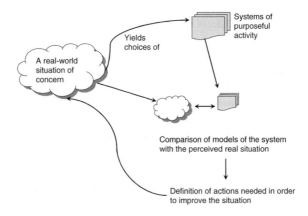

FIGURE 7.1 *Checkland's soft systems methodology*

possible systems can then be used to identify opportunities for improvement when they are compared with the situation that exists. The different world views may be derived following discussions with stakeholders or may be conceived by the analysts based upon their views about the situation. In the SSM, each view is developed and formulated as a sentence. Checkland named these sentences 'root definitions', but we prefer the term 'business perspective'. Different stakeholders may identify different systems based upon their beliefs and values with regard to the business area in question. The differences between these systems may be considered by examining the models representing the systems and considering where they overlap, where they are in conflict with each other or where gaps exist. This approach can lead to the development of a consensus model, where a desired future system is built; this model can then be used to explore possible improvements to the existing situation.

One important element of Checkland's systems thinking that the business analyst needs to bear in mind is that a system, with all of its components working together, will have characteristics that are not the characteristics of any one component. These are known as its 'emergent properties' and reflect that the whole system is more than the sum of all of the parts. For example, if we consider the car as a system that allows one to travel, then the movement along the correct roads and at the correct speed is an emergent property requiring engine, suspension, steering, the driver and a whole host of other parts in order to be successful. The engine alone could not achieve this; all of the parts individually could not achieve this. The business analyst must be aware of the emergent properties in any recommended business changes, since such properties may be undesirable as well as desirable.

DOCUMENTING BUSINESS SITUATIONS

One of the problems with investigating business situations is that they are rarely clear-cut. Therefore, although some of the more standard models for documenting systems, such as organizational charts and business process models, provide a clear view of one perspective, they are not able to cope with the range and variety of issues that may be uncovered. For example, interpersonal, political and cultural issues are rarely documented, even if they are evident, and yet if such issues are not taken into account, recommendations may be rejected and the implementation of solutions may be deeply problematic. Checkland's rich-picture technique provides a free-format approach that allows analysts to document whatever is of interest or significance in the business situation. This often includes details of processes, stakeholders, issues raised and the culture inherent in the situation. Figure 7.2 shows an example of a rich picture.

The rich-picture approach enables the analyst to capture the essence of the situation under investigation without being constrained by notation

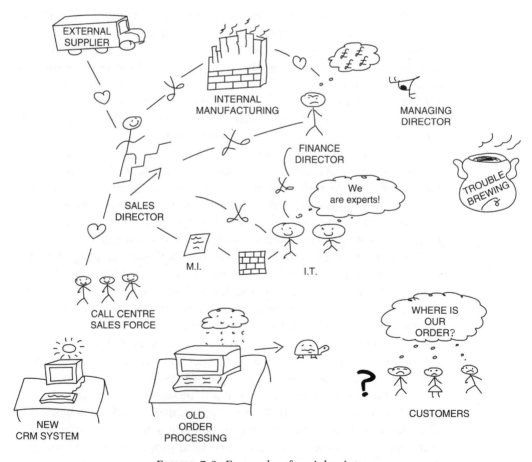

FIGURE 7.2 *Example of a rich picture*

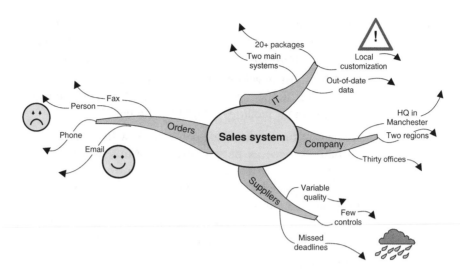

FIGURE 7.3 *Example of a mind map for a sales system*

and format. This allows any useful information, including details about personal issues and connections, to be documented as required. Ideally a rich picture is captured on one page and hence provides a distilled view of all of the aspects to be considered. This helps the analyst to develop a mental picture of the situation and to perceive how the different aspects relate to each other and how they may impact upon any possible solutions.

An alternative or additional method of capturing the findings about the business situation is to use a mind map. These diagrams represent a situation as a form of tree structure: the subject is at the centre, major subsidiary subjects are the tree's branches, sub-issues from those branches are twigs, and so on. Mind maps show summary detail but may also use pictures in order to trigger analysts to remember more information. Figure 7.3 shows an example of a mind map.

Sometimes it can be useful to use both rich pictures and mind maps. The free format of the rich-picture approach allows the analyst freedom to produce a 'mental map' of the situation without worrying about structuring his or her thoughts and ideas. The development of this picture alone can often help the analyst to organize his or her thinking. Following this it may be useful to develop a more organized diagram of the situation in the form of a mind map.

BUSINESS PERSPECTIVES

The starting point in identifying and analysing business perspectives is the stakeholder analysis discussed in Chapter 6. The key stakeholders should be asked how they view, from their own perspective, the purpose and objectives of the part of the organization that is within the scope of the change project. For example:

- Bank tellers handling customers' needs in a branch of the bank may see their area of the business as 'a system to provide customers with an accurate and speedy service, whilst maintaining security of cash'.
- A business development manager in the same branch may perceive 'a system to encourage customers and potential customers to use the investment facilities offered by the bank'.

Notice that the bank tellers, being faced with customers directly, view the customer service as particularly important, whereas the manager views business development as the main priority. We might consider which perspective is 'right', but it is likely that both perspectives are 'right' and in studying the bank's business system analysts must take both into account.

The SSM offers a useful framework for defining and analysing business perspectives, given by the mnemonic CATWOE:

- **C = customer:** the beneficiary of the transformation, the recipient of the system's end product or the person on the receiving end of the system's services.
- **A = actor:** those responsible for performing business activities. Actors could be within the organization (in other words, they represent job roles) or they could be business partners, such as distribution firms or offshore IT suppliers.
- **T = transformation:** the core business processes that are carried out in order to transform an input into an output of value to the customer.
- **W = Weltanschauung or world view:** an encapsulation of the individual's beliefs about the organization or business system, i.e. their views as to why it exists and what it should be doing.
- **O = owner:** the person or group of people who can take major decisions about the business system, who could change its direction or who could ultimately cause it to cease to exist.
- **E = environment:** the conditions and rules under which the system must operate that are outside the control of the owner and that must be regarded as 'givens'. The PESTLE analysis (see Chapter 3) provides a tool for identifying many of the environmental factors here. Internal business policies may also be relevant if they are to be regarded as fixed and unchangeable.

Let us consider our first banking example again and analyse it using CATWOE:

- **Customer:** people with accounts at the branch, or at other branches of the same bank, and who visit the branch to make an account transaction.
- **Actors:** bank tellers, back-office staff and branch management.

- **Transformation:** providing bank counter services, such as cash deposit and withdrawal, answering account enquiries and setting up standing orders.

- **Weltanschauung:** customers continue to deal through a bank branch, rather than by telephone or over the internet, because they value personal service and human contact and find a physical branch convenient.

- **Owner:** the senior management – possibly the chief executive – of the bank.

- **Environment:** government competition policy (P); consolidation of banking sector worldwide (E); not everyone likes the internet (S); electronic funds transfer (T); attitude of financial regulators (L); behaviour of anti-capitalist protesters (E).

When using CATWOE, it is important to begin by understanding the Weltanschauung or world view as this encapsulates the beliefs that underpin the rest of the framework. From this point, it is useful to define the transformation and the customer and then to consider the actors, owner and environment.

Checkland's root definition is developed as a sentence that ties together the CATWOE elements. For the example given above, this would be as follows:

> The branch is a system controlled by the bank senior management (O), where bank tellers, back-office staff and branch management (A) provide bank counter services such as cash deposit and withdrawal, answering account enquiries and setting up standing orders (T) to branch customers who require personal service (C) within constraints imposed by government competition policy, the consolidation of worldwide banking, variable use of the internet, increasing electronic funds transfer and increased regulation by financial regulators (E).

Sometimes the perspectives developed for key stakeholders are so different that further progress is impossible. For instance, if one director of a company said that they were in the grocery business but another asserted that they sold stationery, then clearly it would be difficult to get any further in the analysis unless and until these different views were reconciled or one stakeholder was able to overrule the other. In our experience, however, the differences are more often differences of emphasis and priorities within the same business area. In this case, the implications of the perspectives can be developed using business activity models, and these can then be used to consider what the organization is about and to generate discussion about the nature of any changes.

BUSINESS ACTIVITY MODELS

So what is a business activity model (BAM)? What it is not is a model of the organization's business processes; such models are described in the next chapter. A BAM essentially is a 'conceptual model' (the term used by Checkland) that shows the business activities that we would expect to see in place given the business perspective from which it has been developed.

Developing a BAM therefore requires the analyst to use both analytical ability and creative thought. The analyst needs to ignore as far as possible what is going on in the organization now and instead should consider what should be present based on the business perspective. In effect the BAM develops the business perspective, or root definition, to reveal the activities that comprise the system envisaged by the stakeholder. The principles underlying the BAM approach are as follows:

- There will be one BAM for each business perspective.

- A separate BAM is needed to describe each perspective. These will subsequently be overlaid to form a consensus model, possibly covering all relevant perspectives.

- The BAM aids analysis of the business situation and the identification of improvements.

- The model is not concerned with who carries out the activities or where they are carried out.

All business systems can be described in terms of five types of business activity and the dependencies between them. These activity types are:

- planning activities;
- enabling activities;
- doing activities;
- monitoring activities;
- controlling activities.

We can use these five activity types as a basis for developing a BAM.

Planning activities

These define the rules dictating the types of resource required and how the performance of these resources is to be measured. In a company providing high-quality holidays to customers, the planning activities could include deciding the number of staff required and the skills they should have, deciding the marketing approach, and so on. Within the planning activities, performance expectations should also be set. For example, if we identify a planning activity as 'decide staffing requirements', then we would expect this activity to include defining staff numbers and the required skills. If our Weltanschauung for this organization is based upon a belief about customers wanting high-quality holidays, then this would affect the decisions made about staffing. Customer service would be important; this might mean ensuring there are sufficient staff members so that customers do not have to wait to be dealt with, and the staff would need excellent customer relationship skills. We would expect these factors to be reflected in the performance targets.

Enabling activities

These ensure that the resources and facilities needed by the doing activities are obtained and deployed. Resources include raw materials, infrastructure and staff. For our travel company these could include recruiting and training the staff with the required skills, attracting customers and negotiating rates with hotels. The planning activities would influence how the enabling activities are carried out. For example, we would expect the activity 'recruit staff' to take account of the planning decisions about staffing requirements.

Doing activities

These relate directly to achieving the transformation described in the business perspective. Sometimes they are referred to as 'primary task activities'. They contribute directly to the purpose of the business system. In our travel company the transformation required could be 'convert potential holiday-makers into happy, paid-up holiday-goers'. Doing activities to support this would include booking high-quality holidays and supplying detailed travel details.

Monitoring activities

These collect metrics to check the performance of other activities against the targets and performance expectations set when planning. Such activities could include logging enquiries and holidays booked and comparing these with conversion targets, recording sales against each salesperson and comparing them with individual sales targets. As we are concerned with delivering high-quality holidays, we would also want to monitor the level of customer satisfaction with aspects such as the service provided, the hotels and the airlines.

Control activities

These act on the other activities when monitoring has identified that some action is required. This is usually when performance expectations are not being met, but it could also be when action is felt to be needed, for example if targets are exceeded by a wide margin. Such action may involve changes to any of the activities, including the monitoring activities. For example, if sales targets for a range of products are not being achieved, then possible control actions may range from reconsidering the price, through reviewing the targets to providing additional training to the staff.

Dependencies

In the BAM, activities are connected by arrows. Such arrows represent logical dependency between the activities. This means that for activity B to occur, activity A must have occurred. This relationship allows for the fact that activity B may happen daily even though activity A happens only monthly.

Modelling notation

The good news here is that there is no universally agreed notation for creating BAMs, which leaves analysts free to design their own. Soft systems specialists like to use 'cloud' symbols, as illustrated in Figure 7.4, because these emphasize the essentially conceptual nature of the model.

Business activities should be given an identifier and a title consisting of an imperative verb and a noun, as in 'do something'. The lightning-strike symbol coming out of the control activity in Figure 7.4 shows that the control action that is taken could feed back anywhere into the model; it might, for instance, involve improving the recruitment process, or changing the way selling is done, or even revisiting the strategy. Trying to model all of these possibilities with individual lines would result in an impossibly cluttered model that would obscure rather than illuminate what the organization should be doing.

In the more complete BAM shown in Figure 7.5, we have used ellipses for the business activities, as these are easier to draw than cloud shapes. The core belief underpinning this model is that the travel company believes that customers want quality holidays that deliver a high level of service. Hence, the monitoring activities focus on checking the level of customer satisfaction plus the hotel and airline performance in line with predefined targets. This is in addition to monitoring both sales and

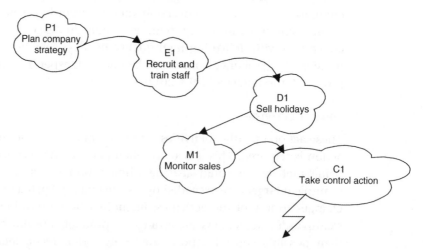

FIGURE 7.4 *Business activity model notation using cloud symbols*

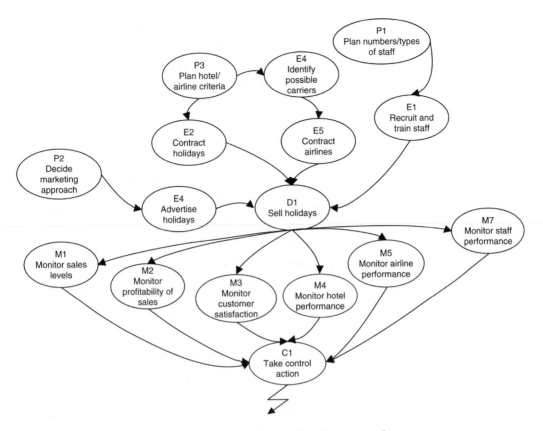

FIGURE 7.5 *Business activity model for a travel company*

profitability levels to make sure that providing quality holidays is also beneficial to the company.

Developing a business activity model

As we have mentioned, creating a BAM involves the use of both business knowledge and creativity on the part of the analyst. The Weltanschauung or world view must be kept in mind when building the BAM, as this comprises the set of beliefs that the model will fulfil. In addition, the following provides a guide to BAM development:

(i) Begin by identifying the main **doing activities**. This can be done by referring to the transformation contained in the business perspective. The activities in the BAM must fulfil the transformation.

(ii) Look for **enabling activities** that need to be in place to provide the resources that will allow the doing activities to function.

(iii) Identify **planning activities**, which need to cover two areas: first, decide upon the resources to be provided; second, define the performance targets that must be met using these resources. You need to consider the Weltanschauung to understand the resources that will be required and the performance expectations.

(iv) Add **monitoring activities** to compare actual performance with planned performance. These monitor the performance expectations defined by the planning activities.

(v) Add **controlling activities** to respond to deviations between actual and planned performance.

(vi) Where environmental constraints are referred to in the business perspective, activities should be added to consider the constraints (planning activities), measure performance in relation to them (monitoring activities) and react to any threat of failure to comply with them (controlling activities).

(vii) Add dependency arrows between the activities showing which activities are **dependent** on others.

(viii) Add lightning-strike **control** arrows from the controlling activities to indicate the control feedback loop.

Producing a consensus model

The BAMs produced up to this point have been derived from an individual business perspective from a key stakeholder. Potentially, therefore, we could at this point have several BAMs, each representing a slightly different view of the organization or business system. Our eventual goal is to derive just one definitive BAM of the activities needed by the business by merging the individual models into one. This model is known as a 'consensus model'.

To arrive at a consensus model, the business analyst must resolve any conflict between the various views that have caused the creation of the different models. In order to achieve this, we must examine the necessity for each activity in each BAM and combine those that are agreed by the stakeholders to be necessary into a consensus model. This is often easier said than done, as each stakeholder has beliefs that underlie his or her viewpoint and may not be able to appreciate the other stakeholders' points of view. Skilful facilitation may be required in order to enable each stakeholder to accept other perspectives as valid.

There are three kinds of consensus that we might consider:

- Global consensus, which assumes there is a neutral model applicable to all organizations of a particular type. For example, all commercial businesses have activities related to purchasing, sales, marketing and finance.

- One hundred per cent consensus, where all the participants agree readily that a given activity, often one that is common to all individual models, is needed.

- Consensus through accommodation, where participants with conflicting viewpoints agree to compromise. The creation of additional activities and/or modification of existing activities may be necessary in order to achieve this kind of consensus or compromise.

The process of creating the consensus model is best carried out in a controlled facilitated workshop environment where views can be expressed openly and conflict resolved in a fair manner. A consensus model workshop should aim to:

- create a tentative consensus model by combining all individual BAM activities, events and dependencies;
- derive a new consensus business perspective for the area of study;
- test the tentative model against the new business perspective, adding, removing or modifying activities as necessary, in order to satisfy the consensus view;
- check the consensus model to ensure that it satisfies fully the new business perspective and the objectives of the area of study and the change project.

By deriving a consensus model in this way, we have identified not only areas of agreement but also differences and areas of misunderstanding. The resulting consensus BAM is a powerful and effective tool for communication, focusing on the activities without the clutter of real-world constraints. The development and discussion of this will provide the business analyst with a vehicle for eliciting and clarifying requirements.

BUSINESS EVENTS AND BUSINESS RULES

One way of analysing a BAM is to consider the business events to which the organization must respond and the business rules that underpin and constrain the business operations. This information is also very useful when redesigning business processes.

Business events

Business events happen in the real world. Customers place orders, suppliers send in invoices and employees resign. All of these events trigger the business system to do something – typically an activity or a series of activities – in order to respond to the event. The approach selected for business activity modelling must have a means of documenting business events and relating them to the activities that they trigger. In effect, the business events tell us when a business activity should be triggered; a business event causes an activity to spring into life. Hence, identifying the business events will help us to think about the processes that form the business system response to them.

There are three types of business event to consider:

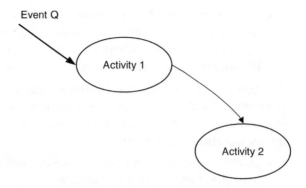

FIGURE 7.6 *Business event triggering activities*

- **External:** these events originate from outside the boundary of the business system. In our travel company, an external event would be a prospective customer telephoning with a holiday enquiry. Other, less welcome external events would include a customer arriving at the company's front door with a complaint or one of our chosen hotels going bankrupt.

- **Internal decision points:** these events are usually internal decisions made by business managers, for example the senior management staff of the travel firm decides to award discounts to holidays that are to be taken within the next month. This event would be the result of an internal decision rather than an external occurrence.

- **Scheduled points in time:** these are the events that occur regularly, for example at the start of each day the travel agency staff members produce travel documents for holidays that begin two weeks before their departure date.

In the BAM, events can be recorded as broad arrows pointing to an activity but, as they do not originate from another activity, they have no source. Some business events may trigger more than one activity and some activities may be triggered by more than one business event. Figure 7.6 shows two activities triggered by one event.

Business rules

For the activities identified in the BAM, there will be rules defining how the activities are to be performed. It is important that these rules are considered when modelling the processing to carry out the activity. Rules are of two main types:

- **Constraints:** these restrict how an activity is performed and may include laws and regulations and – if these cannot be challenged – business policies.

- **Operational guidance:** these rules describe the procedural guidance that dictates how activities should be performed. An example for our travel organization is the guidance on how to calculate discounts on holidays when there is a group booking.

The business rules would emerge in discussion of the activities with stakeholders and should be documented to support the BAM.

CRITICAL SUCCESS FACTORS AND KEY PERFORMANCE INDICATORS

Another useful way of approaching BAM construction is to consider the organization's critical success factors (CSFs) and key performance indicators (KPIs).

The CSFs are the things the organization must be good at in order to succeed and therefore provide some insights into the planning, enabling and doing activities that are needed. For example, 'excellent customer service' may be a CSF, in which case the recruitment, training and retention of good customer-service staff may be needed on the BAM.

KPIs are the things an organization measures to find out how well it is doing. These may be identified by considering the planning activities in the BAM. Checking up on the KPIs should therefore be reflected in the monitoring activities of the BAM.

VALIDATING A BUSINESS ACTIVITY MODEL

Peter Checkland devised a 'formal systems model' for validating a 'human activity system', or in our terms a business system. His formal model was a series of checks that can be applied to see whether the model is complete and at least internally consistent. The checklist consists of the following:

- Objectives and purpose (of the system): these must be explicit.
- Connectivity: the activities in the model must all be connected. If they are not, then they represent separate systems.
- Measures of performance must exist and expected levels of performance must be set.
- Monitoring and control mechanisms: there must be control activities that have the power to change other activities when expectations are not met.
- Decision-making procedures: there must be decision-making procedures that will be influenced by the control actions.
- Boundary: the extent of the system must be clear and communications across the boundary defined explicitly.

- Resources: staff, materials and other resources used by the system must be acquired, allocated, replenished and accounted for.
- Systems hierarchy: it should be possible to decompose the system hierarchically based on the scope of control activity. Any business activity should be within the scope of only one control activity. If not, then additional activities need to be introduced in order to resolve any conflict.

USE OF THE BUSINESS ACTIVITY MODEL IN GAP ANALYSIS

Although the analysis of business problems, and devising solutions, is the subject of other chapters, it is useful to understand how the BAM can be used to identify high-level business problems and issues.

The BAM represents a theoretical (conceptual) model of the activities that we would expect to find in place given the initial business perspective. When we compare the BAM with the current reality in the organization, we will find the following:

- Some activities are in place and are quite satisfactory. Therefore, little needs to be done about these, except perhaps to make sure that they are not lost in our proposed changes.

- Some activities are in place but are not satisfactory. This could be because the processes they represent are poor, there are organization issues associated with them – carried out in the wrong department, for instance – or there are problems with the people involved. It could also be that these activities are supported poorly by the current information systems. In any of these cases, there will be opportunities for business improvement.

- Some activities are not in place at all. In this case, again there will be implications for the organization and opportunities for beneficial change.

SUMMARY

In this chapter we have made the journey from understanding that any business situation may be considered from different perspectives. Each of these perspectives is based upon the core values and beliefs held by different stakeholders.

We have considered how we might model the business by viewing it as a purposeful system with processes that cross departmental boundaries. By taking into account the differing viewpoints of key stakeholders, we have explored how we might develop a model of the business activities, including the key events and the business rules. We have also explained how we might derive a consensus model encompassing the different stakeholder perspectives and how the BAM can provide a powerful analytical tool to identify problems in an organization and opportunities for improvement.

FURTHER READING

Bowman, C. and Faulkner, D. (1996) *Competitive and Corporate Strategy.* Irwin, Homewood, IL.

Checkland, P. (1981) *Systems Thinking, Systems Practice.* John Wiley & Sons, Chichester.

Checkland, P. and Scholes, J. (1999) *Soft Systems Methodology in Action.* John Wiley & Sons, Chichester.

Hammer, M. and Champy, J. (1995) *Reengineering the Corporation.* Nicholas Brealey, London.

Rummler, G. and Brache, A. (1990) *Improving Performance.* Jossey-Bass, San Francisco, CA.

8 Business process modelling

KEITH HINDLE

INTRODUCTION

In this chapter we will examine some of the ideas behind the business process modelling technique and determine why process modelling is becoming so important. We will consider the following four main areas:

- The technique of business process modelling, including the production of an overview process map as well as high-level and detailed process models.

- The benefits of the process modelling approach, primarily in identifying problems and weaknesses in current business processes and developing solutions to those problems.

- The strategic use of business process modelling to help ensure that process improvements provide benefits to the overall organization and are aligned with the business strategy.

- The business process management approach, where we examine how business process modelling is combined with software facilities to give considerable control over the resulting processes.

WHAT IS BUSINESS PROCESS MODELLING?

A business process model is a diagram showing the steps that a business carries out in order to respond to a business event or trigger and achieve a specific goal or objective. Figure 8.1 provides an example: a sales organization has a business trigger 'Customer places order' and there is a business process in place to deal with this trigger, in other words to handle the order request. This process has a specific goal: to ensure the customer receives the ordered goods.

The three important concepts here are the business event, the process and the process goal. The concept of the business event was discussed in the previous chapter; this section considers the process and process goal concepts and sets out a common understanding for using these terms.

Process goals or objectives

Two other factors to consider when we examine a business process are the questions 'Who?' and 'Why?' These questions relate to the customers who

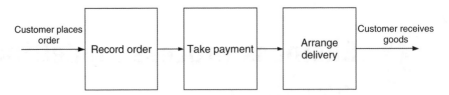

FIGURE 8.1 *Outline business process model*

benefit from the process, because a business process will have at least one customer and sometimes more. By understanding who the customer is and asking what they want from the process, we can find out exactly how the customer benefits from the process and then define our objective or goal.

Business processes

The word 'process' is used widely by analysts to indicate some kind of transformation. By this we mean that there is an input that the process transforms into an output, as shown in Figure 8.2.

This very generic concept can be applied at many different levels, either internally within an IT system or within a much larger business system. This approach to the definition of a business process allows us to identify and define processes in a top-down manner by treating the processes initially as black boxes. We are interested in the boundary of the process, and its inputs and outputs, but initially we are not interested in the internal activities required to carry out the process. At the early stage of analysis, we can identify the boundaries of the process once we know who the customer is and what they want from the business system.

However, at this point we may have little understanding of how the business process operates internally in order to give the customer what they want.

External and internal views

Much traditional analysis concentrates on an internal view where fact-finding is carried out in a top-down manner: senior management provide the big picture, which is then filled in by the staff lower down the departmental hierarchy. The emphasis here is on 'what we do' rather than

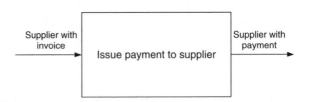

FIGURE 8.2 *The process concept*

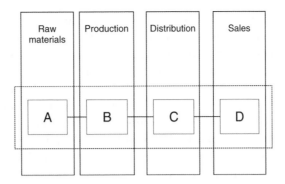

FIGURE 8.3 *Process versus functional view of a business*

'who is the customer and how do they benefit?' The resulting functional decomposition reflects how the organization is structured rather than the logical dependencies of the work undertaken. Staff members are often very mindful of where they belong in an organizational structure and as a result may be unaware of the cross-functional dependencies and interactions that are more apparent from the alternative process view. This alternative view focuses on the event and the goal.

The functional and business process views can be considered as diametrically opposed. The functional approach often produces a silo orientation where people work within the boundary of their particular business unit and strive to achieve the goals of their business unit. The process view, as shown in Figure 8.3, cuts across the silos and shows clearly that the functions must work together if the process customer is to get the level of service that they need.

This does not mean, however, that the process view should completely replace the functional view. There are good reasons for grouping staff into centralized specialist departments, including the development of areas of expertise, the provision of career progression and the definition and adoption of standards. A good example is the finance function that is a specialist area within most organizations and employs and develops specialist skills and standards.

THE IMPORTANCE OF PROCESS MODELLING

In this section we will examine why businesses have turned to process modelling and then look at the benefits of process modelling from the business analysis and IT perspectives.

Business performance

It is a truism to say that businesses operate under intense pressure due to increasing competition, globalization, innovation and demands for short-term results from shareholders. As a result, businesses are constantly looking for ways to operate either more efficiently or more effectively. It does seem odd, however, that business processes have been allowed to get so bad. How has this happened?

The main reason is lack of integration. For centuries, organizations have been getting more efficient by becoming more specialized. As firms get larger, they become more difficult to manage and so they are divided up into semi-autonomous units. Each unit is given objectives that together should support the overall objectives of the business. Unfortunately it is very difficult to coordinate the work of the different units effectively, so the units tend to go their separate ways. As an example, we need look no further than the development of IT systems. Until recently, both the politics of the situation and the technical difficulties ensured that computer systems were normally developed department by department. As a result, we commonly experience difficulties when we try to get those systems to work with each other. As organizations started to realize the significance of business processes, they could see real problems in the way that their work flows were organized. Methods of working had often evolved rather than been designed in a rational way. Over the years, they had changed to take account of new business conditions and needs, reorganizations and takeovers. There was often a lack of integration, and no one had responsibility for the objectives of the process as a whole.

Business process modelling allows us to document and understand how the processes currently operate across the organization and see how they could be integrated. When people study the model of their processes, they can they see how their part fits into the bigger picture; they also understand the effects of what they do on other parts of the process. This is an important element of process modelling, as it allows us to visualize and understand what is taking place. Once we all understand the problems, we can identify and agree on ways of improving how we work. Improved business performance is necessary to the organization's existence, but poor processes can continue for some time unless there is a stimulus – often a legal or compliance requirement. The legal requirements for organizations are becoming increasingly strict, with the introduction of new legislation such as Basle II, Sarbanes-Oxley and the Freedom of Information Act. Where there are legal constraints, a business must demonstrate that it has the legally compliant processes in operation. If the current processes are not compliant, then the organization will have to change them rapidly or stop operating.

Process modelling and IT

Different organizations have different attitudes about their IT systems. Some love them, recognizing that they could not be without them. Other organizations are not so appreciative: they may complain about the systems and feel that they are not getting value for money from their IT investment. The problem often stems from a misalignment between what the business is trying to achieve and what the systems actually do. This could result from a simple misunderstanding of the business users' requirements, or there could be a more fundamental lack of knowledge on the part of IT about the strategy and objectives that the business has adopted.

The business process can be seen as the environment in which the IT system operates, as shown in Figure 8.4. However, few IT systems operate in isolation and there may be interfaces to several other systems, some of which may be supporting different parts of the overall business process.

Understanding the entire business process is very useful for the business analyst when defining IT requirements. The business analyst will often talk to the prospective system users and ask them what they want from the new IT system. If we talk to the users individually or to a team from the same area within the organization, we may be provided with an isolated view of the requirements. This situation also runs the risk of accepting localized responses at face value. If, on the other hand, we understand the bigger picture, then we can confirm the stated requirements against the support required for the process. Analysing and revising the business process is more fundamental than merely considering the IT system provision. In many situations, a change to the business process may solve the problem and eliminate the need for a new or enhanced IT system.

IT management staff need to demonstrate that investments in IT actually help the business. No organization can afford to invest in technology without business justification. The positioning of IT at the core of business operations in many organizations serves to intensify this concern and has led to the heightened interest in business IT alignment, whereby the business objectives, strategy and tactics both drive and are supported by the IT provision. This alignment may not be easy to deliver, however, if business objectives and strategy are defined at a high level but the IT systems are working at a lower operational level. The business

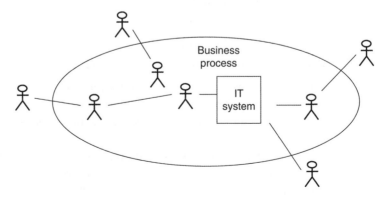

FIGURE 8.4 *Business process and the embedded IT system*

process helps business managers to understand how these two levels need to operate in tandem. Business objectives may specify, for example, the customer sales required in order to meet profitability targets. Management will then have to judge, among other things, the pricing and level of customer service and customer satisfaction necessary in order to achieve those sales. The business processes will then have to be designed to provide the specified level of service within the cost limitations that will allow adequate profit margins. Business process design allows us to integrate the required IT support and define the requirements in line with the business objectives and measures relevant to the process. If we are able to demonstrate clearly the cause and effect links from IT to process performance to achievement of business objectives, then we can justify the investment in IT and gain the support needed from senior management.

THE BUSINESS PROCESS MODELLING TECHNIQUE

Although the fundamental concepts of business process modelling are well established, business process modellers and business analysts use various different notation sets. Consequently, there are many techniques available, ranging from the swim-lane diagrams and activity diagrams of the unified modelling language (UML) to the more complex approaches supported by tools such as Aris, Case Wise and Enterprise Modeller. It is beyond the scope of this chapter and this book to describe, compare and contrast all the business process modelling approaches in detail. Our approach is to highlight a standard technique for business process modelling and illustrate this with some straightforward examples. There is an increasing realization of the value of swim-lane diagrams, and so we will consider this technique in some detail.

When developing business process models, it is worthwhile remembering some simple guidelines. Process models should:

- be multi-levelled;
- be developed from the outside in;
- be performance-related;
- be developed in an iterative manner;
- provide understanding to all involved.

Business process models are often large and complex, and it is easy to become confused by all of the detail, both as a developer and as a reader of the models. Sometimes the models are unnecessarily complex because they have been developed as a stream of process steps covering every element of a large process or because the process steps have been defined in too much detail. Process models of this nature do not help our understanding and so we need to find a better way. To avoid the overcomplicated models, we can develop high-level versions of the model first and build a hierarchy of increasingly detailed models. We begin with the organizational process model showing all of the key processes carried out in the organization. Once we have the business's confirmation that this is an accurate, albeit summarized, description of the overall process, then we can take each individual process area and go into further detail. The summary provides an overall roadmap that helps us to understand the detailed view more easily. This overview map can show the relationships between all the different business processes within the organization. Effectively, this overview outlines the context in which any one process operates, showing the dependencies between the inputs from and outputs to other processes.

Building the overview model

Earlier in this chapter we introduced the idea of the customers who are looking for particular results from the business process. An excellent way to begin modelling an overview business process is by considering what that process is supposed to achieve and for whom. One way of doing this is to consider what Michael Porter called the 'value proposition' offered by the organization to the customer. The value proposition considers issues such as the benefit we offer to customers, why customers buy from us rather than from our competitors, and the value of our product or service.

The value proposition for the customer should be expressed in unambiguous terms so that we can be clear as to whether that result has been achieved. If we think of all the stakeholders who wish to benefit from the process, then ensuring that they are all satisfied requires all aspects of the process's performance to be defined and measured. As the potential customers may include shareholders as well as purchasers of the product or service, the measures may relate to costs and use of internal resources as well as delivery timescales and quality standards.

An overview process map shows a set of related processes in a single diagram. Each process is a box and the arrows between them show their interdependencies. The map in Figure 8.5 shows the processes for the internal lending library of a consultancy company. The library provides a service to in-house staff ('Loan item – personal') and consultants working on client sites ('Loan item – remote'). The loan processes cannot take place unless the person requesting the loan is a registered borrower. Once the loan has been made, the subsequent process would normally be 'Accept returned item' but failure to do this within the specified time period would result in the process 'Issue reminder'.

Although we will not have full details about each process at this point, we can find out the events that trigger each process, the customer of that process and the results required. For example, if we consider 'Register borrower':

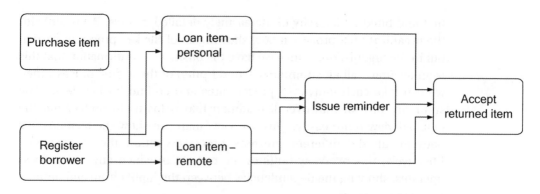

FIGURE 8.5 *Overview process map for a library service*

- The process will take place each week on receipt of information from HR detailing all the staff changes. This will allow the library to both add and delete borrowers.
- The customers will be the member of staff who is registered and the HR department that wants new employees to be added and employees who have left to be deleted.
- The results required are the successful addition or removal of employees, possibly within a prescribed timeframe.

As the analyst starts to model a particular process, the overview process map is extremely useful in identifying the boundaries of that process as it helps the analyst to define where the process begins and where it ends. If we use the example of the lending library, the overview process map shows us what each process incorporates and what is part of the following process. For example, the 'Issue reminder' process concludes with the sending of the reminder; it does not include the acceptance of the returned item. If we consider the 'Loan item – personal' process, then the customer here is the borrower and the process objective is achieved when the borrower has successfully completed the loan transaction. The measures applied to this process typically will be concerned with the speed and accuracy of the loan transaction.

Another approach that examines the linkage between processes and provides an overview of the organization's business processes is Michael Porter's value chain. Porter perceived a business as a chain of related activities, each of which added value to a product or service. In Figure 8.6 we can see raw material entering the value chain on the left, where it is stored by 'Inbound logistics'. The latter supply the material to 'Operations', where it is manufactured into finished goods. The finished goods are stored in the warehouse and distributed to customers by 'Outbound logistics' in response to requests from 'Marketing and sales'. Finally, the 'Service' activity supports customers during their purchasing and after

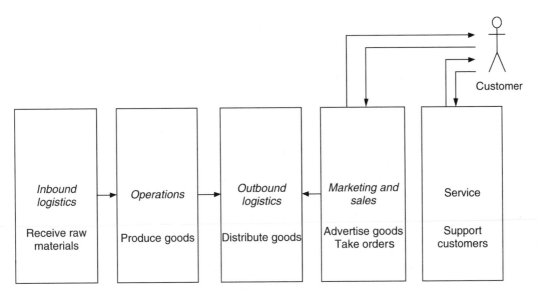

FIGURE 8.6 *Example value chain*

they have received the goods. The customers are looking for value from the products they receive from the organization. Each activity along the chain must add value over and above the costs that it incurs, and ultimately the value chain should deliver the value proposition to the customer. Applying this principle along the value chain allows us to identify the primary value-adding activities plus those that do not add value and should be eliminated or improved. The value-chain concept also helps us to consider two factors: the value proposition offered by the value chain and how well the value chain is able to deliver that value proposition.

Figure 8.6 shows only what Porter calls the 'primary activities'. In addition, Porter identified four areas of support activities as part of his generic value chain; these are shown in Figure 8.7.

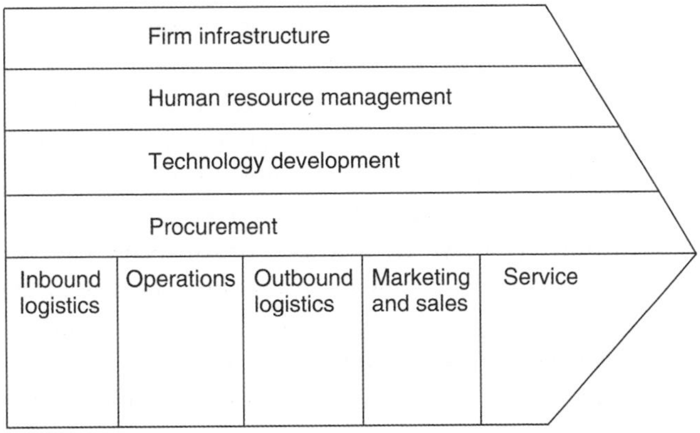

FIGURE 8.7 *Porter's generic value chain*

This representation is termed 'generic' because Porter found the activities shown to exist in all the organizations he studied. However, the form and relative significance of the activities will vary from one type of business to another. For example, the heart of a manufacturing business is 'Operations', where the production and assembly take place; in another organization, 'Marketing and sales' may predominate.

Figure 8.7 differentiates between the primary activities (as shown in Figure 8.6) and support activities. The latter are activities that do not directly add value themselves but help the primary activities to do so. Thus, a business analyst working on a production control information system is operating in the 'Technology development' row and investigating the potential for technology to support the activities of 'Operations'. The aim here is to deliver a production control system that will make the 'Operations' activity more flexible and less error-prone. This in turn will ensure that the customer receives the correct goods of the required quality and the organization will deliver the value proposition it has promised. The value chain concept is very close to that of an overview process map. In each case, they are:

- externally oriented, concentrating on how to meet a customer's needs;
- composed of sub-processes or steps;
- analysed in order to improve their effectiveness.

Thus, the value chain can be regarded as the highest level of process within the business. In fact, there may be a number of value chains within a single organization. A systems integration company could have a series of value chains – one for strategic consultancy, one for IT systems development and one for application management – and each of these value chains would differ significantly from the others.

When planning a process improvement initiative, it is best to start at the top. By identifying what value chain to improve, we are aware of the value of the improvement to the business as a whole and how well that value chain supports the evolving strategy. Once the high-level process has been chosen, the next step is to determine which sub-processes are most in need of improvement. This may require several levels of decomposition before we arrive at process definitions that are specific enough to be analysed and improved. The advantage of this top-down approach is that we are identifying at a high level what is good and what needs improvement. We need to concentrate on the weak areas, but as we improve those weak processes or sub-processes we need to be aware of the context in which they operate. The overview process map, or value chain, provides this context and we are able to check how improvements to the lower-level process may have repercussions on other related processes. This approach helps us to avoid the problem of sub-optimization, where an improvement in one area causes problems elsewhere.

End-to-end process modelling

The end-to-end process model takes a business event and shows the individual steps that make up a particular process and who carries them out. The process model concludes when the goal of the process has been achieved. We use swim-lane diagrams to demonstrate the process modelling techniques. The swim-lane diagramming technique uses a set of simple rules that cover:

- the overall layout;
- the symbols used;
- the sequencing of the symbols;
- the naming of the steps.

First we identify who takes part in the process. This enables us to identify the business actors or roles. The steps carried out by each actor are shown in a separate band or swim lane, and arrows are used to show the flow of the work between the different swim lanes. Swim lanes usually appear on the diagram in the same sequence as the actors' involvement in the process, although there is an informal convention to place the customer swim lane at the top. As a result, the action on the model goes from left to right on a horizontal layout, following the time axis, and from top to bottom as the different actors get involved. These left-to-right and top-to-bottom flows mirror the way in which many people read text, at least in the western world, and tends to be intuitive.

The symbols used on the model should be limited so that they require as little explanation as possible. There should be no need to use separate symbols for documents, displays or files as you would find on traditional flowcharts. The final guideline covers naming of both processes and process steps. In each case, use the verb–noun format to describe what the process or step does. Where possible, use specific verbs, avoiding words such as 'manage' and 'handle'. A good example is 'Find book', as this indicates the state of the process after the step has been completed – the book has been found. The term 'Handle payment' is not specific enough: by the end of the step the payment may have been handled, but what does that tell us? The major advantage of a diagram of this type is that each actor can easily see his or her own contribution to the overall process. We highlighted earlier the need to involve the business in the development of the process model; a clear, visual diagram helps to engage the business actors during this task and increases everyone's understanding.

Figure 8.8 shows the expanded process 'Loan item – remote'. This process involves two actors – the 'Borrower' (or customer) and the 'Librarian' – and so we have two swim lanes. We place the customer at the top of the diagram, as this is usually where the process begins and/or ends. The start and end points of the process are shown clearly. The first step takes place when the borrower rings the librarian to check whether an item

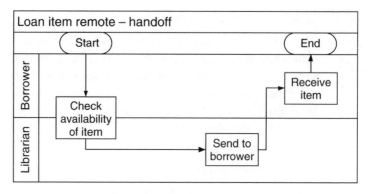

FIGURE 8.8 *End-to-end process model*

is available for loan. This conversation involves both actors simultaneously, so it is represented by a box that straddles the boundary between the two swim lanes. Once the check shows that the item is available, the process moves on to the next step, 'Send to borrower'. The final step occurs when the borrower receives the item. However, this diagram is a simple view, as the steps to deal with an item that is not available are not shown. We need to consider what will happen if the item is not available. In Figure 8.9 the borrower is able to reserve such an item, and an additional step and flow are added to the diagram.

The alternative paths are shown using a decision diamond. This structure is not essential, as an alternative approach would be to use the structure shown in Figure 8.10.

The follow-on action from 'Reserve item' will be carried out in the 'Accept returned item' process. Each time a borrower returns an item, a check is made to determine whether another borrower has reserved the item. The librarian will recognize that the item is on the reserved list and will trigger the 'Send to borrower' step in the 'Loan item' process to issue it

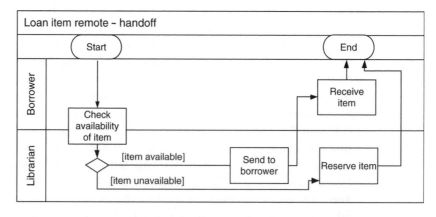

FIGURE 8.9 *Process model with alternative paths*

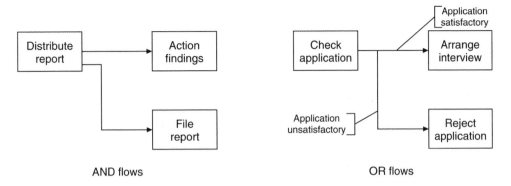

FIGURE 8.10 *Flow conventions*

to the reserving borrower. This flow is added to the process model, as shown in Figure 8.11.

As we are trying to provide a summarized view of the process at this stage of the analysis, the steps reveal minimum detail. A rule of thumb is to show a separate step for a piece of work done by an actor at a particular point in time. Each step should be shown as a single step, receiving an input from the preceding actor and handing over to the succeeding actor. The flow of work from one actor to another is known as a 'handoff'. It is important to analyse where this occurs, as handoffs often cause problems. We shall revisit this later in this chapter.

Detailed process analysis

The swim-lane diagram shows the shape of the end-to-end process, including the flow of the work. This may be sufficient to identify problems with the as-is process, but often we have to go into more detail in order to really understand how the process works and what is going wrong. One possibility is to develop a detailed diagram, as shown in Figure 8.12.

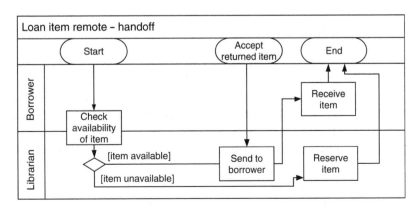

FIGURE 8.11 *Process map with link from other process*

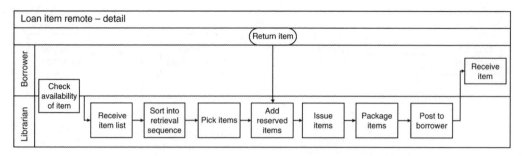

FIGURE 8.12 *Detailed swim-lane diagram (partial)*

This diagram provides more detail about the 'Send to borrower' step of Figure 8.11 by showing us all of the detailed steps carried out by the 'Librarian' actor. The receipt and transmission of information are included, because they can significantly affect the timing of the process. It is at these points, for example, that we may find queues building up.

An alternative approach is to analyse each process step from the end-to-end process model. We might consider the following aspects for each step:

- inputs;
- the trigger that initiates the step;
- outputs;
- costs relevant to this particular step;
- measures;
- detailed breakdown of steps;
- rules to be followed.

The multi-level approach described here reflects the difficulty inherent in developing a clear and useful process model in one pass. As the lower levels reveal more detail, it is inevitable that the higher-level views will have to be updated and the analysis will be iterative.

IMPROVING BUSINESS PROCESSES

One of the main reasons for building business process models is to help us to identify problems with the existing process before producing an improved version. These two versions are called the 'as-is' and the 'to-be' process models. With all process modelling work, it is important to look ahead and keep in mind why we are modelling this process. Usually the aim is to change the process in order to improve it, but this will not happen unless we take the people involved with the process along with us. Process modelling is about shared insight; we cannot simply tell people that they must change and expect them to accept the change immediately. What we can do is to give them the information from which they can draw their own conclusions. It may be that change is possible because we have identified the problems and know how to overcome them; or change might be inevitable because if we do not change, then our competitors will take over our customers. Process modelling is an excellent way of involving the people affected and getting them to understand the business realities.

Identifying problems with the as-is process

One of the frequent problems found with processes involves handoffs, where one actor passes the work to another actor. Figure 8.13 shows two handoffs, one from the 'Manager' to the 'Clerk' and the other from the 'Clerk' to the 'Manager'. The step 'Calculate results' has two handoffs in this diagram, one preceding and one succeeding.

Clear representation of handoffs is a major advantage of this diagramming technique when we are trying to improve processes. Handoffs account for many of the problems experienced by traditional processes, as they can cause delays, communication errors and bottlenecks. For example, once a piece of work arrives at its destination, it may have to wait in a queue until an actor is free to deal with it. Analysis of as-is processes commonly shows that transactions spend more than 80 per cent of the elapsed time simply waiting. It has even been estimated that in some processes the transactions are being actively processed for less than 10 per cent of the elapsed time, with more than 90 per cent of the time being spent in transit or in queues. Queues form at handoffs because the two actors do not synchronize their work. In some situations, attempts to optimize work in one step can actually make the performance of the whole process worse. For example, batching of transactions will help a particular step to be carried out more efficiently but the delay caused by waiting for the batch to build up may slow down the overall progress.

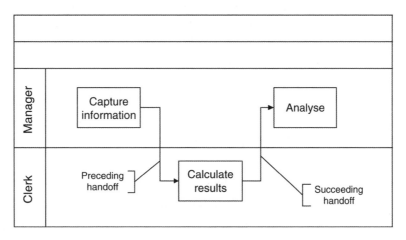

FIGURE 8.13 *Handoffs on the high-level process model*

A further cause of delays at handoffs is the inadequate resource capacity to handle the throughput. Queues can behave oddly, especially when the transactions are coming in a random fashion. Queuing theory tells us that attempts to increase the utilization of the workers under these circumstances will cause the queues to build up dramatically. The production system on the shop floor of a factory is a specific example of a process in which the queues, in this case of physical components that are being produced, are very visible as they are handed over to the different machine operations, such as milling and turning. Although a process in a bank, for example, may seem very different from a process in a factory, both processes face the same kinds of problem where handoffs occur. There are other problems with handoffs, often because the transaction is going from one system to another. These could be large information systems or small spreadsheets developed by individuals. The result is that the data within the transaction needs to be reformatted and rekeyed to suit the needs of the receiving software. This not only takes time and effort but also can introduce errors. Subsequent correction of the errors soaks up extra time and resources.

As-is processes may have been in use for some considerable time. During their life, they have been changed in a piecemeal fashion to reflect changing business needs. Nobody will have looked at the process as a whole; as a result, there are significant inefficiencies and inconsistencies. Steps are still carried out despite the fact that they are no longer needed. The same work may be carried out twice, and the same data captured and stored redundantly. Previously, organizations were less aware of the need for effective processes and hence there was less emphasis on carrying out processes in a standard way. Remote locations such as branch offices and depots were allowed flexibility in the way that they interpreted and implemented their processes. This may have worked in a decentralized business, but now that there is greater control and centralization all the different parts of the business are expected to operate in an integrated fashion. The more relaxed approach also placed less emphasis on measurement and control, whereas we now measure the level of customer service or the level of service that we received from our suppliers.

Improving the business process

Improving the business process is about removing the problems that have been identified in the as-is process. It is also about challenging the assumptions upon which the current process is built and that may limit the process. Improving a process may involve:

- simplifying it;
- removing bottlenecks;
- changing the sequence in which the steps are carried out;
- changing the way in which the steps are carried out;
- extending the boundaries of the process.

Simplifying a process can be achieved by eliminating unnecessary parts. Certain steps within a process may have been required when the process was first introduced but, as a result of changes to the business, have now become redundant, such as reports that are still produced despite the fact that nobody uses them any more. Eliminating these steps not only reduces the running costs and resources used by the process but also reduces the number of handoffs and their delays. Another example of simplification is where a number of steps carried out by different actors are combined into a single step for one actor only. As well as reducing the number of handoffs, this can also result in other improvements. There is greater scope for giving the actor a more meaningful task to carry out compared with the subtasks carried out previously. For example, it may be better if the actor is given more responsibility for checking the output produced instead of having the production and the validation split across different actors. The problem with the latter is that it includes a handoff and hence delays when errors are identified and the transaction has to be recycled.

Bottlenecks result when there is a mismatch in the capacities of related steps. For example, step A can handle 100 transactions per hour, which are then passed on to step B, which can deal with only 90 transactions per hour. In a simple example like this, it is easy to see that the resources needed by step B will have to be increased. Real-life processes are often very complex and require detailed analysis; in these cases it can be useful to use sophisticated process modelling tools as they provide simulation facilities that help us to examine the performance and resource requirements of proposed process designs.

As-is processes often reveal their origins. Although they may be supported by computer-based information systems, you do not need to look too closely to see that these systems are updated versions of the paper-based processing of years ago. Unfortunately, the processes may have unwittingly and unnecessarily carried through the limitations of that approach. Typically, there was only one copy of the paper transaction, which meant that only one person could be working on the information at any one time. As a result, the process steps were sequential, even though there might be no logical dependency between the steps. Modern workflow technology can free us from this limitation. Even if the transaction starts life in paper form, it can be scanned and electronic copies sent to several actors simultaneously, so long as they can work independently. As a result, the elapsed time for the overall process can be reduced significantly. This use of workflow technology is only one example of carrying out the steps in different ways. Another example is the use of computer systems to automate the flow through a process as much as possible. We are seeing this with the connection of web-based front ends to back office systems. The main problem with this approach is that we need to link up not only one but several back-office systems. As these systems were often developed to meet the needs of users operating in separate independent silos, the systems were not designed to cooperate. More software, the enterprise application integration (EAI) layer, is required to allow the necessary communication. Once that is in place, we can do away with the manual intervention at the interfaces and move to straight-through processing (STP).

Our final approach to improving an as-is process is to identify how the boundary of the process can be stretched by starting it earlier and finishing it later. This might seem to be contrary to some of the simplification ideas discussed above, but it can help to improve the service to the customer. Imagine we are defining a help-desk process, 'Solve customer problem'. It is tempting to assume that the process starts when the customer contacts the help desk with a problem. The help-desk analyst usually will need some details of the problem in order to identify its cause. If the customer does not have that information available, then the analyst will have to ask the customer to obtain it. If that is difficult, then the customer may have to wait until the problem occurs again, when they can then collect the required information. It would be more effective to regard the process as starting when the customer first picks up the problem. If at that point the necessary information was collected, then the frustration of reporting the problem only to be told that the help desk cannot help will be avoided. Taking this example a stage further, automatic diagnostic tests within the customer equipment might be able to identify faulty components before they affect the customer. If the maintenance engineers were notified of such problems, then the equipment could be modified without any reduction in service to the customer. Not only would the customer be happier with the equipment – 'It never goes wrong!' – but also the organization would receive fewer calls to the help desk.

Business processes are complex, a fact we realize when we try to understand and improve them. Although we can examine the flow through a process and determine how that can be supported by an IT system, there are many other factors that can affect the success of a process. Most processes involve people, and there are many reasons why individuals do not work at peak efficiency. They may not have been trained properly to carry out their step, they may not understand how their step fits into the overall process and then when something unusual happens they cannot deal with it, or staff motivation may be poor. It is important, therefore, to ensure that the processes, the people and the organization structure work in harmony in order to optimize performance.

PLANNING THE BUSINESS PROCESS IMPROVEMENT INITIATIVE

The term 'business process' can mean different things to different people. Senior management might think of 'supplier management' as a process, while an operational manager would be more familiar with smaller chunks of processing, such as 'place supplier order'. Although we can model processes at any level, there is a danger that we concentrate on a low-level process in isolation. The management staff of a functional area may realize that one of their processes is inefficient and, therefore, needs improving. At first sight it would seem that any improvement is to be welcomed, but a little more thought identifies pitfalls. First, how do we know that the money is best spent on this process? There may be other processes that are in a worse state or that would provide far greater benefits for the same investment. Second, there is always the possibility of sub-optimization. By improving one process in isolation, we might actually cause some degradation in the performance of other dependent processes. Although the local picture may be positive, with the immediate benefits outweighing the immediate costs, the broader picture across all the related processes may not look so good. The big picture would take into account all of the associated consequent effects and identify the dis-benefits. The third factor concerns the alignment between the process improvement and the high-level strategy of the organization. Short-term improvements may not look quite so sensible once we know the medium- to long-term plans of the business.

Business process modelling should not be regarded as a tactical exercise to improve the performance of individual processes. Instead, there should be linkage with the business objectives and strategy, possibly through an approach such as the balanced scorecard technique, as described in Chapter 3. The balanced scorecard first identifies what the organization wants to achieve financially. In order to achieve the stated revenues and profits, the organization must satisfy its customers' requirements, so the next level down in the scorecard is the measurement of customer satisfaction. That in turn depends on the performance of the processes that influence customer satisfaction, such as speed and accuracy of order delivery. As we indicated previously, processes and process modelling show in detail the steps necessary to meet higher-level business objectives. Once we have defined the processes, we can go on to identify not only the information and IT requirements but also the skills and competences of the people that will run those processes.

ADVANCED PROCESS MODELLING CONCEPTS

Modelling is an intrinsic part of design and subsequent development. Business analysts are familiar with modelling techniques. Increasingly, computer-aided software engineering (CASE) tools can use the information from the models to produce either program code or database schemas. The same is now happening with business process models. Workflow packages, for example, have to be told the sequence of steps that make up a process. This can be specified as a process model that directs what the package does. This approach is at the heart of business process management (BPM).

BPM is much more than modelling followed by the automated execution of that model. For instance, the designer of the process will want to find out how good that design is in terms of how well it will perform. Instead of implementing the process in the hope that it will perform satisfactorily, some modelling software can simulate the behaviour of the process so that we can assess in advance how well the redesign will work.

In order to do this, we will have to supply the software with the following details:

- the resources that will be available to carry out particular process steps;
- how long each step will take to deal with each type of transaction;
- the number of transactions of each type;
- the number of transactions that will go down particular paths in the process.

Based on this information, the software can predict what the process will do when presented with a typical set of transactions. This entails calculating how long each transaction will take at each stage, finding out where the queues will form if there is a shortage of resources to carry out a particular step, and determining how long on average the process will take to handle an input from start to finish. Often, initial process designs will not provide the desired performance. The designer then has to refine the design, perhaps by providing more resources to critical steps or by removing work that is not essential. In this way, the designer can experiment with the simulated process until it meets the stated requirements.

Once the process is in use operationally, the business process management system (BPMS) that controls the process collects data about the actual performance, a key aspect of the specification of a process. Therefore, we will need to collect actual measures to demonstrate the quality of the process. The balanced scorecard approach outlines a cause-and-effect chain between lower-level factors such as process behaviour and higher-level impacts on customer satisfaction and the financial performance of the business. If the processes do not perform as they should, then the business will not meet its revenue and profit targets. The performance measures are an early-warning system, pointing out what needs to be improved.

The introduction of BPMS potentially changes the nature of process modelling. Before BPMS, process models were aimed at people. Business analysts, for example, use BPMS to understand the business context in which a proposed IT system will operate and then go on to define the system's requirements. The business staff members who carry out the process can understand their role and how they interact with other actors involved in the process. With a BPMS, on the other hand, the model is being used by software to define the implementation of the process. Just as in the case of code generation, the models need to be defined with rigour and precision, otherwise the BPMS software will not know how to implement the process.

The growing importance and scope of process modelling highlight the need for increased standardization. If a process-modelling package produces a model that will be fed into a BPM package to implement the process, then both packages will have to adopt the same modelling conventions. As processes get larger and cross organizational boundaries, for example between suppliers and their customers, the modellers in the two organizations will find it easier to collaborate if they are using the same modelling techniques. Another factor is the prospect of integrating web services into business processes, hence the increased activity from the standards groups such as the Business Process Management Initiative (BPMI). It is not the remit of this book to examine this area in detail, but business analysts should be aware of standards such as business process modelling language (BPML) and business process execution language (BPEL), as they will be increasingly important in the future.

SUMMARY

Organizations need to operate effective and efficient business processes if they are to be successful in meeting their customers' needs. The emphasis on improving processes has increased over the past decade or so and currently many organizations devote a great deal of effort to analysing existing processes and designing new processes. Business process modelling is recognized as a key skill for business analysts, as it is an area where they are expected to help deliver business improvements for the organization.

FURTHER READING

Burlton, R. (2001) *Business Process Management: Profiting From Process.* Sams Publishing, Indianapolis, IN.

Davis, R. (2001) *Business Process Modelling with ARIS: A Practical Guide.* Springer-Verlag, London.

Hammer, M. (1998) *Beyond Reengineering: How the Process-Centered Organization is Changing Our Work and Our Lives.* HarperCollins, New York.

Hammer, M. and Champy, J. (1995) *Reengineering the Corporation: A Manifesto for Business Revolution.* Nicholas Brealey, London.

Harmon, P. (2003) *Business Process Change.* Morgan Kaufmann, Boston, MA.

Rummler, G.A. and Brache, A.P. (1990) *Improving Performance: How to Manage the White Space on the Organization Chart.* Jossey Bass Wiley, San Francisco, CA.

Sharp, A. and McDermott, P. (2001) *Workflow Modeling Tools for Process Improvement and Application Development.* Artech House, Boston, MA.

USEFUL WEBSITES

Business Process Management Group: www.bpmg.org
Business Process Management Initiative: www.bpmi.org

9 Requirements engineering

MALCOLM EVA

INTRODUCTION

> When I actually meet users ... I find that they certainly have needs, but that these do not appear in an organized form at all. The needs come out in a rush, a mixture of complaints, design decisions, interface descriptions, current situations, and from time to time specific human–machine interface requirements. It is sometimes possible to isolate chunks of this as definite functions. In short, there seems to be a gap between theory and practice. Theory says that on the one hand we'll find people who state what they want, and on the other, people who make things to please the first bunch of people. Instead, all the people and tasks and documents seem to be muddled up together.
>
> Alexander and Maiden (2004)

Most analysts involved in defining user requirements will probably recognize Ian Alexander's description. Requirements, apparently regarded by users as the uncomplicated bit of a new systems development, are actually the most problematic aspect. And yet as we see below, the time allocated for these is far less than for other phases. Requirements engineering, while an apparent oxymoron, is the industry's response to the problem of requirements for new IT/IS systems not being met and, indeed, not being offered clearly in the first place. Tight timescales and tight budgets – both the result of constraints on the business – place pressures on the development team to deliver a product. However, without the due time to understand and define the requirements properly, the product that is delivered on time may not be the product that the business thought it was asking for. Applying the process of requirements engineering should help to rectify that problem.

THE PROBLEMS WITH REQUIREMENTS

Studies carried out into IS project failures during the 1980s and 1990s tell a common story. Many of the projects and unsatisfactory systems suggest the following conclusions:

- A large proportion (over 80 per cent) of errors are introduced at the requirements analysis stage.

- Very few faults (less than 10 per cent) are introduced at the development stage – developers are programming things correctly but often not programming the right things.
- Most of the project time is allocated to the development and testing phases of the project.
- Less than 12 per cent of the project time is allocated to the requirements analysis phase.

These findings are particularly significant because the cost of correcting errors in requirements increases dramatically the later into the development lifecycle we find them. However, the study quoted above identifies requirements analysis as the most error-prone stage of the development lifecycle.

Typical problems with requirements have been identified as:

- lack of relevance to the objectives of the project;
- lack of clarity in the wording;
- ambiguity;
- duplication between requirements;
- conflicts between requirements;
- requirements expressed in such a way that it is difficult to assess whether they have been achieved;
- requirements that assume a solution rather than state what is to be delivered by the system;
- uncertainty among business users about what they need from the new system;
- business users omitting to identify requirements;
- inconsistent levels of detail;
- users and analysts taking certain knowledge for granted and failing to ensure that there is a common understanding.

The first point often results from a lack of terms of reference for the project. These are key to ensuring that everyone involved in defining the requirements understands the objectives, scope and constraints within which the project is to be carried out. The terms of reference should also identify the business authority for the project, thus ensuring that there is an ultimate arbiter to handle any conflicts between business users and their requirements. The eighth difficulty, that the users are uncertain of their needs, is by no means uncommon in a world of new business practices and new technology. The business analyst is the person who must help the users to visualize precisely what they need the new system to perform and then to articulate it.

Another source of difficulties for the business analyst is recognizing the different viewpoints behind each user. Depending on their roles in the organization, one user might see the business system as revolving around the product, another may think in terms of finding a marketing solution, and a third may see the system as being customer-focused. All three are describing their perceptions of the same system, but each sits in his or her own silo, viewing the business from that one viewpoint. It is up to the business analyst to draw the threads together in order to view the system as a whole and to meet all three perspectives as well as possible.

The philosopher Wittgenstein proposed an ambiguous animal in his Philosophical Investigations (1953) that illustrates this point well. The view of the animal is of its head in profile, showing two long protuberances which look like a bill – or could they be ears? – and a dimple on the other side of its head. The animal's eye is unambiguously visible in the centre. If the creature is viewed as looking to the left, it is clearly seen as a duck with a bill; if it is seen as looking towards the right, however, it is clearly a rabbit with its long ears. What it is not, though, is both together. Wittgenstein christened this ambiguous animal a duckrabbit, to make its identity clear.

The business analyst will encounter many duckrabbits during his or her career: a sales director who sources products to satisfy customer demands sees the company as a sales organization, while a finance director who has invested heavily in an in-house manufacturing capability will see a manufacturing organization. They are describing the same company, but one sees a duck and one sees a rabbit. Is the company there to provide satisfaction to its customers (a duck) or to sell its manufactured products (a rabbit)? The analyst or requirements engineer needs to understand all of these valid perspectives, or Weltanschauung (as described in Chapter 7), to be sure of capturing more than a one-sided view. Recognizing the existence of a duckrabbit, or simply multi-Weltanschauungen, helps us to anticipate scoping issues and potential requirements conflicts before they arise.

Another problem that business analysts face is an apparent inability on the part of the business users to articulate clearly what it is they wish the system to do for them. Some users, perhaps due to uncertainty, may even be reluctant to state their requirements. Very often they are deterred from doing so because the nature of the requirement is not susceptible to a straightforward statement. These issues may be due, at least in part, to the problem of tacit knowledge; we shall explore some of those issues in the section 'Requirements elicitation' on page 143.

THE PLACE OF REQUIREMENTS ENGINEERING AND THE SYSTEMS DEVELOPMENT LIFECYCLE

It is helpful to understand the place of requirements engineering in the overall lifecycle of a systems development project. A systems development lifecycle sets out the stages that are undertaken in the process of developing an IT system. The lifecycle covers the entire life of a system from feasibility study to operation. One of the principal models for systems development is known as the 'waterfall lifecycle'.

The waterfall lifecycle

The waterfall lifecycle was originally published in 1970 by W. Royce. Since this time many variations have evolved. However, the fundamental principles of the model persist. The systems development process is shown as a number of sequential stages, with each stage being completed before work begins on the following stage. The outputs from one stage are used as inputs to the next. An overview version of this lifecycle is shown in Figure 9.1.

The requirements engineering approach is used primarily in the 'Feasibility study' and 'Analysis' stages of this lifecycle.

Several variations of this lifecycle have been developed, for example to extend the lifecycle to include the operation and maintenance stages for an IT system and to reflect the lifecycle where a system is to be implemented in phases.

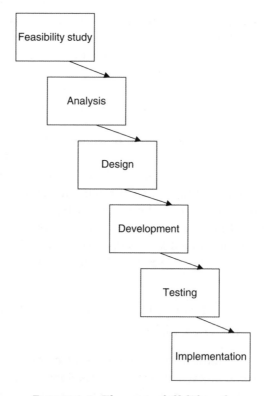

FIGURE 9.1 *The waterfall lifecycle*

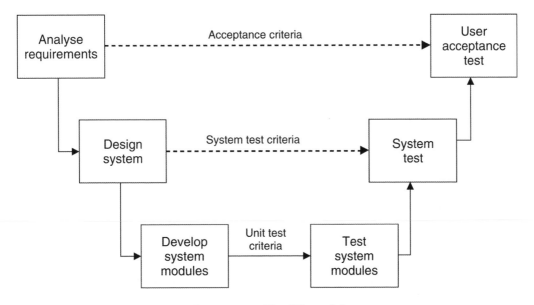

FIGURE 9.2 *The 'V' model*

One of the most popular variations is known as the 'V' model, where the stages from analysis to development are explicitly linked with the testing stages. A simplified version of this lifecycle is shown in Figure 9.2.

The major focus for requirements engineering in this model is the 'Analyse requirements' stage. We can see that the requirements documentation is passed to the next stage, 'Design System', and provides the basis for this work. An additional, and particularly useful, feature of the 'V' model is the inclusion of sideways links to the testing phases. The model in Figure 9.2 shows that the deliverables from the requirements analysis provide a basis for the user acceptance testing of the system.

The range of systems development lifecycles available also includes the evolutionary development approach based on the spiral model and the unified process used in object-oriented development. Further information about these lifecycles may be obtained from good project management and systems development texts; some references are provided at the end of this chapter.

A PROCESS FOR REQUIREMENTS ENGINEERING

The business analyst must be rigorous in understanding and documenting requirements in order to avoid the mistakes identified in the section 'The problems with requirements' on page 137. In order to ensure this rigour, the business analyst should follow a process or roadmap that includes all of the key steps required to develop a rigorous requirements document. Figure 9.3 illustrates the requirements engineering process. The rest of this chapter explains and expands on the entries in the process.

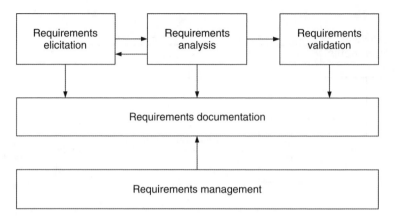

FIGURE 9.3 *Requirements engineering process*

The requirements document is at the heart of the process and can take a number of forms. Typically the document will include a catalogue of requirements, with each individual requirement documented using a standard template. One or more models showing specific aspects such as the processing or data requirements may supplement this catalogue. The standard template used to document each requirement is illustrated in the section 'Documenting the requirements' on page 149.

There are often situations where the catalogue is not sufficient on its own. One such situation is where there are numerous business rules to be documented, for example when validating an insurance claim. Where this is the case, an alternative approach is to document the requirement to validate an insurance claim at an overview level in the requirements catalogue and then express the detail using another, more appropriate technique. One possibility is to use a decision tree as shown in Figure 9.4. The business analyst must ensure that the document and any such supporting documentation are easily understood by two key groups: the business users who will need to validate the documentation, and the developers who will use the requirements document during the design and development phases of the lifecycle.

When we gather requirements, they are often explained to us with a lack of clarity and completeness, as described by Alexander at the beginning of this chapter. Before the requirements are formally entered into the catalogue, the business analyst needs to list them and subject them to careful scrutiny. This scrutiny will involve organizing the requirements into functional groupings and checking that each requirement is well formed. This is the 'analysis' phase in the process model; here, the business analyst has a gatekeeper role, ensuring that only those requirements that pass the scrutiny will be entered in the document.

One truism that everyone who works in systems development recognizes is that 'stuff happens'. Changes occur throughout the development cycle

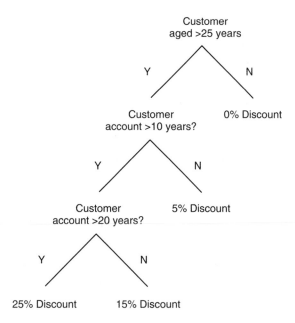

FIGURE 9.4 *Example decision tree to support a requirement 'Calculate customer discount'*

and procedures need to be in place to deal with them. Drivers for change include new project personnel generating new ideas, revisions to company policy or strategy, and external changes to the business environment. Whatever the reason, the business analyst must record, analyse and action the changes and, hence, ensure that every requirement is fully traceable from the initial recording to sign-off during user acceptance testing. Traceability and the use of CASE tools to support requirements management is discussed on page 156.

The requirements document should be analysed and checked by the business analyst for completeness and consistency. Once the document is considered to be complete, it must be reviewed by business representatives and confirmed to be a true statement of the required system; at this point, the document is said to be 'signed off'. This process of review and sign-off is known as the requirements validation stage. During this stage the reviewers examine the requirements and question whether they are well defined, clear and complete. The review will be similar to that undertaken in the analysis stage, but the business rather than the analysts is required to carry out the validation.

ACTORS

There are some participants we expect to see in the requirements process. They represent three broad stakeholder groups:

- the business;
- the user community;
- the system development team.

The project sponsor represents the needs of the business. The sponsor has the following responsibilities:

- to agree the project initiation document that approves the requirements analysis study;
- to deliver the business benefits predicted in the business case;
- to make funds and other resources available for the project;
- to accept the deliverables at the end of the project;
- to approve and sign off the requirements document as a true statement of the business's needs for the new system;
- to rule on any conflicting requirements where the business analyst cannot negotiate agreement.

The user community is represented by the following:

- Domain expert or subject-matter expert: this person's role is to give high-level advice on the requirements, particularly when they concern more than one business function or are for a new business process or product that the company does not yet fully understand. They bring breadth of understanding to the process and should have experience and knowledge of industry best practice.

- End users: by definition, these will be the individuals or groups who will need to use the system and, accordingly, for whom the system is designed. They should be able to define their requirements in detail, providing specific clear information. They are required to describe current procedures and documentation, highlight any difficulties they experience with current processes, and identify new requirements for the system. They will be able to assist with the specification of non-functional requirements that apply to their tasks, although some aspects may need the involvement of more senior management, for example decisions about archiving information and the length of retention of data. There are likely to be several end-user roles, each of which needs to be considered when analysing the requirements. One of the end-user roles may be the 'customer', for example where an internet-based system is to be implemented; in this case, care needs to be taken to ensure that the requirements are gathered accurately and appropriate techniques, such as focus groups, are used to acquire the relevant information.

The system development team is represented by the following:

- Requirements engineer (usually a business analyst): the analysts carry out the requirements engineering work and their key objective is to ensure that the requirements are documented clearly and completely. They discuss the requirements with the users and are responsible to the sponsor for the quality of the submitted requirements document.

- Developer: the developer will be able to check the technical feasibility of some of the requirements and help the analyst to appreciate the implications of the users' expectations. The developer is able to produce prototypes of the requirements, to help users visualize in greater detail what they need, or to confirm our understanding of what we have been told.

REQUIREMENTS ELICITATION

Nowadays, the rationale for developing or enhancing systems includes a need to help the organization gain a competitive advantage, to support new business processes, or to support a business process re-engineering exercise. The more straightforward approach of using the current procedures as a basis has declined. Hence there is a strong likelihood that the business users will be not at all clear about what they need the system to provide.

Requirements elicitation is a proactive approach to understanding requirements. It involves drawing out the requirements from the users, helping them to visualize the possibilities and articulate their requirements. The requirements emerge as a result of the interaction between analyst and user, with much proactive elicitation on the part of the analyst.

Tacit knowledge

When developing a new system, the business user will pass on to us their explicit knowledge, i.e. their knowledge of procedures and data that is at the front of their mind and that they can articulate easily. A major problem when eliciting requirements is that of tacit knowledge. By tacit knowledge, we mean those other aspects of the work that a user is unable to articulate or explain. The term derives from the work of Polanyi (1966), whose thesis is expressed succinctly in the maxim 'We can know more than we can tell.' In terms of understanding requirements, there are a number of elements to tacit knowledge that we must be aware of and recognize when we encounter them.

Some common elements that cause problems and misunderstandings are as follows:

- Skills: when explaining how to carry out actions, using words alone is extremely difficult. For example, consider how you might convey the correct sequence of actions that would be necessary to turn right at a roundabout on a dual carriageway. To build an automated vehicle that could travel along roads without a driver would need all of this information, but a driver would not be able explain this accurately during an interview.

- Taken-for-granted information: even experienced and expert business users may fail to mention information or clarify terminology, and the analyst may not realize that further questioning is required. The gap in your understanding may not emerge until user acceptance testing or even post-implementation, and this may be costly and complex to correct. This issue has been identified as a cause of many systems failures.

- Front story/back story: this issue concerns a tendency to frame a description of current working practices, or a workplace, in order to give a more positive view than is actually the case. The business user may do this in order to avoid reflecting badly on the staff or the organization. An analogy could be the swan gliding gracefully across the smooth surface of a lake (front story) while below the surface its feet are paddling frantically to sustain the gentle momentum (back story). This problem can occur because we are perceived to be reporting to the management of the organization. Therefore the business users may feel that we should be given the favourable front-story version of how the business or department works. It is important that we build good working relationships with the business users and encourage them to trust us so that we are able to obtain details of the back story of the reality of the business operation.

- Future systems knowledge: if the study is for a green-field develop-ment, with no existing expertise or knowledge in our organization, how can the prospective users know just what they want? We cannot ask them to demonstrate what they do not understand, and yet we must draw from them precisely what they need the system to provide.

- 'Your finger, you fool!': this is based upon an apocryphal story about a 17th-century European explorer who landed on an island and asked a native inhabitant the name of a prominent mountain. He pointed at the landmark he was asking about, but the islanders did not recognize the gesture of pointing. The inhabitant assumed that what he was being asked to identify was the outstretched finger. This illustrates the difficulty of an outsider assuming a common language for discourse and common norms of communication. Without an extended period of detailed investigation of the organizational culture – an ethno-graphic study – how can external analysts be sure that they have a common understanding? If they do not have this, then the scope for misrepresentation of the situation can grow considerably.

- Intuitive understanding, usually born of considerable experience: decision-makers are often thought to follow a logical linear path of enquiry while making their decisions. This is so of medical diagnosticians, geological surveyors looking for specific mineral bearing rock, investment brokers and experts in all sorts of fields. In reality, though, as improved decision-making skills and knowledge are acquired the linear path is often abandoned in favour of intuitive pattern recognition. Ask specialists why they made a particular judgement and you may hear some logical steps, but there will often be a stage where they give a shrug and an answer such as 'Well, you just know, don't you?' This response reflects that at least part of the answer has been made using 'intuition'; this is where knowledge has been applied at a tacit level rather than explicitly.

With the exception of 'front story/back story', these issues all occur because of the application of an individual's tacit knowledge. However, there are situations where an organization possesses tacit knowledge, and it is important that this is recognized and understood. Examples of organizational tacit knowledge include the following:

- Norms of behaviour and communication: these evolve in every organization rather than fit into what is decreed from above. Any new system that threatens to conflict with these norms may face resistance.

- Organizational culture: without an understanding of the culture of an organization, the requirements exercise may be flawed.

- Communities of practice: these are discrete groups of workers related by task, department, geographical location or some other factor and that have their own sets of norms and practices, distinct from other groups within the organization and the organization as a whole. A community of practice is likely to have its own body of tacit information, which it is not accustomed to sharing openly. If a systems development project involves cross-functional requirements or is company-wide, then the understanding of the various communities of practice is an important part of the elicitation.

Table 9.1 shows levels of both tacit and explicit knowledge.

TABLE 9.1 *Levels of tacit and explicit knowledge*

	Tacit	Explicit
Individual	Skills, values, taken-for-granted, intuitiveness	Tasks, job descriptions, targets, volumes and frequencies
Corporate	Norms, back story, culture, communities of practice	Procedures, style guides, processes, historical data

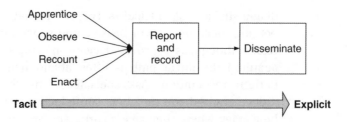

FIGURE 9.5 *Tacit to explicit knowledge*

Tacit knowledge can be made more explicit. To do this, we need to use techniques to assist business users to articulate tacit knowledge. Once the users have articulated the tacit knowledge, it is important to ensure that it is documented and disseminated to the other members of the project team.

Requirements elicitation techniques

There are a number of techniques available to the analyst to help elicit knowledge and requirements from all levels of the organization. The most useful and accessible techniques are discussed in Chapter 5. A process for eliciting tacit knowledge is shown in Figure 9.5.

Techniques described in Chapter 5 that specifically support the process above include the following:

- Apprentice: shadowing, protocol analysis.

- Recount: storytelling, scenario.

- Enact: prototype, scenario role-play.

It is important that business analysts have a toolkit of techniques so that they can tailor their approach when eliciting requirements. Table 9.2 matches some of the most popular elicitation techniques with the knowledge types that a business analyst is likely to have to handle. This mapping of techniques to knowledge types provides a good indication of where certain techniques can be particularly useful and where they are of less use.

TABLE 9.2 *Techniques and knowledge types (after Maiden and Rugg 1996)*

Technique	Explicit knowledge	Tacit knowledge	Skills	Future requirements
Interviewing		✓		✓
Shadowing	✓✓	✓✓	✓✓	✗
Workshops	✓✓	✓✓	✗	✓✓
Prototyping	✓✓	✓✓	✓✓	✓✓
Scenario analysis	✓✓	✓✓	✗	✓✓
Protocol analysis	✓✓	✓✓	✓✓	✗

✓✓, very relevant; ✓, relevant; ✗, not relevant.

BUILDING THE REQUIREMENTS LIST

As we uncover the requirements from our various users, we need to document them. This is best done in two distinct passes: building the requirements list and developing an organized requirements catalogue.

The requirements list is quite simply what it says – a list containing every requirement that has been stated or elicited. The list tends to be an informal document and can be presented as three columns, as shown in Table 9.3.

TABLE 9.3 *Example requirements list*

Requirement	Source	Comments
1 The company needs to reduce the amount of paper moved between departments	IN	Real requirement? See also requirement 5
2 The system must capture customer payments	IN	
3 The customer file must be password-protected	FD	Non-functional? Is this a solution?
4 We need the information quicker	JK	Quantify
5 We must be able to record customer details, amend them and delete old customers	JK	Need breaking into three requirements?

The requirements list is produced following an initial interview or workshop and is developed further once more requirements have been identified. The requirements identified at this stage will vary considerably; some may be detailed and specific, while others will be defined only at an overview level or may represent several potential requirements. The requirements list helps to ensure that everything that is raised is documented and the source identified.

Once some requirements have been elicited and entered on to the requirements list, the next step in the requirements engineering process can begin: analysing the individual requirements.

REQUIREMENTS ANALYSIS

Requirements analysis is concerned with ensuring that all of the requirements identified during requirements elicitation have been developed into clear, organized, fully documented requirements. As this process is carried out, many additional questions will be raised, and the analyst may need to investigate the requirements further using requirements elicitation techniques. Thus, an iterative cycle of requirements elicitation and analysis develops.

The analyst needs to examine each requirement on the list to see whether it is well formed and SMART (specific, measurable, achievable, relevant, time-framed). The filters to apply are as follows:

- Are the requirements as captured ambiguous? We need to consider here the problems of terminology and jargon. Common sources of confusion are:
  - synonyms – two words with the same meaning across different departments;
  - homonyms – the same word being used differently across departments.

- Is the meaning clear?

- Is the requirement aligned to the project and business objectives, or is it irrelevant?

- Is the requirement reasonable, or would it be expensive and time-consuming to satisfy? Imagine a client asking an architect to build a large swimming pool into a new house design without increasing the cost. Business users sometimes ask for an additional feature without appreciating the cost implications.

- Do any requirements conflict with one another, such that only one may be implemented? When such a conflict is identified, the business analyst is responsible for helping to negotiate a resolution. If the two sources are adamant, and neither will give way, then the decision needs to be passed up to the sponsor or even escalated to the project board.

- Do the requirements imply a solution rather than state a requirement? Business users often express a requirement in terms of the technological solution, rather than in terms of what the business needs. For example, a requirement may dictate that a specific package should be used before any recommendations about system enhancement or replacement have been made.

- Are they atomic, or are they really several requirements grouped into one entry? For example, 'The reservations clerk must be able to record a booking. They must also be able to amend or cancel bookings.'

- Do several requirements overlap or duplicate each other?

There are several potential outcomes from this exercise, as follows:

- Accept the requirement as it stands and document it in full in the requirements catalogue (see the section 'Documenting the requirements' on page 149).

- Reword the requirement in order to remove jargon and ambiguity.

- Merge duplicated/overlapping requirements.

- Take unclear and ambiguous requirements back to the business users for clarification.

Requirements that are in conflict, unrealistic or out of alignment with the business objectives still need to be documented in the requirements catalogue in order to ensure that an audit trail is kept of all requirements raised and any subsequent action taken. This does not mean that they will be implemented in the new system, as that decision comes later, but that they should be considered for implementation.

DOCUMENTING THE REQUIREMENTS

The requirements catalogue is the central repository of the business users' requirements, and all of the requirements should be documented here. There are two major types of requirement: functional and non-functional.

Functional requirements are concerned with the functions that the system must provide, i.e. what the system must do. Examples of functional requirements are:

- record customer details;
- provide a report of all outstanding invoices;
- convert order amounts payable into US dollars on request.

Non-functional requirements are concerned with the performance and level of operation of the system, in other words how well the system will perform in certain areas. Common non-functional requirements are:

- response times or transaction time;
- availability;
- adherence to conditions of legislation;
- privacy/security;
- volumes of data that can be handled;
- frequencies of transactions;
- backup and recovery;
- usability;
- archiving.

Non-functional requirements must be defined clearly and specifically so that they can be measured and tested. For example, if there is a usability requirement, then the statement 'The system must be easy to use' is not sufficiently clear and measurable. Such a statement raises the question 'How easy is "easy"?' Does this mean easy for a novice or for a technical expert? The requirement needs to be defined in measurable terms, such as 'The function must be capable of being used by a novice with half an hour's training', or 'The transaction should be completed with no more than 10 keystrokes, and with an error rate of no more than 1 in 50 transactions.'

The requirements catalogue

Each requirement that has been analysed is documented using a standard template. Figure 9.6 illustrates such a template.

Project/system	Author		Date
Requirement Id	Requirement Name		
Source	Owner	Priority	Business activity
Functional requirement description			
Non-functional requirements	Description		
Justification			
Related documents			
Related requirements			
Comments			
Resolution			
Version No.	Change history Date Change request		

FIGURE 9.6 *Requirements catalogue template*

A template such as this provides a standard agreed form for describing each requirement, a set of acceptance criteria for testing, and information about related requirements and documents. In addition, the ability to record different versions of each requirement enables one to track changes to the requirements.

The entries in the template are as follows:

- **Requirement identifier:** an identifier allocated by the project (possibly the project reference plus a number) for reference and retrieval. This is particularly important if the template is kept electronically.

- **Requirement name:** a simple explanatory name.

- **Source:** the business user or users who requested the requirement, or the document where the requirement was raised. It is possible that there will be many sources of a requirement. Recording the source of a requirement helps ensure traceability.

- **Owner:** the one business user who accepts ownership of the individual requirement, will agree that it is worded and documented correctly, and will sign it off at acceptance testing when satisfied.

- **Priority:** the level of importance and need for a requirement. There are several approaches to prioritizing requirements, from the simple 'mandatory', 'desirable' and 'nice to have' to more complex approaches such as MoSCoW:
  - Must have: a key requirement without which the system has no value. These requirements are sometimes said to form the 'minimum usable subset'.
  - Should have: an important requirement that must be delivered but, where time is short, could be delayed for a future delivery. This should be a short-term delay. These requirements are mandatory, as it is anticipated that they would be delivered, but in the short term the system would still have value without them.
  - Could have: a requirement that would be beneficial to include if it does not cost too much or take too long to deliver but that is not central to the project objectives.
  - Want to have (but will not have this time): a requirement that will be needed in the future but is not required for this delivery. In a future release, this requirement may be upgraded to a 'must have'.

The priority is not awarded when the requirement is first documented: that will happen at a later meeting with the business users.

- **Requirement description:** a succinct SMART description of the requirement in a clear and unambiguous way. A useful approach is to describe the requirement using the following structure:
  - actor (or user role), e.g. the sales clerk;
  - verb phrase;
  - object (noun or noun-phrase).

An example is 'The sales clerk must be able to view the customer name, account number and credit limit.' Avoid the use of words such as 'and', 'although', 'except', 'unless', 'when' and 'until', as they suggest that there may be a number of requirements included within the description. In addition, if a descriptive sentence contains multiple clauses, it becomes more complex to read and follow and increases the likelihood of misunderstanding. Where the requirement incorporates complex business rules or data validation, these may be defined more clearly if techniques that specifically address the particular area of complexity are used. For example, a decision table or decision tree may be more useful to define complex business rules, and data-validation rules may be defined in a data catalogue. If a supplementary technique is used to specify or model the requirement, then there should be a cross-reference to the related document.

- **Business activity:** a simple phrase to group together requirements that support a specific activity, such as sales, inventory and customer services. If the scope of the project was an HR department, then business activity headings might be 'Recruitment', 'Appraisal' and 'Staff development'. The business activity can provide a basis for organizing the requirements catalogue, so that all requirements concerned with a particular business activity, such as 'Recruitment' in the HR system, can be grouped together.

- **Associated non-functional requirements:** these are constraints or performance measures with which the functional requirements must comply.

- **Justification:** not all of the requirements that are requested will be met. This may be due to time and budget constraints or may be because the requirement is dropped in favour of a conflicting requirement. Often, the requirement is not met because it adds little value to the business. The justification sets out the reasons for requesting the requirement. If possible, it should be related to a tangible benefit, but at this early stage this is not always possible. If the requirement is for a core function, then the justification might be that without that facility there can be no system. For example, a sales system would be useless without the requirement 'Capture new customer order'.

- **Related documents:** this refers to any document that provides further information about the requirement. Examples of such documents are interview notes, workshop minutes, use case descriptions, sections of a functional specification, a sample report layout and an input document. A cross-reference to another document may help with the traceability of the requirement. The related document entry should develop as the analysis and design of the system progress.

- **Related requirements:** requirements may be related to each other for several reasons. Sometimes there is a link between the functionality required by the requirements or a high-level requirement is clarified by a series of more detailed requirements. For example, a manager may raise a high-level requirement, which is defined further by the clerks who perform the work. The lower-level expression may take the form of several discrete requirements that together satisfy the higher-level expression. Thus, a sales-office manager may tell us that he or she needs the system to satisfy a customer order (requirement 1). The clerks who deal with the order transactions tell us that in order to do that they must be able to:

– record a new customer (requirement 2);
– interrogate the parts record (requirement 3);
– interrogate stock levels (requirement 4);
– identify substitutes for out-of-stock items (requirement 5);
– allocate stock (requirement 6);
– reserve stock out of a future delivery (requirement 7);
– enter the order details to create a record (requirement 8).

The catalogue entries will cross-refer requirements 2–8 to requirement 1. This helps with change control and traceability. If a requirement is subject to a change, then it is possible that one or more related requirements will also be affected. By identifying them in the catalogue, there is less chance that an important impact will be overlooked.

- **Resolution:** this reflects how and when the requirement is to be addressed, including where the requirement is not to be included in the system. This entry will be one of the last to be completed for each requirement, as it is often dependent upon the decisions made by business management about the content of the system. Recording the resolution also aids the traceability of the requirement.

- **Change history:** the entries in this section provide a record of all the changes that have affected the requirement. This is required for configuration management and traceability purposes.

This template suggests the most common aspects described about requirements. However, there may be other attributes about each requirement that an organization might wish to keep, for example an estimate of the cost of delivering the requirement would help to construct the business case.

Modelling approaches

As we mentioned earlier, the requirements catalogue is the central repository of the requirements. However, although it should be a complete record and provides the basis for the delivered system, it is not a document that is easily read and assimilated. Most requirements catalogues run to several hundred requirements, and it is not possible to understand what the system will do by reading so many individual entries. What is missing is any sense of cohesion, a diagram that allows us to appreciate exactly what this system will deliver, and a narrative explaining the sequence and connections between the systems functions. In order to address this, the analyst should supplement the documentation with one or more models of the system defined in the requirements catalogue.

The first model that should be included is a simple scoping model to provide a baseline for the high-level requirements for the development. A common model for this purpose is a use case diagram, which simply shows the functions, or use cases, inside the system boundary, and those actors responsible for using them. There is no indication of flow, sequence, input or output, but simply the scope of the new system. It is good to do this early because the individual use cases can become the starting point of a scenario analysis to uncover further lower-level requirements. Use case diagrams are explored further in Chapter 10.

To supplement this diagram, it helps to provide a model showing a narrative of the system. Dataflow models, interaction diagrams or business process models (see Chapter 8) are easily read models that show the processes that the system is to perform. When checking the requirements catalogue for completeness, one can cross-refer the catalogue entries with the model in order to be sure that a requirement is specified for each part of the process.

Process models serve a number of purposes:

- They can prompt further questions for the business users if they uncover a gap in the analyst's or business users' understanding.

- The inputs, outputs and processing can be cross-referenced to the catalogue entries.

- It is often easier for developers to follow the logic of a model than to assess separate catalogue entries.

- It is easier to check for completeness of the requirements set.

The requirements document

The requirements document should provide a complete picture of the requirements and should define clearly what we want the system to include. An effective requirements document should comprise the following elements:

- a glossary of terms to define each organizational term used within the requirements document. This will help manage the problem of local jargon and will enable the analysts to clarify synonyms and homonyms for anyone using the document;

- a scoping model such as a use case diagram;

- the requirements catalogue;

- a process model comprising diagrams such as business process models, dataflow diagrams and interaction diagrams.

VALIDATING REQUIREMENTS

Once the analysts deem the requirements document to be complete, then the business representatives need to agree that it is an accurate statement of the system requirements. The document is then said to be 'signed off'. A review group needs to be defined that will be responsible for checking the document and confirming its suitability. The review group should include the owners of the individual requirements or their representatives. These reviewers focus on the issues that the requirements analysis stage considered earlier. Hence, they should look for any ambiguity, lack of clarity, conflicting requirements, misalignment with the business objectives and a lack of testable measures. It is the business's responsibility – and last opportunity – to be satisfied with the requirements before accepting them.

There may be some additional reviewers who represent specific areas and have a particular remit for their review. An example is the project office review perspective, which would focus upon conformance to standards laid down by the project office.

When all the reviewers are satisfied with the document, it will be signed off and any subsequent changes will be subject to formal change control procedures.

The format for the review may comprise a meeting where the document is subject to a 'structured walkthrough'. If the requirements document is large, then it may be necessary to hold several meetings. Some organizations use electronic reviews, where the document is distributed, and reviewers are required to respond, via email. Whichever approach is used, there are some participant roles that should be involved in each review:

- project sponsor;
- subject-matter (domain) expert;
- reviewers, including the requirements' owners;
- presenter (business analyst);
- chairperson for the review.

The outcome of the review should be an agreement that the entire requirements document is complete, consistent, conformant and a true reflection of what the business requires to be delivered. This may be agreed outright, but more typically some changes or enhancements are needed before the business is ready to sign off.

MANAGING CHANGES TO REQUIREMENTS

One inevitable fact about a requirements document is that it will change over time. These changes may come about because:

- a key stakeholder has changed;
- the scope of the development has altered through budget constraints;
- the system must comply with new regulation or legislation;
- changes in business priorities have been announced;
- a response is needed to a competitor's development;
- there are compatibility issues with new technology that is to be installed;
- users and analysts have understood a requirement better after some detailed analysis, for example using scenarios or prototyping, and amended the original requirement accordingly.

An important feature to help guide the management of requirements is traceability. Traceability means that any user who has asked for a requirement can find out how it has been designed and implemented. There are two forms of traceability that need to be built in:

- Forward traceability, which enables the business to see how requirements that have been raised are carried forward to implementation, or not, as the case may be. This will link the source notes from interviews or workshops to the entry in the requirements catalogue, through to the functional specification, or design, and from there to the delivered functionality.
- Backward traceability, which begins at a piece of functionality that has been implemented and links it back to the functional specification, from there to the catalogue, and finally back to the source that requested it.

Documenting and tracking requirements can take a great deal of effort, and some analysts may find electronic tools beneficial. With the numbers of requirements that even a fairly small project can generate, and the numbers of changes that can impact upon the catalogue, trying to maintain it on paper can be very onerous. There are a number of specialist support tools on the market, known as computer-aided requirements engineering (CARE) or computer-aided software engineering (CASE). However, in the absence of a specific tool, a suite of office software, including a spreadsheet or simple database, can carry out some of the core functions of such a tool. These functions include:

- maintaining cross-references between requirements;
- storing requirements documentation;
- managing changes to the requirements documentation;

- managing versions of the requirements documentation;
- restricting access to the requirements documentation.

The major aim of requirements management is to ensure that each requirement is tracked from inception to implementation (or withdrawal) through all of the changes that have been applied to it. An electronic tool is vital if we are to achieve this.

SUMMARY

Requirements engineering is the approach by which we ensure that sufficient rigour is introduced into the process of understanding and documenting user's requirements and ensuring traceability of changes to each requirement. This process comprises the stages of elicitation, analysis (which feeds back into the elicitation) and validation. All of these contribute to the production of a rigorous, complete requirements document. The core of this document is a repository of individual requirements that is developed and managed during the requirements engineering process. If an organization places insufficient emphasis on defining requirements, it is to the detriment of the implemented systems and leaves business users unable to do their jobs effectively. Requirements engineering is an approach by which we can deliver systems that truly meet business needs.

REFERENCES

Alexander, I. and Stevens, R. (2004) *Writing Better Requirements*. Addison-Wesley, Harlow.

Maiden, N.A.M. and Rugg, G. (1996) ACRE: selecting methods for requirements acquisition. *Software Engineering Journal*, **11**, 183–192.

Polanyi, M. (1966) *Tacit Knowledge in Managerial Success*. University of Chicago Press, Chicago.

Wittgenstein, L. (1953) *Philosophical Investigations*. Blackwell, Oxford.

FURTHER READING

Alexander, I. and Maiden, N. (2004) *Scenarios, Stories and Use Cases*. John Wiley & Sons, Chichester.

Cadle, J. and Yeates, D. (2004) *Project Management for Information Systems*. FT Prentice Hall, Harlow.

Gause, D. and Weinberg, G. (1989) *Exploring Requirements: Quality before Design*. Dorset House, New York.

Hay, D. (2003) *Requirements Analysis*. Prentice Hall, Upper Saddle River, NJ.

Kotonya, G. and Sommerville, I. (1998) *Requirements Engineering.* John Wiley & Sons, Chichester.

Kulak, D. and Guinney, E. (2000) *Use Cases, Requirements in Context.* Addison Wesley, Boston, MA.

Robertson, S. and Robertson, J. (1999) *Mastering the Requirements Process.* Addison-Wesley, Harlow.

Skidmore, S. and Eva, M. (2004) *Introducing Systems Development.* Palgrave Macmillan, Basingstoke.

Yeates, D. and Wakefield, T. (2004) *Systems Analysis and Design.* FT Prentice Hall, Harlow.

10 Modelling the IT system

DEBRA PAUL AND JAMES CADLE

INTRODUCTION

This chapter introduces some of the most commonly used techniques for modelling IT systems. These techniques are used mainly during the analysis stage of the systems development lifecycle (see Chapter 9). Models are extremely useful in helping to clarify understanding and, if cross-checked with other models, ensuring the completeness of the analysis. A model shows only one view or perspective of a system, but it does show this view very clearly. This induces the analyst to ask further questions, often those that have not been identified previously. The techniques we describe here have been selected from two standard approaches to systems modelling: the unified modelling language (UML) and the structured systems analysis and design method (SSADM). The selected techniques model two distinct views of the IT system: the functions that the system will provide and the data to be stored within the system.

MODELLING SYSTEM FUNCTIONS

The saying 'one picture is worth 10,000 words' applies directly to the definition of IT system requirements. It is extremely difficult, if not impossible, to write textual statements that are completely unambiguous. However, this is not the case with a model that has been drawn using defined notational standards; each box and line makes a clear statement about the system under investigation. Some models are understood more easily than others by business users. The view of a system that is often most accessible to business users depicts the functions that will be provided and the actors that are involved in using those functions. A function may be defined as a set of actions that the business users want the IT system to support in order to achieve a specific goal. For example, a function might be 'Record customer'; the actions here would include the following:

- Accept the customer details.
- Validate the customer details.
- Store the customer details that have been entered.

A widely used approach to modelling system functions is the use case model.

In the UML, a use case is something that an actor wants the IT system to do; it is a 'case of use' of the system by a specific actor and describes the interaction between an actor and the system. Each use case will have a stated goal and will contain a description of the actions that the system must perform in order to achieve this goal. The use case model will consist of a diagram showing the actors, the use cases and the associations between them, plus a set of use case descriptions. The following elements are found in the use case diagram:

- **Actors** are whoever or whatever expects a service from the system. They are usually user roles, but also they may be external systems or time. On the use case diagram, actors are shown interacting with the use cases. As they are external to the system and outside its control, defining the system actors and the use cases they are associated with helps us to define the system boundary. Actors are usually shown as matchstick figures, but if the actor is another system it can be shown by a rectangle with an <<actor>> stereotype before the name of the system. Some analysts prefer to show all actors, including the job roles, as rectangles because business users can feel that matchstick figures trivialize the diagrams. Time can also be an actor and may be shown as a rectangle or matchstick figure.

- Each **use case** is shown as an oval and represents a function that the system will perform in response to a trigger from the actor. We use the 'verb–noun' convention to name use cases, for example 'Set up project' or 'Book room'.

- The **system boundary** is indicated by drawing a large box around all of the use cases, but with the actors outside the box. This illustrates clearly the boundary of the system and is very useful when agreeing the scope of the system.

- **Associations** indicate which actors will need to interact with which use cases. Lines are drawn linking actors with the appropriate use cases.

The use case diagram in Figure 10.1 shows part of a project control system. We might create a diagram such as this during a workshop or following some interviews with the business users.

Use case diagrams are particularly useful during a workshop because they are easily understood by business users and provide an excellent framework for the discussion. The detail of the interaction between an actor and a use case is documented in a use case description. This lists the steps that take place during the interaction and is usually a textual description. The detail of any processing carried out within the use case may be documented using a variety of techniques. For example, we could

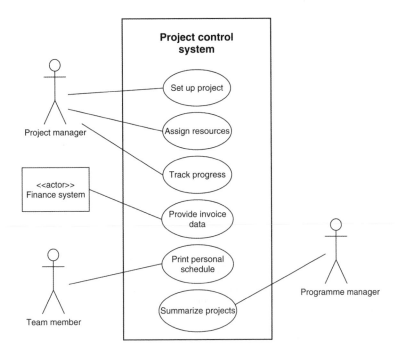

FIGURE 10.1 *Use case diagram for project control system*

use activity diagrams from the UML or other more established techniques such as decision tables.

The <<include>> and <<extend>> constructs

When exploring the use cases, it often emerges that some processing elements are repeated. For example, in the project control system many of the use cases start by identifying the project concerned. As it stands, the steps involved in identifying the project would have to be included in each use case, and a great deal of duplication would result. Instead of this, the project-identification elements can be written as a separate use case and then 'included' in a number of others. This is represented in Figure 10.2, where the <<include>> stereotype is shown on a dotted line with an arrowhead pointing to the included use case.

It may also emerge during more detailed investigation and specification that there are some optional elements to the use cases that require a significant amount of processing and may be so large that they overwhelm the original use case. In this situation, a separate use case can be created to 'extend' the original use case. For example, after the project manager tracks progress, he or she may also print a progress report; in Figure 10.3, this has been split off into a separate use case. The new use case is said to 'extend' the original use case, and this association is shown by a dotted line with an arrowhead that points back to the original use case.

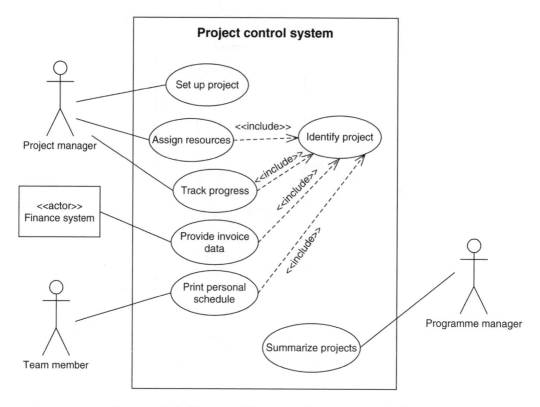

FIGURE 10.2 *Use case diagram showing <<include>>*

The <<include>> and <<extend>> concepts allow use cases to be connected to each other. This is the only way in which use cases are linked, as these diagrams are not intended to show the flow or sequence of the processing.

MODELLING SYSTEM DATA

Modelling the data to be stored within the IT system is vital. A data model allows the stakeholders who will need to use the system or obtain information from it to agree the data that will be recorded and retrieved. It will also provide the basis for the database design in a bespoke development or help in the evaluation of a packaged application. Data modelling is a useful tool for the business analyst. It helps the analyst better understand the data required to support process improvements and provides a mechanism for communicating the data requirements forward into the design and build of an IT system. The entity relationship modelling technique is used extensively to model the data to be held in IT systems. The UML approach to modelling data, known as class modelling, is also used widely. In this section, we look at both of these techniques.

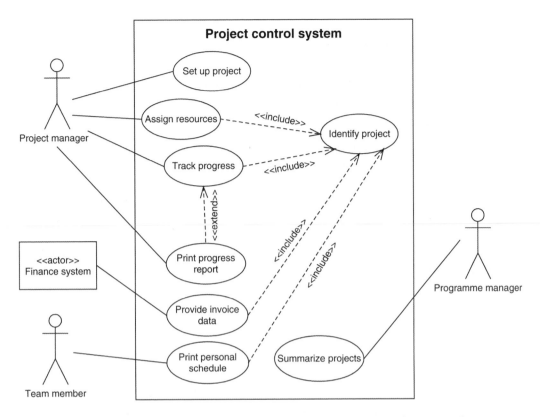

FIGURE 10.3 *Use case diagram showing <<include>> and <<extend>>*

Entity relationship diagrams

Regardless of whether or not they are computerized, organizations require clear and accurate knowledge of the data structures that underlie their information requirements. Chapter 11 explains the use of data as a resource and the importance of managing that resource.

Data is the raw building blocks of all information systems, and the objective of data modelling is to express this structure in a concise and usable way. Data modelling is concerned with identifying and understanding:

- the data items (attributes) that the organization (or system) needs to keep;
- the grouping of the attributes (into entities);
- the relationships between entities.

The notation we use here is used widely in Britain. There are other notations in use, but the principles of data modelling are very much the same, whichever notation is used.

An entity is something that the enterprise recognizes in the area under investigation and wishes to collect and store data about. An entity might be:

- physical, e.g. order, customer, supplier;
- conceptual, e.g. booking, appointment;
- active, e.g. meeting, course.

Entities are represented on the model by a box. Each entity has a meaningful name, normally a noun, which is always singular. It is important to distinguish between the 'entity type' and the 'entity occurrence'. For example, if the entity type is 'Book', then the entity occurrence is a specific instance of a book, such as *Business Analysis* or *Data Analysis for Database Design.* The physical equivalent of an entity type is a table, and that of an entity occurrence is a record. We usually talk about 'entities' as an abbreviation of 'entity types' but refer specifically to entity occurrences. Individual occurrences of an entity must be uniquely identifiable. For example, each customer or order must have a unique identifier, such as 'account-number' or 'order-number'.

Attributes

Entities contain and are described by attributes or, more accurately, attribute types. For example, the entity 'Book' might be described by the attributes 'title', 'author-name', 'publisher' and 'price'. Attributes may also be called data items. An attribute's physical equivalent is a field. A specific entity occurrence should be uniquely identifiable by the value of an attribute or combination of attributes. For example, a member may be identified by the attribute 'member-number' or a specific book may be recognized from the combination of the two attributes 'author' and 'title'. This identifying attribute or combination of attributes is termed the key to the entity. The initial entities and some attributes will be identified from the interview notes, documents and observations made in the fact-finding and investigation of the current system. Existing file or database content and information needs also give pointers to system entities and their attributes.

Relationships

A relationship is a relevant business connection between two entities. A relationship is represented on a data model by a line linking the associated entities. Relationships may be:

- one-to-many (1:m);
- many-to-many (m:m);
- one-to-one (1:1).

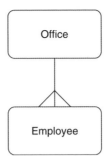

FIGURE 10.4 *Diagram showing one-to-many relationship*

One-to-many relationships

Relationships are often of the degree one to many (1:m). For example, an employee is allocated to exactly one office, but each office must have one or more employees allocated to it. We express this by saying that there is a relationship of one to many between an office and an employee. The 'many' aspect of a relationship is represented by the crow's-foot symbol on the end of the relationship line (Figure 10.4).

In a simple order-processing entity model, there appears to be an obvious one-to-many relationship between customer and order. A customer will place one or many orders, but a particular order will be placed by only one customer.

One-to-one relationships

If each office was allocated to only one employee and each employee was allocated to only one office, then the relationship between office and employee would be one-to-one. These relationships are not permitted in some methodologies. It is usually suggested that the two entities are merged and that one of the identifiers is selected to identify the merged set, typically the identifier that is created first.

Many-to-many relationships

Many-to-many (m:m) relationships occur frequently. For example, an employee may be contracted to work on many projects, and a project may have many employees contracted to it (Figure 10.5).

Many-to-many relationships are normally decomposed into two one-to-many relationships with the definition of an additional link entity (Figure 10.6).

This allows all the contract details with which an individual employee is associated to be accessed as detail entity occurrences. It also allows access from the project entity to all the contracts associated with a specific project occurrence. Attributes of the original relationship can now be recorded as attributes of the link entity, for example the date the employee

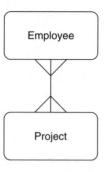

FIGURE 10.5 *Diagram showing many-to-many relationship*

was contracted to the project and the duration of each contract. Note that the name of the link entity is normally the noun form of the verb that described the relationship, and thus the contracted relationship is replaced by a 'Contract' entity.

If we look at an order-processing example, there appears to be a many-to-many relationship between the entities 'Product' and 'Order'. An order may be for more than one product, and we would expect most products to be on more than one order. This is solved by introducing a link entity ('Order line') that has a one-to-many relationship with both the original entities.

Many-to-many relationships can be problematic, for at least two important reasons:

- They may mask omitted entities. Two examples have already been given above.

- Most database management systems (DBMS) do not support many-to-many relationships.

Optionality

More detailed information about the business rules that underpin the data model is represented by including optionality in the relationship between

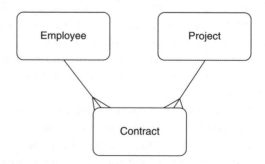

FIGURE 10.6 *Diagram showing resolved many-to-many relationship*

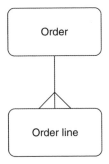

FIGURE 10.7 *Diagram showing fully mandatory one-to-many relationship*

two entities. This describes whether the entities at both ends of the relationship must always coexist or whether one entity can exist without the other entity. The example in Figure 10.7 shows two entities joined by a relationship that is represented by a solid line. This indicates that both entities must exist and that neither can be entered without the other; this is a fully mandatory relationship. The example shows that each order input to the system must always have at least one order line.

The complete opposite of this level of optionality is where the relationship is fully optional. This means that both entities can exist completely independently of each other. In the example in Figure 10.8, the relationship is shown as a dotted line. This indicates that an order can be placed without a customer call being made, and a customer call need not result in an order.

The remaining two alternatives show how relationships really need to be considered in two directions: from the 'one' end of the relationship, known as the parent or master entity, to the 'many' end of the relationship, known as the child or detail entity. The first situation is where a parent entity can exist without any child entities but a child entity must have a parent. In the example in Figure 10.9, we can see that a customer may not have placed any orders yet, but an order must always be placed by a customer.

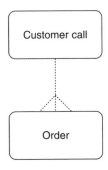

FIGURE 10.8 *Diagram showing fully optional one-to-many relationship*

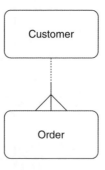

FIGURE 10.9 *Mandatory parent entity with optional child entities*

The second situation is the opposite of this, such that the parent entity must be linked to at least one child but the child entities can exist without a parent. The example in Figure 10.10 shows that an order need not be related to any complaints but a complaint must be linked to at least one order.

Relationship names

The nature of the relationship between two entities is clarified by relationship naming and identification. A relationship link phrase is constructed from the perspective of each entity. In the example in Figure 10.11, a sales region may or may not contain one or more customers.

This reads from the 'Sales region' end as:

each sales region may be responsible for one or more customers

and from the 'Customer' end as:

each customer must be allocated to one and only one sales region.

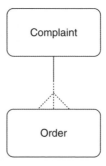

FIGURE 10.10 *Optional parent entity with mandatory child entities*

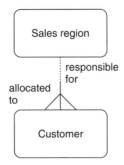

FIGURE 10.11 *Named relationship between entities*

Exclusive relationships

In an exclusive relationship, the participation of an entity occurrence in one relationship precludes it from participating in another. This is indicated by an exclusivity arc (Figure 10.12).

In Figure 10.12, the diagram uses the exclusivity notation to show that:

- each employee must be allocated to one and only one sales region **or** to one and only one office;
- each office must be occupied by one or more employees;
- each sales region must be defined for one or more employees.

The exclusive relationship may extend to more than two alternatives. The lower-case letter identifies which relationships are participating in the exclusivity.

Entity relationship diagram for the sales system

If we put these examples together, we can build an entity relationship diagram that reflects the data requirements for our system (Figure 10.13).

Class models

A class model shows graphically the classes in a system and their associations with each other. These models have similarities to entity

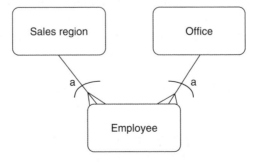

FIGURE 10.12 *Exclusive relationships*

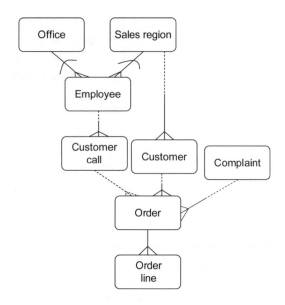

FIGURE 10.13 *Entity relationship diagram for a sales system*

relationship diagrams and apply many of the same principles. In a business system, a class model captures information about the particular things involved in the organization's operations, for example projects, customers and team members for a project control system.

Objects

An object is something that we wish to hold data about because this data is needed within the system we are analysing. For example, an object might be account number NX112G AK506 and we may wish to hold the following information about this object:

- Account number: NX112G.
- Name: Mr H. Hillman.
- Credit limit: £8000.
- Amount payable: £3500.

Objects are sent messages that invoke them to respond in some way, typically by changing data. For example, a message might be sent to the object 'NX112G' to change Mr H. Hillman's credit limit.

Classes

To build a model of the system data, we consider classes of objects rather than individual objects. We explained earlier the difference between entity types and entity occurrences. Similarly, in object class modelling we have classes that provide the generic definition of the data items or attributes, and objects that are the instances of a particular class. Thus, account NX112G is an object of the class 'Account'. The class 'Account' has attributes such as 'accountNumber' and 'creditLimit' and, as we saw above, the object 'NX112G' has values associated with these attributes. When we define a class, we also include operations that the account is subject to. These might include 'updateCreditLimit' and 'recordAmount'. All of the accounts in the system will contain these attributes and be subject to the same operations. A class, therefore, is a template for its object instances in the same way that an entity type is the template for its entity occurrences. Every object is an instance of some class that defines the common set of features (attributes and operations) that are shared by all objects in that class.

In the UML, classes are represented by rectangular boxes with three sections (Figure 10.14). The name of the class is shown in the top part and is a noun. The first letter is capitalized, for example 'Account', 'Payment' or 'Transaction'. If the name has more than one word, then each word is joined and capitalized in the class name, for example 'OrderLine'.

The attributes – the individual items of data about the class – are stored in the middle section. The attribute names are usually shown in lower case with constituent parts shown with capital letters. The first letter of the attribute name is not capitalized, for example 'name', 'dateLastPayment' or 'creditLimit'.

Operations are stored in the bottom part of the class and are invoked by messages being sent to the class by other classes. It is usual to name the operation in the class with the same name as the message. The detailed content of the operation – what the class will do when that operation is invoked – will be defined in the method associated with the operation; this is usually left to the later stages of the development process.

Attributes held within a class are accessible only to the operations of that class, as they are hidden from all other classes in the system. This is known as encapsulation and is an important principle of the object-oriented approach. Any other part of the system that needs to access or modify the data of that class has no need to understand how it is structured. It simply sends a message and the receiving class responds appropriately.

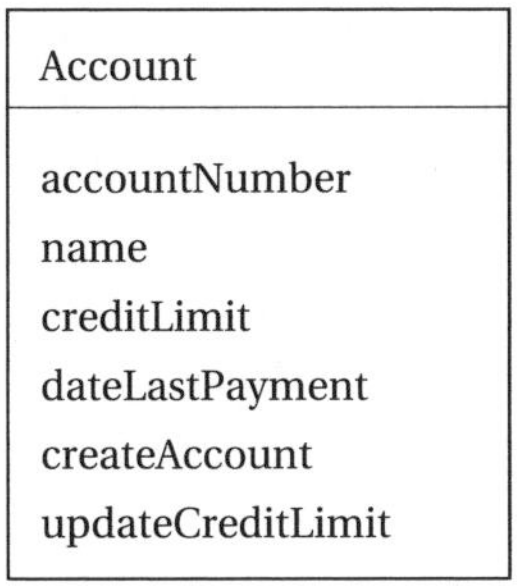

Account
accountNumber
name
creditLimit
dateLastPayment
createAccount
updateCreditLimit

FIGURE 10.14 *Definition of the class 'Account'*

FIGURE 10.15 *Association between two classes*

For example, in Figure 10.14 the object class 'Account' has the operation 'updateCreditLimit', which may take place when the customer requests a new credit limit. To enable this to take place, a message is sent to the object 'Account' to 'updateCreditLimit', and the parameters of 'account-Number' and 'newCreditLimit' are also sent to indicate the account in question and the new credit limit amount. In the class 'Account', we have defined an operation called 'updateCreditLimit' to respond to the message of the same name. This operation has been specified as 'replace creditLimit with newCreditLimit', which uses the value passed in the message to update the credit limit on the appropriate account.

Associations

As in entity relationship modelling, we now need to establish how different classes are linked to each other and the nature of these connections. We call the connections between classes 'associations'. For instance, a 'Project' class must have an association with a 'ProjectManager' class so that the system will be able to list the projects for which a manager is responsible. Figure 10.15 shows this association.

We have stated already that classes interact. This is done by the messages moving along the association lines defined in the class model. If there is no association between classes, then the classes cannot communicate directly.

The class model reflects the business rules that will govern the classes and the operations performed on them. Multiplicity is used to show the business rules for an association between classes. For example, the multiplicity of the association shown in Figure 10.16 indicates that a project manager may manage many projects but an individual project may have only one project manager.

FIGURE 10.16 *Association with one-to-many multiplicity*

The multiplicity entries can be extended to show the minimum and maximum values in the association. This is shown using two dots between the minimum and maximum values. For example, the asterisk in the example in Figure 10.16 is a simplification of the range 0..* and the '1' is a simplification of 1..1.

The 'JobSheet' to 'Task' association shown in Figure 10.17 shows that an instance of task has an optional association with a job sheet. In addition, this shows that although there may be no job sheets associated with a task, there is also a maximum of one job sheet for a given task.

In the example in Figure 10.18, the class 'Employee' has a mandatory association with 'Allocation', which is the assignment of someone to a project. There must be at least one instance of 'Allocation' for each instance of 'Employee', although the asterisk indicates there is no upper limit. An allocation is for only one employee.

In some circumstances the actual minimum and maximum values may be defined. For example, if we assume there is a business rule that no more than 20 people can be allocated to a project, then this would be modelled as shown in Figure 10.19.

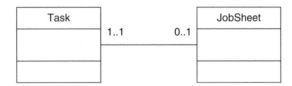

FIGURE 10.17 *Association with one-to-zero-to-one multiplicity*

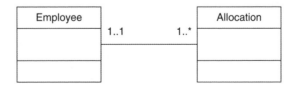

FIGURE 10.18 *Association with one-to-one-to-many multiplicity*

FIGURE 10.19 *Association with one-one-to-20 multiplicity*

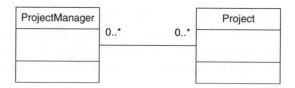

FIGURE 10.20 *Association with many-to-many multiplicity*

The class model supports associations where the multiplicity is many to many. For example, Figure 10.20 shows that a project may have many project managers, and each project manager may control many projects. It is likely – but not necessarily so – that this would occur over a period of time. The zeros on this diagram indicate that a project manager may be newly appointed and thus has not yet been allocated a project, and a project may be set up without the project manager being known.

In some circumstances the association between the classes also holds information. If we consider the example in Figure 10.20, we would probably want to know which project manager was in charge of a project during a particular period. To do this, we create an association class called 'Assignment' to hold the start and end dates for each project manager. Figure 10.21 shows this additional class.

In this example, there is only one instance of the class 'Assignment' for each combination of 'Project' and 'ProjectManager'. If there were more than one – for example, if a project manager could be reassigned to a project that they had previously left – then it would be necessary to convert this association class into a class in its own right.

Generalization and inheritance

The 'ProjectManager' class that we have been considering has been defined for the narrow requirements of the project control system. However, during analysis it turns out that the organization also needs to

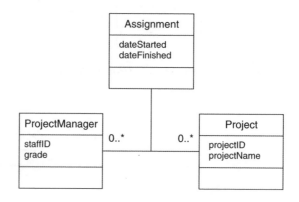

FIGURE 10.21 *Association class*

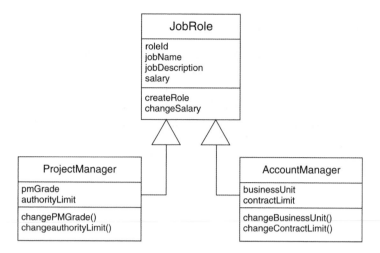

FIGURE 10.22 *Generalization structure*

keep information on contracts – managed by account managers – and more information on job roles in general.

Some of the data kept about 'ProjectManager' and 'AccountManager' will be common to the more general class 'JobRole', whereas some data will be specific to the two existing classes. It also appears that although some operations are common to all job roles, some are relevant only to project managers or account managers. The UML handles this situation through a concept known as generalization; this is illustrated in Figure 10.22.

Both specializations are said to inherit the attributes and operations of the generalization. So, the class of 'JobRole' has the attributes 'roleId', 'jobName', 'jobDescription' and 'salary'; 'ProjectManager' has 'pmGrade' and 'authorityLimit' in addition to the 'JobRole' attributes; and 'AccountManager' has the additional attributes of 'businessUnit' and 'contractLimit'.

SUMMARY

This chapter has provided an introduction to some of the key techniques used to model system requirements. The benefit of using models is that they provide an unambiguous view of the system, albeit from a particular perspective. Another benefit is that these views may be compared and cross-checked. So, we might develop a use case diagram and cross-check it against a model of the data in order to identify any gaps such as missing data items or use cases. The models also help us to generate further questions and improve our understanding of the business requirements of the system.

FURTHER READING

Arlow, J. and Neustadt, I. (2002) *UML and the Unified Process*. Addison-Wesley, Boston, MA.

Skidmore, S. and Eva, M. (2004) *Introducing Systems Development*. Palgrave Macmillan, Basingstoke.

Yeates, D. and Wakefield, T. (2004) *Systems Analysis and Design*. FT Prentice Hall, Harlow.

11 Managing the information resource

TONY JENKINS

INTRODUCTION

As a business analyst, you will already know how important it is to understand the processes, the people and the organizational context, both current and future, that organizations use to achieve their objectives. Another important parameter we need to discuss is that of the use of data and information to support effective business processes. This chapter is about information resource management or, as it is more usually known, data management, and how it affects your role as a business analyst. Over the years it has been found that the process view often dominates business analysis. There is a lot of focus, as we saw earlier, on business process and standards for that approach. We are not suggesting that this is a wrong perspective, but it is only one of several perspectives, and it is important that we do not allow the process view to dominate the picture for the business analyst.

Let us start by considering how we might define the terms 'information'. In the previous chapter, we considered what we meant by the term 'data' and looked at some techniques for modelling this data. Information is obtained when we put data, which might well appear as values in a table in a database, into context. For example, if we see two data items, 1 and 0, then we need to understand what the 1 and 0 are representing. For example, are they representing:

- the final score in a football match?

- the number of children in a family?

- the temperature of something?

The only way we can know is by understanding the context of the data. The context of the data is often held in an electronic form separate from the data. The term that we use for that contextual information is metadata. In the example we have just used, the metadata would tell us what 1 and 0 represented. If they were football goals, then the metadata would tell us which of those numbers represented home goals and which represented away goals. The metadata would tell us what date the goals were scored on and which teams scored those goals. We could go further and look to see which league they were in. Knowing what game they were playing would be useful as well – for example football might be different from rugby, where 1–0 might not be a legal score. So, once we understand the context of data, then we have information.

As another example, consider a text phrase such as 'He made a killing!' To give the phrase any context, we would need to know whether the 'killing' we were talking about was some sort of murderous act or whether it was a reference to some success on one of the world's stock markets. We would also need to know when that statement occurred, who the author was and so on. We refer to all those contextual pieces of additional 'data about the data' as metadata.

The role of data management is not only about managing the raw data. It is also about managing all the contextual metadata that goes with the raw data.

We believe that data, as the basis for the organization's information, has all the necessary requirements to be treated as a resource. For example, data is essential for the achievement of business objectives and to the successful daily workings of an organization. In addition, we know that data can be obtained and preserved by an organization, but only at a financial cost. Finally, we know that data can, along with other resources, be used to further the achievement of the aims of an organization. As a business analyst, you will need to consider how to handle this valuable resource in the work that you do.

MANAGING DATA RESOURCES

If data is not managed effectively:

- people maintain and collect data that is not needed any more;
- the organization has historic information that is no longer used;
- the organization holds a lot of data that is inaccessible to potential users;
- information is disseminated to more people than it should be;
- the organization uses inefficient and out-of-date methods to collect, analyse, store and retrieve the data;
- the organization fails to collect data that it needs.

Additionally, we do not always know whether information is derived from good quality data because there are no measures in place against which to compare the data. For example, poor quality data often arises because of poor checks on input and/or updating procedures. Once inaccurate or incomplete data has been stored in the computer system, any reports produced using this data will reflect these inaccuracies or gaps. Additionally, there may be a lack of consistency between internally generated management information from the operational systems and from other internal locally used systems. It is not unusual to find people relying on local spreadsheets to give them the right results rather than the corporate systems that should be the main trusted source. Dealing with this proliferation of small cheap desktop systems is an important issue for organizations as they try to rationalize and improve overall data quality.

One way of improving the quality of data is to use a central data management function that establishes policy and standards, provides expertise and makes your role as a business analyst much easier as you come to look at the data aspects of new projects. The BCS Data Management Specialist Group (DMSG) defines data management as 'the corporate service that assists the provision and operation of business information systems by controlling and or coordinating the definitions (format and characteristics) and usage of useful, reliable and relevant data'. Note that this definition talks about information systems and not only IT systems. So, the BCS is saying that it is important to manage all of the data within an organization, and not only the data held in database systems managed by the IT department.

It is probable that as part of an early scoping decision for a data management function, the information systems based on IT become the first focus of attention. However, as a business analyst you should expect the scope of data management to extend to incorporate non-electronic forms of data. In fact, it is common for business analysts to be involved in extending the scope of data management into new areas such as document and text management. There are further scope issues that are important for business analysts to understand. Data management is not concerned only with large operational databases; it is much wider in scope and incorporates an interest in many areas. This includes non-structured data that is not held in conventional database systems, for example formats such as text, image and audio. It could also be that a decision is made to establish data management with a remit to cover important non-electronic formats, such as paper files and records. As an example, this might include cabling diagrams, information on building layouts and classic typewritten or even handwritten administrative documents. When document management is seen as a strategic direction for an organization, life for the business analyst will become easier in future projects, as all the data needed is held electronically, with standardized metadata defined.

Whatever the project situation, understanding how the data management function can help you in your business analysis will be important. Never assume that its scope is concerned simply with 'databases' and therefore not relevant to your work. An additional advantage for you as a business analyst is that the data management team may well provide a business information support service. Because it manages the metadata, this team can answer questions from you or the business about the meaning, format and availability of data internal to the organization. The team is also able to understand and explain what external data might be needed in order to carry out the necessary business processes and will take the necessary action to source this. Examples of external data include financial information such as market rates, general information such as that available in business telephone directories, and reference code information available from organizations such as the Post Office.

If there is no data management function within the organization, then the business analyst's work may be more complex, as some of the data management responsibilities may fall on the analyst. When improving the efficiency and effectiveness of business processes, it is important to understand the data aspect of the business process improvement activity. In particular, when redesigning the processes, it may be beneficial to consider reusing data and metadata across different areas of the organization. The ability to do this may be supported by a corporate information model – sometimes known as a corporate data model – to help support reuse, a major role of a data management function.

The conclusion is that it is important to work in collaboration with the data management function. This will help to ensure that as the new processes are implemented, they are implemented with the minimum amount of redefinition and/or re-creation of data. Additionally, a significant element of business process improvement should concentrate on improving data quality through the use of the techniques and practices of data management.

SUPPORT FOR THE SYSTEMS DEVELOPMENT LIFECYCLE

One of the benefits of having a data management function in place is its ability to support projects of all types and at all stages of the systems development lifecycle (see Chapter 9). It is expected that the data management team will be able to help with queries such as those concerning data definitions, availability and quality.

At a strategic level, for example when thinking of information systems strategy, it is very important that the organization makes use of the knowledge of shared data that the data management team has as it moves forward into developing such a strategy. The alignment of IT systems with the business needs will be helped by a detailed knowledge of the information resource.

If a project is concerned with analysing the business system, then the existence of metadata and a corporate data model will simplify the tasks of business process improvement and help analysts to understand the existing business processes. The corporate data model usually contains a large number of entity types. An extract from a corporate data model is shown in Figure 11.1

If some data analysis work is required, then the data management team can help by providing, for a particular project, relevant metadata definitions and views of the corporate information model. In effect, a

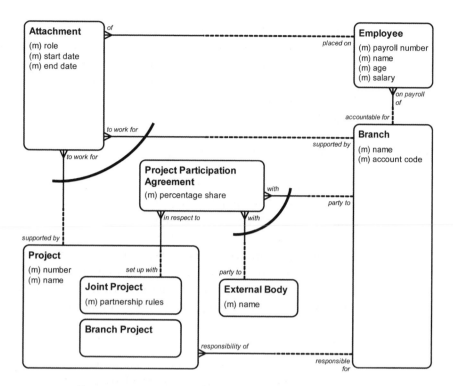

FIGURE 11.1 *Extract from a Corporate Data Model*

section is cut from the corporate model, which is created and maintained by the data management team, and made available to the project team. During requirements elicitation and analysis, the data management team can assist project teams with project-specific data modelling and give advice on the use of various techniques to model data.

When a project reaches the detailed design phase, the data management function can provide technical expertise on database management systems and on how to convert initial logical models of data into physical, product-specific implementations. During testing phases the data management team can also help to ensure test quality; during implementation, the data management team will be concerned particularly with support for data migration tasks, if any are necessary.

Once the development project has ended, there will be a need for an ongoing relationship between the data management team and the IT service management teams that are looking after IT services and systems once they have gone live and are available for business use.

Many projects have failed because poor quality data has not been addressed during the project or because a particular project has gone ahead with the creation of its own data and metadata, without consultation with other projects or with the central data management team. As we stated earlier, if a data management team does not exist, then business analysts, particularly during the early stages of an IS project, will need to be aware of the issues that can arise and be able to resolve them. It is strongly recommended that business analysts work closely with the data management team, as the team will simplify many aspects of the analyst's work and ensure a consistency of approach to, and a sharing of, data and metadata across multiple business process improvement projects.

VALUING AND CLASSIFYING DATA

Data is a resource and an asset and has value. This is more obvious in some organizations than in others. Organizations that are providers of data to other organizations – for example Yell, Dun & Bradstreet and Reuters – can value data as an output in terms of the price that they are charging external organizations to receive that data. Also, we can think of value in terms of what our data would be worth to another organization. We can also value the data in terms of what it is worth to the owner organization. There are a number of suggested ways of doing this:

Valuing data by availability

One approach often used is to consider which business processes would not be possible if a particular piece of data were unavailable and how much that non-availability of data would cost the business. So, for example, if we had no data available about a customer and we wanted to make a decision about whether to accept a large order from that customer, then we would have to look at a risk evaluation approach to decide whether we could go ahead with that order without the customer data. The cost of doing the evaluation and the likely cost of getting our decision wrong would give us a way of valuing the customer data.

Valuing lost data

Another approach that is often used is to think about the costs of re-obtaining some data if it was destroyed. Here, we are assuming that we did have the data at some point in the lifecycle and that it has been destroyed, overwritten or lost or we are no longer sure of the quality. We can calculate how much it will cost us to recapture that data, hence deriving a value.

The data lifecycle

Another way of valuing data is to think about the data lifecycle. This involves thinking about how data is created or obtained in the first place, how we then make the data available to people to use, and how we retire the data, through either archiving or physical destruction. It may be that some data is provided from an external source and then held internally or that data has to be created by the organization's internal systems. In these two cases, the lifecycle is different and the processes that take place for data capture will be entirely separate.

It is important to work closely with the business in understanding data value and on defining specific lifecycles for the various types of data that you have been asked to investigate. For any particular project you might be involved in, you will need to think carefully about these data aspects and how to value them. The more highly valued the data, the more effort that needs to be expended on ensuring the integrity, availability and confidentiality of the data.

Classifying data

Data can be classified as operational, tactical or strategic. Operational data is necessary for the ongoing functioning of an organization and can be regarded as the lowest, most specific level, for example detailed data on orders, invoices, payments or hours worked. Without operational data, we could not keep up to date our view of how the organization is functioning. Many of the transactional processes that we run in modern organizations using IT systems are entirely dependent on operational data. Business analysts need to understand what operational data is collected in order to identify where tactical and strategic data may be derived.

Tactical data is usually needed by second-line management or higher and typically is concerned with summarized data and historical data, such as year-to-year or quarterly data. Often, the data used here appears in management information systems, where we might, for example, require summary data from a number of operational systems in order to deal with an accounting requirement. The data required here usually has an element of history. This makes it different from operational systems, where typically data that is no longer required for immediate operational needs is deleted or overwritten by new versions. It has become more and more the situation since the mid 1990s that tactical data has been moved away from transactional IT systems into special-purpose systems known as analytic or business intelligence systems. These systems provide the type of reporting and querying required by tactical management.

At the highest level we have a need for strategic thinking and, hence, much more data is required from external sources. Strategic data is often concerned with longer-term trends and comparison with the outside world, and so providing the necessary data for a strategic support system involves bringing together the operational and tactical data from many different areas with relevant external data.

An alternative classification distinguishes between organization-wide data, functional-area data and service-specific data. Organization-wide data is data that is of use across the whole organization and that needs to be managed centrally and kept consistent. For example, if we have customer data, then this is probably going to be used by a number of different business areas and should be kept consistent at one central point.

Historically, the proliferation of customer data in many different formats has led to huge quality and duplication problems for organizations. Other organization-wide data may be standard reference data; for example, if we want to keep data on exchange rates between different currencies or reference data for postcodes, then this should be held centrally. Note that both of these examples may well be externally sourced and, therefore, will need to be managed actively to ensure that the data is up to date and accurate.

The next level comprises functional data, which should be shared across a complete business function. This involves sharing data instances, for example individual customer records, and also ensuring that consistent metadata across that functional area, such as standard address formats, is being used.

The final level we call IT service-specific data. Here we are considering data that is valid for one IT service and does not need to be shared with other IT systems. For example, we might find within stock control that logistics data about arrivals at the warehouse is needed by only one IT service within the stock-control area and, therefore, the data and the related metadata would be local to that particular service. We can see that the latter is becoming less and less common in integrated organizations, as data tends to be defined and shared at a functional level and, where necessary, at an organizational level. One of the roles of the data management team is to identify all the possibilities for both data sharing and the reuse of metadata, ensuring that as much of that strategy as possible is enforced.

SUPPORTING BUSINESS ACTIVITIES

We described in Chapter 7 the use of the business activity model in business analysis and explained the five different types of activity: plan, enable, do, monitor and control. From a data point of view, each of those various categories of activity puts different requirements on the data resource and the management of that resource. Let us take each separately and think about the data requirements.

For **planning**, it is very common for us to need past historical data and external data in order to carry out 'What if?' forecasting or prediction. So, for example, we might want to see what the impact might be, based on past data, of a price increase for a service. To do that, we need to look into the previous impact of price changes, the profit margins that we could obtain and external prices from other organizations. As a result of that, we can build some predictive models and carry out 'What if?' calculations. Traditionally this has been spreadsheet work, but it is important that it is all based on accurate, easily accessible and consistent data if the task is to be worthwhile.

Enabling means making the necessary resources available for the 'doing' business activities to be carried out. As data is one of those resources, making data available will form part of the enabling activities. It would be important to consider where data is to be sourced, how we can ensure that the data is consistent and up to date, and how the data can be made available in a useful form.

The **doing** set of activities defines the main day-to-day processes carried out that justify the planning, enabling, monitoring and controlling activities. This is where we need to make sure that the data is as easy to use as possible. We need to investigate what data resources are needed to support these activities and how we are to ensure that they all remain accurate, up to date and rapidly available.

In the **monitoring** set of activities, it is important to access the performance data related to the doing activities. Monitoring will involve comparing the data that has been obtained from the actual doing activities with the targets that were set at the planning stage; hence, monitoring activities require good data support.

Control as the final set of activities relates to taking action as a result of the monitoring activities, so that we can improve the planning, enabling and doing types of activity. Many possible outcomes result from control activities. The data helps us to define the total picture and identify the best courses of action.

Business intelligence projects

As a business analyst, you may work on projects that are entirely or partially about business intelligence or analytics issues. These types of project are concerned with understanding the way in which an organization is performing through detailed analysis of the underpinning operational data that exists in all organizations. For example, it may be useful to do 'What if?' predictions, so we might work with the business to obtain a mathematical formula linking price and profit, or price and sales. If this model is then used to extrapolate into the future, the business will be able to understand the impact on sales of a 5 per cent cut in prices. Such systems have been known, historically, as 'management information systems', 'executive information systems' and 'decision support systems'. The general term 'business intelligence' (the UK term) or 'analytics' (the North American term) is used as a general descriptor for such systems. The systems are created for the benefit of strategic and tactical management and rely on large amounts of data to identify trends and to make predictions for the future. The business intelligence terminology includes terms such as 'data warehousing', 'online analytical processing', 'data mining' and 'data mart'. All of these terms refer to concepts, tools and systems used in the business intelligence area.

A data warehouse refers to an environment where data is stored not only in its latest version but also with a history of that data, so that we can look at trends over time. Data warehouses are usually populated by updating them regularly from consistent underlying operational systems. The data in the warehouse can be analysed at multiple levels through summarization or aggregation and through mining of the data in order to find patterns. Data marts contain extracts from the central warehouse of data of particular relevance to one subject area. The subject area may relate to a functional area, so, for example, we might decide to pull all the data concerned with people from the warehouse into one data mart. That data can then be further explored and manipulated by strategic and tactical management within the HR function of the organization.

Data mining is the exploration and organization of patterns in data by the use of intelligent, coordinated tools. Usually, the basis for mining systems is the data warehouse information at the lowest, or atomic, level. Warehouses and marts make use of base-level data such as a particular order's details, but they are also interested in summary data such as the number of orders for a particular product in a particular week. One of the great advantages of this sort of system for tactical and strategic business intelligence is that precalculated totals based on a number of views are already in place within the warehouse and/or marts. Data mining needs the base-level data because the mining is aiming to find, for example, unexpected patterns within a set of transactions in a financial institution that might imply fraud. One of the major applications of data mining is in predicting credit-worthiness based on patterns in past transactional histories of the applicant.

Online analytical processing uses software that allows 'What if?' and more complex statistical analyses to be carried out online rather than by offline query submission and reporting. It enables one query to be followed up with a further query, prompted by the result from the first query. This is the sort of transactional system-breaking query work that previously was discouraged in operational systems because of the resources required and the subsequent damage to the transactional response times. It makes use of statistically based tools to analyse what has happened in the past and to predict what could happen in the future.

There is a strong emphasis on separating the data in transactional systems, often at the operational level, from the data used by strategic and tactical management. This is often a physical technology separation, where data warehouses and data marts are populated with data from operational systems on a regular basis. These specialist systems can then be used to answer the complex queries put together to support both the management of business performance and the general monitoring and control requirements of any business.

One of the impacts of business intelligence projects on process modelling is that it is very difficult to use process models in a traditional way, because much of the decision making is not automated. For example, after running one query, it is not possible to predict what the next query will be from a tactical or strategic level user. However, process modelling is useful in helping us understand:

- which data will be required by the process;
- the operational system sources of the data;
- the areas where new data might need to be created in order to support the business intelligence work of the tactical or strategic user.

One of the reasons why many projects are taking place in this area is that organizations are attempting to control the spread of small databases and associated spreadsheet-based trending and predictive models, which have sprung up inside many strategic and tactical user areas. The danger here is that we have inconsistent and overlapping data held on local databases and spreadsheets. Another impact on the business analyst is caused by the move of some of the large enterprise resource planning (ERP) vendors into business intelligence by including data warehouses within their software offerings.

A particular aspect of business intelligence systems is that of customer relationship management (CRM). Many business analysts are involved in improving CRM systems by supporting the business in analysing the historic behaviour of customers through the use of business intelligence concepts, techniques and systems.

As a business analyst, you can often help to ensure that the project structure for these business intelligence system activities is correct. It is good practice to regard the achievement of a corporate data warehouse as a programme objective, with the process of obtaining individual compatible data marts seen as projects within that programme. It is also essential to ensure that all of the relevant stakeholders are involved in the analysis and management of the data resource. Typical stakeholders would include:

- the operational system owners, both business and IT;
- the operational data owners, again both business and IT, as we need to understand the metadata for the operational systems in order create new metadata for the data warehouse;
- the data management team;
- technical architects, who can ensure that the project is moving in an architecturally sound direction;
- domain experts from the business who understand the needs of the project and the meaning of the data that they need for their strategic and tactical analysis.

DATA ADMINISTRATION

Data administration is a major aspect of the data management function and encompasses several important areas. These range from defining standards for defining data to managing the migration of data. The key areas of data administration are described below.

Standards

One of the critical aspects of data administration is to ensure that standards for metadata are in place so that we know, for example, what metadata we are going to keep for different underlying data types. Different details are kept about structured tabular data than are kept in the metadata for other areas. So, for example, in a structured data area we would want to keep information about entities (such as customer), attributes (such as customer ID or credit limit) and relationships (such as the fact that a customer can place many or no orders). Note that these types of business rule may need to be documented further, and we may want to capture other data-related business rules, such as the rule that states how a particular calculated attribute is obtained from other basic attributes. We may also want to keep information that constrains attributes to domains, telling us what values are possible. If we had a grading scheme for examinations, for example, then we might want to say that the domain of that particular attribute could be only one of the characters 'a', 'b', 'c', 'd', 'e' or 'f'.

When we think about what we should keep as metadata, whatever the data type, then we may well say that ownership is a critical item, as are some sort of unique identifier, a description in business meaningful terms, and a format. For example if the particular piece of data has to be all upper case. We probably want to keep track of the custodian or steward – a person in the IS department who takes responsibility for the day-to-day management of the data.

When we are involved with data administration, we expect to find in place standards for naming. So, for example, if we want to create a new type of data in a future system, then we need to use names that meet these standards. An example standard might be 'all upper case, no underlining, no abbreviations'.

Another critical service that data management teams can provide is the resolution of synonyms and homonyms. With synonyms, we have the situation where the same underlying data is known by different names within systems in the organization, causing confusion when tactical and strategic management want to assemble or integrate data from several different systems. For example underlying product identification might be known as the 'product number' in one system and as the 'product code' in another. A similar issue arises with homonyms, where the same name is used to describe essentially different data. As an example, consider the use of the term 'profit', regarded in one system as a percentage of turnover and in another as an absolute figure relating income to expenditure. If these problems occur between systems, further problems can occur in assembling data for further analysis in a business intelligence system. It is much less common to find these problems within individual systems, but they can occur within functional areas and are very likely to occur when an organization-wide view of data is needed.

In addition to the standards for data access and for the security of data, we would also expect that the data management team had put in place standards for maintaining data integrity.

Another benefit that a business analyst might find from a data management function would be in the field of reference data. It may well be that certain types of data, such as postcodes and names of countries, are needed across a variety of systems and need to be consistent. It is part of the responsibility of a data administration team to manage reference data on behalf of the whole business and to make sure that the same reference data is used by all systems in the organization. From a business analyst's point of view, this will give an extra resource to use in projects.

Data ownership

The next way in which data administration can assist the business analyst is by making sure that responsibilities for data ownership are taken seriously by the business and the IS department. One of the most successful ways of doing this is to get the business and the IS department to sign up to a data charter, a set of procedural standards and guidance for the careful management of data in the organization by adherence to corporately defined standards. Responsibilities of a data owner are often defined in such a charter and may include:

- agreeing a business description and a purpose for the data;
- defining who can create, amend, read and delete occurrences of the data;
- authorizing changes in the way data is captured or derived;
- approving any format, domain and value ranges;
- approving the relevant level of security, including making sure that legal requirements and internal policies about data security are adhered to.

Data dictionary

It may well be that the data management team has established a data dictionary or information repository where metadata is held. The creation and management of this resource is considered to be a fundamental aspect of a formal data management function and gives the business analyst a great deal of valuable input without having to research individual stores of data in the organization. One of the great advantages of having a tool available to access this resource is that if it is web-enabled and has a helpful user interface, then everyone, including analysts and business users, can see the definitions of data, the formats in which the underlying systems hold the data and the ownership of the data. This facility enables a data management function to fulfil another of its objectives – to disseminate metadata throughout the organization. This means that the problem of business users being unaware of the existence of data in those areas not directly under their control is eliminated, leading to a great deal of data and metadata reuse.

Data migration

Data migration occurs where a new system is replacing a number of existing systems and it is necessary to carry across into the new system good quality data from the existing systems. There are two types of data migration of interest to projects here: data migration into data warehouses or marts (which we discussed earlier) and data migration to a new transactional operational system. In both cases, it will be beneficial if data migration standards, procedures and processes are laid down by a data management function. Data migration tools may have been purchased already on behalf of the organization by the data management team. Without this support, it is easy to underestimate the amount of effort required, particularly if data consolidation has to take place between multiple source systems and the quality of the existing system data is known to be questionable.

Change control

Another area that the data management function takes responsibility for is that of change control and configuration management for metadata. As a result of this, the business analyst can be reassured that no changes can take place to metadata without proper authorization and that earlier versions of metadata still exist if it is necessary to access them, typically to support historic analysis in business intelligence projects. It is expected that data management teams will use change management procedures and configuration management procedures compatible with those defined in the IT Infrastructure Library created by the Office for Government Commerce.

Data architecture

Similarly, we would expect the data management function to have a standard approach to data distribution policy. By this we mean the decision about whether the data should be held:

- centrally for all organizational units to access via networks;
- locally, with the relevant data for a particular geographical location held at that location, but with access from other areas across the network;

- using data replication, where multiple local copies of the data are refreshed from the centre on a regular basis.

The whole strategy on centralized versus distributed data will almost certainly have been devised as part of a data architecture initiative, which again is the responsibility of the data management team.

DATA MODELLING

As a business analyst, you may well have used processing and business activity models. These have been covered in earlier chapters. In Chapter 10, we explained two approaches to modelling the data for a system. Understanding the data is very important in order both to understand the existing processes better and to assist with the development of new processes. Two possibilities arise: that the business analyst is an expert in data modelling and that the business analyst can call on support from a data management team to carry out the data modelling.

A data model presents a logical view of the data requirements. This means that it does not dictate the technical environment in which it will be implemented. In fact, it can be translated into a number of different technical designs based on various types of database management systems, such as Oracle, DB2 and SQL Server. Choosing the physical implementation is beyond the scope of the business analyst's role.

It is common to find business analysis and data management teams working together using the same data modelling tools and supported by an underpinning data dictionary or information repository. These tools, sometimes referred to as computer-aided software engineering (CASE) tools, provide useful support for the business analyst, particularly where the tools used by the analyst and the data management teams provide differing views on the common metadata held in the repository.

Data modelling is an extremely useful tool for the business analyst. We do not consider it essential that the business analyst is a data modelling specialist, but an understanding of data modelling techniques is important, as is the ability to follow standards laid down by data management teams.

TECHNOLOGY FOR CAPTURING AND STORING DATA

It is important that business analysts are aware of technology developments in the data management area because this knowledge may help in decision making processes about, for example, the cost effectiveness of a project. Although analysts do not need to be aware of all the technology options that are developing, they should expect this expertise to be available from within the data management function working with them, typically on the creation of a business case.

An area where technology moves very rapidly is the storage of data. Analysts may need to consider different storage media and be aware of the size and cost implications associated with this. The main reason for understanding the developments in this area is that they bring within the range of the possible many types of data storage that were once considered too expensive. For example, storage of real-time video, which uses an enormous bandwidth, was regarded as too expensive until the start of the 21st century. The same is true of the scanning of large numbers of paper documents, particularly where those documents are not text-based and contain detailed diagrams or pictures. Understanding technology developments with regard to the electronic storage of data is critical to understanding the opportunities for the business to exploit the information resource effectively by making the best use of new technology.

It will also be very important to work with the data management team on effective measures for data capture. The aim here is to capture data as quickly and as accurately as possible. We need to ensure that we have data capture processes that require the minimum amount of keying and exploit the advantages that graphical user interfaces provide in terms of minimizing the number of keystrokes needed, hence decreasing the opportunity for errors during data capture. We would expect the data management team to have laid down standards for, and to provide expertise on, effective methods of data capture in various environments, including non-structured data capture using mechanisms such as scanning documentation. The developments in data capture and data storage technologies may result in an organization's information resource residing in a multimedia database, where tabular data is stored alongside other forms of data such as scanned documents and video.

Once the data has been captured and stored, the next aspect to consider is the retrieval of the information. The whole area of searching within scanned text and other non-structured data, such as video, still images and sound, is a major area of expansion, and you may find that you are going to be working on projects in this particular area. Techniques such as automatic indexing and the use of search engines to give efficient access via keywords to relevant parts of a document are essential technologies that have been implemented widely, particularly on the internet. Many business analysts work on internet-based projects, where they define requirements for websites or other web-based applications for their organizations. Expertise on the use of data within websites should exist within the data management team.

SECURITY, GOVERNANCE AND RELATED ISSUES

When defining requirements for computer systems, it is vital that business analysts consider non-functional requirements related to data management, in particular in the following areas:

- recovery of lost or corrupted data;
- controlled access to data;
- policies on archiving of data.

Sometimes you will find these aspects defined – appropriately perhaps – using the abbreviation CIA (confidentiality, integrity, availability). For any business process that we are working on, we would expect the data, whether electronic or non-electronic, to have the right levels set for confidentiality, particularly in terms of data privacy, which for personal data would be very important. For other data, confidentiality is often about preventing accidental leakage of commercially sensitive data. It is the business analyst's responsibility to consider, as part of defining business improvements, the requirements for data confidentiality and how they may be met.

Data integrity is concerned with ensuring that the data is of a high quality and uncorrupted. This topic is also about preventing uncontrolled data duplication and, hence, avoiding any confusion about which version of the data is valid. There are several approaches that may assist with this. Various technology devices, such as database locking, are used to prevent multiple inconsistent updating of data. In addition, prevention of illegal updating may be achieved through access-control mechanisms.

Availability of data is concerned with minimizing the time when business users are unable to access their data. To achieve this, it is important to ensure that databases are:

- secure;
- hosted on highly reliable equipment;
- connected via highly reliable networks.

The second aspect of availability is the need to be aware of which data exists so that effective use may be made of the data. The data management function can help to ensure that data knowledge is spread as widely as possible throughout the organization, for example via an intranet.

A key part of business analysis work is to be aware of, and ensure compliance with, government legislation and organizational policies. For example, if a new system contains personal data, the analyst will have to consider whether it needs to be registered under the Data Protection Act. If the analyst is working with government or quasi-government organizations, he or she may well find that their work is subject to the rules and regulations of the Freedom of Information Act.

Various financial issues have arisen in organizations in the USA and the UK since the millennium leading to new legislation, such as the Sarbanes-Oxley Act in the USA (which has a much wider reach than just the USA). This has led to new requirements for accounting standards and practice, to which many organizations need to adhere, and as a result a greater emphasis on the accuracy and quality of data and their management.

Many business analysts are involved in projects that have been driven by the need to conform to new legislation.

SUMMARY

The data held by an organization is a key resource that supports the business operations and can help to deliver competitive advantage. Business analysts need to appreciate the importance of this resource to organizations and should have an appreciation of the techniques and tools used in the modelling, recording, storage and management of data.

REFERENCES

Central Computer and Telecommunications Agency (1994) *Data Management*. TSO, London.

FURTHER READING

Brackett, M.H. (1994) *Data Sharing Using a Common Data Architecture*. John Wiley & Sons, New York.

Rhind, G. (2003) *Global Sourcebook for Address Data Management*. Gower, Aldershot.

12 Making a business and financial case

JAMES CADLE

INTRODUCTION

A business case is a key document in a business analysis project. It is where the analysts or consultants present their findings and propose a course of action for senior management to consider. This chapter considers the purpose, structure and content of a business case and provides some guidance on how to assemble the information and to present the finished product. One thing worth remembering here is that, to some extent, a business case is a sales document aimed at getting people to make a decision. Therefore, some of the key rules of successful selling apply: stress the benefits, not features; sell the benefits before discussing the cost; and get the 'buyers' to understand the size of the problem or opportunity before presenting the amount of time, effort and money that will be needed to implement a solution.

THE BUSINESS CASE IN THE PROJECT LIFECYCLE

A question often asked about the business case is 'When should it be produced?' This issue is addressed in Figure 12.1.

As Figure 12.1 shows, a business case is a living document and should be revised as the project proceeds and as more is discovered about the proposed solution and the costs and benefits of introducing it. In addition, of course, organizations and the environments in which they operate are not static, and so the business case must be kept under review in order to ensure that changing circumstances have not invalidated it. The initial business case often results from a feasibility study, where the broad requirements and options have been considered and where ballpark estimates of costs and benefits are developed. The ballpark figures must, however, be revisited once more detailed analysis work has been completed and a fuller picture is available of the options available. It should also be examined again once the solution has been designed, when much more reliable figures should be available for the costs of development. The business case should next be reviewed before the solution is deployed because the business circumstances may have changed and it may now not be worth proceeding to implementation.

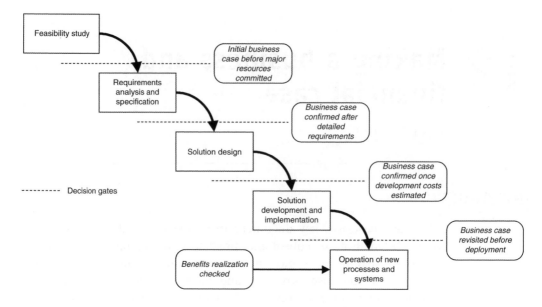

FIGURE 12.1 *The business case in the project lifecycle*

Finally, once the proposed solution has been in operation for a while, there should be a post-project review to determine the degree to which the predicted business benefits have been realized and to identify actions to support the delivery of these benefits.

Figure 12.1 refers to each of these review points as 'decision gates'. The concept here, now used widely in project management, is that projects should pass certain tests – not least those relating to their business viability – before they can be allowed to proceed to the next stage.

IDENTIFYING OPTIONS

The first step in putting together a business case is to identify and explore the various options that exist for solving the business issue. There are two kinds of option:

- **Business options** explore what the proposed solution is intended to achieve in business terms – for example, 'Speed up invoice handling by 50 per cent' or 'Reduce the number of people we need to staff our supermarket'.

- **Technical options** consider how the solution is to be implemented, often through the use of IT.

At one time, it was thought that these two elements should be considered separately and that we should deal first with business options, the aim being to avoid the technical 'tail' wagging the business 'dog'. Nowadays, however, most changes to business practice involve the use of IT in some form, and it is often the availability of technology that makes the business solutions possible. For example, one way of reducing the need for staff in a supermarket would be to enable customers to scan their purchases themselves using 'smart' barcodes. For this reason, it is difficult to keep business and technical options separate, although it remains true that business needs, rather than the use of technology for its own sake, should drive the options process.

The basic process for developing options is shown in Figure 12.2. Identifying options is probably best achieved through some form of workshop, where brainstorming and other creative problem-solving approaches can be employed. Modelling techniques such as business activity modelling (see Chapter 7) and business process modelling (see Chapter 8) are also useful to help us generate options. The aim is simply to get all of the possible ideas on the table before going on to consider which are most promising. Even if some of the ideas seem a bit far-fetched, they may provide part of the actual solution or stimulate other people to come up with similar but more workable suggestions. Another way of identifying options is to study what other organizations – possibly the organization's competitors – have done to address the same issues.

Once all the possibilities have been flushed out, they can be subjected to evaluation to see which are worth examining further. Usually, some ideas can be rejected quite quickly as being too expensive, taking too long to implement or being counter-cultural. The criteria for assessing feasibility are examined in more detail in the section 'Assessing project feasibility' on page 198.

Ideally, the shortlist should be reduced to three or four options, one of which will usually be that of maintaining the status quo, the 'do nothing' option. The reason for restricting the list to three or four possibilities is that it is seldom practical, for reasons of time or cost, to examine more than this in enough detail to be taken forward to the business case. Each of the shortlisted options should address the major business issues but offer some distinctive balance of the time they will take to implement, the budget required and the range of features offered. Sometimes, however, the options are variations on a theme, with one dealing only with the most pressing business issues and others offering various additional features. This situation is illustrated in Figure 12.3.

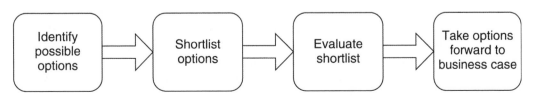

FIGURE 12.2 *Process for developing options*

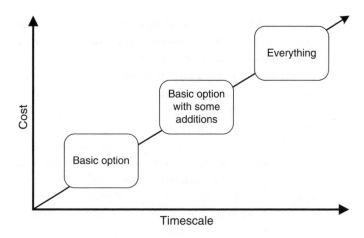

FIGURE 12.3 *Incremental options*

In Figure 12.3, the bottom option deals only with the most pressing issues, as quickly as possible and at minimal cost. The next option adds some additional features to the solution but costs more and takes longer. The last option is a comprehensive solution but takes the longest and costs the most.

One option that should always be considered – and that should usually find its way into the actual business case – is doing nothing. Sometimes this really is a viable option and might even be the best choice for the organization. Often, however, there is no sensible do-nothing option, as some form of business disaster may result from inaction. In this case, the decision-makers may not be aware that action is imperative, and so spelling out the risks and consequences of doing nothing becomes an important part of making the business case.

ASSESSING PROJECT FEASIBILITY

There are many issues to think about in assessing feasibility, but all fall under the three broad headings illustrated in Figure 12.4.

Business feasibility issues include whether the proposal matches the business objectives and strategy of the organization and – if it is a commercial firm – whether it can be achieved in the current market conditions. There is the question of whether the proposed solution will be delivered in sufficient time to secure the desired business benefits. The proposal must fit with the management structure of the organization and with its culture, because lack of cultural fit is often a cause of projects not meeting the expectations held for them. The solution must be capable of implementation within the physical infrastructure of the organization if that is a constraint. Although the proposal may be for major process

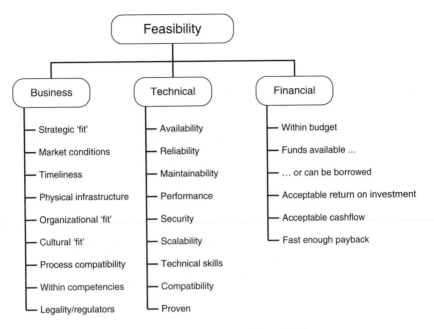

FIGURE 12.4 *Aspects of feasibility*

change, it may still have to interface with other processes that are not changing, and so compatibility with other areas must be considered. Whatever is proposed must be within the competencies of the organization and its personnel, or there must be a plan for the development of these competencies. Finally, many sectors are now heavily regulated and the proposed solution must be one that will be acceptable to the regulators and not infringe other law or treaty obligations.

In assessing **technical feasibility**, one is usually, although not always, considering IT. The proposed solution must meet the organization's demands in terms of system performance, availability, reliability, maintainability and security. It must be questioned whether the solution is scalable, up or down, in the event that the circumstances of the organization change. The organization must possess the technical skills to implement the solution or supplement these with help from outside. Few IT systems are now completely standalone, and so the issue of compatibility with other systems must be considered. If the solution involves an off-the-shelf software package, then thought should be given to the amount of customization that would be required and whether this would cause technical difficulties. Finally, some thought should be given as to whether the proposed solution is proven or places excessive reliance on leading-edge – that is to say, unproven – technologies. Many organizations would prefer a less ambitious but reliable solution to a more advanced solution that comes with a lot of technological risk.

Financial feasibility is about whether the organization can afford the proposed solution. There may already be a budget imposed. The organization needs either to have the required funds available or to be in a position to borrow them. Every organization will have some rules or guidelines about what constitutes an acceptable return on its investment; methods of calculating this are considered in the section 'Investment appraisal' on page 209. Even if a project pays for itself in the end, it may have unacceptably high costs on the way and so cash flow must also be considered. Finally, all organizations specify some time period over which payback must occur; in the case of IT projects, the payback periods are often very short, sometimes within the same accounting year as the investment.

Another tool that can be used in assessing feasibility is a PESTLE analysis. PESTLE examines the environment outside an organization, or perhaps within an organization but outside the area being studied. It can be used to assess feasibility as follows:

- **Political:** is the proposed solution politically acceptable?
- **Economic:** can the organization afford the solution?
- **Sociocultural:** does the solution fit with the organization's culture?
- **Technological:** can the solution be achieved, technically?
- **Legal:** is it legal, and will the regulator allow it?
- **Environmental:** does it raise any 'green' environmental issues?

A final tool that can be employed to assess the feasibility of an option is a force-field analysis, illustrated in Figure 12.5.

With a force-field analysis, we consider those forces inside and outside the organization that will support adoption of the proposal and those that will oppose it. We need to be sure that the positive forces outweigh the negative forces. The forces may include the PESTLE factors mentioned already, the elements identified in Figure 12.4 and also the key stakeholders in the organization (see Chapter 6). If we conclude that the

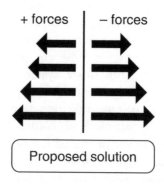

FIGURE 12.5 *Force-field analysis*

negative forces are too strong, then the proposal is not feasible and must be abandoned or recast in a way that gets more positive forces behind it.

In considering the feasibility of options, we also need to think about their impacts and risks. Because these form part of the business case itself, we discuss them in the next section.

STRUCTURE OF A BUSINESS CASE

Organizations differ in how they like to have business cases presented. Some like large weighty documents with full analyses of the proposals and all the supporting data. Others prefer a short sharp presentation of the main points. We have come across one organization that mandates that business cases be distilled into a single A4 page. If this sounds cavalier, remember that the people who have to make the decisions on business cases are busy senior managers, with time at a premium. Whatever the size, the structure and content of most business cases are similar and tend to include the following elements:

- introduction;
- management summary;
- description of the current situation;
- options considered;
- analysis of costs and benefits;
- impact assessment;
- risk assessment;
- recommendations;
- appendices, with supporting information.

We shall examine each of these elements in turn.

Introduction

This sets the scene and explains why the business case is being presented. Where relevant, it should also describe the methods used to examine the business issue and thank people who have contributed to the study.

Management summary

In many ways, this is the most important part of the document, as it is possibly the only part that the senior decision-makers will study properly. It should be written after the rest of the document has been completed and should distil the whole of the business case into a few paragraphs. In an ideal situation, three paragraphs should suffice, covering:

- what the study was about and what was found out about the issues under consideration;

- a survey of the options considered, with their principal advantages and disadvantages;
- a clear statement of the recommendation being made and the decision required.

If you cannot get away with only three paragraphs, try at least to restrict the management summary within one or two pages.

Description of the current situation

Here, we explain precisely the current situation and where the problems and opportunities lie. As long as it is consistent with explaining these issues properly, it is good to keep this section as short as possible, since senior managers often complain of having to read pages and pages to find out what they already know. Sometimes, however, the real problems or opportunities uncovered are not what management thought they were when they instituted the study. In this case, more space will have to be devoted to explaining the issues and exploring the implications for the business.

Options considered

In this section, we describe the options considered and explain, as briefly as possible, why we are rejecting those options that we do not recommend. More space should be devoted to describing the recommended solution and why we are recommending it. As we saw earlier (see Figure 12.3), there may well be a series of incremental options, from the most basic option to an option that addresses all of the issues raised.

Analysis of costs and benefits

Cost/benefit analysis is one of the most interesting – and most difficult – aspects of business case development. Before we examine the subject in detail, it is worth mentioning that it is good psychology to present the benefits before the costs, since the decision-makers will then appreciate the benefits before they are hit with the costs of achieving them. In other words, what we are presenting is actually a benefit/cost analysis, even though by convention it is always referred to as a cost/benefit analysis.

Although cost/benefit analysis is interesting, it does pose a number of challenges, including:

- working out in the first place where costs will be incurred and where benefits can be expected;
- being realistic about whether the benefits will be realized in practice;
- placing a value on intangible elements such as 'improved customer satisfaction' and 'better staff morale'.

The last point brings us to a discussion about the types of cost and benefit that we need to deal with. Costs and benefits are incurred, or enjoyed, either immediately or in the longer term. They are also either tangible, which means that a credible – usually monetary – value can be placed on them, or intangible, where this is not the case. Combining these elements, we find that costs and benefits fit into one of four categories, as illustrated in Figure 12.6.

Costs tend to be mainly tangible, whereas benefits are often a mixture of tangible and intangible. In some organizations, managers will not consider intangible benefits at all, making it difficult or impossible to provide an effective business case. How, for instance, does one place a value on something like a more modern company image achieved through adopting a new logo? In theory, it should be possible to put a numerical value on any cost or benefit; the practical problem is that one seldom has the time, or the specialist expertise – for example, from the field of operational research – to do so.

If intangible benefits are allowed, then it is very important not to overstate them or, worse, to put a spurious value against them. The danger here is that the decision-makers simply do not believe this value, which then undermines their confidence in other, more soundly based values. With intangible benefits, it is much better to state what they are and even to emphasize them but to leave the decision-makers to put their own valuations on them.

Another pitfall in cost/benefit analysis is basing them on assumptions. For example, we might say something like 'If we could achieve a 20 per cent reduction in the time taken to produce invoices, then this would amount to 5000 hours per year or a cost saving of £25,000.' This will prove acceptable to the decision-makers only if the assumption is plausible. If possible, use assumptions that are common within the organization, and always err on the side of conservatism – that is, under-claim rather than over-claim.

Having stated these key issues, let us look at some of the places where costs and benefits might arise and how we might go about quantifying

	Immediate	Longer-term
Tangible	Tangible and immediate	Tangible and longer-term
Intangible	Intangible and immediate	Intangible and longer-term

FIGURE 12.6 *Categories of costs and benefits*

them. We shall use the four categories of costs and benefits described already.

Tangible costs

- **Development staff costs:** in many projects, particularly those that involve developing new processes or IT systems, these will be a major cost element. To work them out, we need a daily rate for the staff concerned – probably available from the HR or accounts department – and an outline project plan showing when and how the resources will be required. If external consultants are being used, then the costs here will be subject to negotiation and contract.

- **User staff costs:** these are often forgotten but can be significant. User staff will have to be available for the initial fact-finding in order to test any systems involved and to be trained in the new systems and methods of working. Again, daily rates can be used in combination with an outline plan of the amount of user involvement.

- **Hardware:** if IT is involved, there may well be a need to purchase new hardware. For this, estimates or quotations can be obtained from potential suppliers.

- **Infrastructure:** this includes things such as cabling and networks. Again, estimates will be required from suppliers.

- **Packaged software:** estimates of the cost of this can be obtained from package vendors, probably based on the proposed number of users. Where tailoring of a package is envisaged, estimates of the effort and cost involved can also be requested.

- **Relocation:** this can be quite tricky to cost out. The costs could include those of the new premises, either rented or bought, refurbishment, new furniture and the actual moving costs. There may also be costs associated with surrendering existing leases and so on.

- **Staff training and retraining:** to work this out, we need to know how many people need to be trained and what they need to learn. Ideally, this requires some form of training-needs analysis. If there is insufficient time for that, then we could make a broad assessment of the training needed and multiply the delivery time for one course by a factor of 10 to get a ballpark estimate of the course development effort.

- **Ongoing costs:** once any new systems are in place, they will require maintenance and support. Quotes for this can be obtained from the vendors. If this is not possible, then a very rough rule of thumb is to allow support costs of 15 per cent of operational costs in the first year after installation and then 10 per cent thereafter. However, this is very crude and real quotes are much to be preferred if possible.

Intangible costs

- **Disruption and loss of productivity:** however good a new process or system is in the long run, there is bound to be some disruption as it is introduced. The level of disruption is very difficult to predict when implementing any business change. Also, if parallel running of old and new IT systems is used to smooth the transition, then there will be a tangible cost involved.

- **Recruitment:** this ought to be tangible, but organizations often have little idea of the total cost involved in recruiting a member of staff. Elements of this cost, such as agency fees, will be tangible, but if new staff members or skills are needed, there will be costs involved in getting the new staff and inducting them into the organization.

Tangible benefits

- **Staff savings:** this is the most obvious saving, although many organizations are now so lean that it is hard to see where further reductions will come from. In calculating the savings, we need the total cost of employing the people concerned, including things such as National Insurance, pensions and other benefits, and sometimes the space the people occupy. The HR or accounts department should be able to supply this information. Do not forget, though, that if people are to be made redundant, then there will be one-off redundancy costs that must be set against the ongoing saved staff costs.

- **Reduced effort and improved speed of working:** short of removing posts altogether, the savings may be of time to free people for other work. This should be a tangible benefit, but only if the effort before the change has been measured and compared with the expected situation after the change – if not, this will have to be treated as an intangible benefit.

- **Faster responses to customers:** this is the ability to respond faster to customers' needs. Again, a pre-change measurement would need to have been made to quantify any possible benefits.

- **Reduced accommodation costs:** these may already have been factored into the cost of employing staff (see 'Staff savings' above), but smaller computers may also save space and, perhaps, people may be able to work from home some or all of the time. The facilities or finance department should have some idea about the cost of accommodation.

- **Reduced inventory:** new systems – especially 'just-in-time' systems – usually result in the need to hold less stock. The organization's finance and logistics experts should be able to help in quantifying this benefit.

- **Other cost reductions:** these include reductions in overtime hours worked, being able to avoid basing staffing levels on peak workloads, reductions in travel time and costs between sites, and reductions in consumption of consumables.

Intangible benefits

- **Increased job satisfaction:** this may result in tangible benefits such as reduced staff turnover or reduced absenteeism, but we cannot prove in advance that these things will happen.

- **Improved customer satisfaction:** this is intangible unless we have sound measures to show, for example, why customers complain about our products or services.

- **Better management information:** it is important to distinguish between better management information and simply more management information. Better information should lead to better decisions but is difficult to value.

- **Greater organizational flexibility:** this means that the organization can respond more quickly to changes in the external environment, through having more flexible systems and staff members who can be switched to different work relatively quickly.

- **More creative problem-solving time:** managers freed from much day-to-day work should have more time to study strategic issues.

- **Improved presentation or better market image:** new systems often enable an organization to present itself better to the outside world.

- **Better communications:** many people report poor communications within their organization as a problem. Improving communications would clearly be beneficial, but again how would one place a value on this?

Avoided costs

One special form of benefit worth thinking about is what we might call 'avoided costs'. For example, in the run up to 2000, many organizations were faced with the costs of making their computer systems 'millennium-compliant'. IT departments often instead suggested the wholesale replacement of systems, thereby avoiding the costs of adapting the old systems. In such a case, an investment of, say, £2 million in a new system might be contrasted with an avoided cost of £1 million simply to make the old legacy systems compliant. There are often situations where an organization has to do something and has already budgeted for it and that budget can be offset against a more radical solution that would offer additional business benefits.

Presenting the financial costs and benefits

Once the various tangible costs and benefits have been assessed, they need to be presented so that management staff can see whether and when the project pays for itself. As this is a somewhat complex topic, it is examined separately in the section 'Investment appraisal' on page 209.

Impact assessment

In addition to the costs and benefits already mentioned, for each of the options we need to explore in the business case any impacts that there might be on the organization. Some of these impacts may have costs attached to them, but others may not and are simply the things that will happen as a result of adopting the proposed course of action. Here are some examples:

- **Organization structure:** it may be necessary to reorganize departments or functions to exploit the new circumstances properly, for example to create a one-stop shop for customers or to create more generalist rather than specialist staff roles. This will be unsettling for the staff and managers involved, and a plan must be made to handle this.

- **Interdepartmental relations:** the relationships between departments may change and there may be a need to introduce service level agreements or similar to redefine these relationships.

- **Working practices:** new processes and systems invariably lead to changes in working practices, and these must be introduced carefully and sensitively.

- **Management style:** sometimes, the style that managers adopt has to change. For example, if we de-layer the organization and give front-line staff more authority to deal with customers, then their managers' roles will change as well.

- **Recruitment policy:** the organization may have to recruit different types of people and look for different skills.

- **Appraisal and promotion criteria:** it may be necessary to change people's targets and incentives in order to encourage them to display different behaviours, for example to be more customer-focused.

- **Supplier relations:** these may have to be redefined. For example, if an organization was outsourcing a lot of the IT services, then this would work much better with a cooperative customer/supplier relationship than with the adversarial situation that too often seems to exist.

Whatever the impacts, the business case needs to spell them out and also make clear to the decision-makers what changes will have to be made in order to exploit fully the opportunities available and the costs that these changes will incur.

Risk assessment

No change comes without risk, and it is unrealistic to think otherwise. A business case is strengthened immeasurably if it can be shown that the potential risks have been identified and that suitable countermeasures are available. A complete and comprehensive risk register (sometimes called the risk log) is probably not required at this stage – that should be created when the change or development project proper starts – but the principal risks should be identified. For each risk, the following should be recorded:

- **Description:** the cause and impact of the risk should be described, for example 'Uncertainty over the future leads to the resignation of key staff, leaving the organization with a lack of experienced personnel.'
- **Impact assessment:** this should attempt to assess the scale of the damage that would be suffered if the risk occurred. If quantitative measures can be made, so much the better, otherwise a scale of 'small', 'moderate' or 'large' will suffice.
- **Probability:** how likely is it that this risk will materialize? Again, precise probabilities can be calculated, but it is probably better to use a scale of 'low', 'medium' or 'high'.
- **Countermeasures:** this is the really important part, the question being what can we do either to reduce the likelihood of the risk occurring or to lessen its impact if it does occur? We may also try to transfer the risk's impact on to someone else, for example through the use of insurance.
- **Ownership:** for each risk, we need to decide who would be best placed to take the necessary countermeasures. This may involve asking senior managers within the organization to take the responsibility.

If there seem to be too many risks associated with the proposal, then it is a good idea to document only the major risks – the potential show-stoppers – in the body of the business case and to put the rest in an appendix.

Recommendations

Finally, we need to summarize the business case and make clear the decisions that the senior managers are being asked to take. If the business case is for carrying out a project of some sort, then an outline of the main tasks and timescales envisaged is useful to the decision-makers. This is best expressed graphically as a Gantt/bar chart, as illustrated in Figure 12.7.

Appendices and supporting information

If detailed information needs to be included in the business case, this is best put into the appendices. This separates out the main points that are put in the main body of the case from the supporting details. If supporting statistics have to be provided, then they too should go into the appendices,

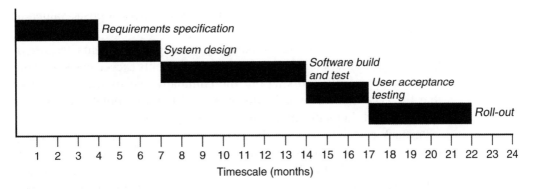

FIGURE 12.7 *Gantt/bar chart for proposed project*

perhaps with a summary graph or chart in the main body. The detailed cost/benefit calculations may also be put into the appendices.

INVESTMENT APPRAISAL

In this part of the business case, the financial aspects – in other words, the tangible costs and benefits – are contrasted so see whether and when the project will pay for itself. The simplest way of doing this is to use a 'payback calculation', which is in effect a cash-flow forecast for the project. An example of a payback calculation is given in Table 12.1.

TABLE 12.1 *Payback calculation*

Item	Year 1	Year 2	Year 3	Year 4	Year 5
Hardware purchase	200,000	—	—	—	—
Hardware maintenance	30,000	30,000	30,000	30,000	30,000
Software purchase	150,000	—	—	—	—
Software support	30,000	30,000	30,000	30,000	30,000
Staff savings	150,000	150,000	150,000	150,000	150,000
Cash flow for year (savings less costs)	−260,000	90,000	90,000	90,000	90,000
Cumulative cash flow	−260,000	−170,00	−80,000	+10,000	+100,000

In Table 12.1, the costs are as follows:

- Immediate costs of £200,000 for hardware and £150,000 for software for a new system.
- Ongoing costs of £30,000 per year for hardware maintenance and £30,000 for software support and upgrades.

The tangible benefit will be the removal of some clerical posts, valued at £150,000 per year.

In the first year, the costs considerably outweigh the benefits because of the large capital expenditures, but thereafter benefits exceed costs by some £90,000 per year. By working out the cumulative positions, we discover that the accumulated benefits finally exceed the accumulated costs after year four and thereafter build up at £90,000 per year.

Payback calculations have the virtue of being easy to understand and relatively easy to construct, although getting reliable figures can sometimes be a headache. If interest rates and inflation are low, payback calculations provide a reasonable forecast of what will happen. However, they do not take account of what accountants call the 'time value of money'. This is the simple fact, which we all understand from personal experience, that money spent or saved today is not worth the same as it will be next year or in five years' time. In part this is the effect of inflation, but even with low or zero inflation there are other things that we could do with the money besides investing in this project. We might, for instance, leave it in the bank to earn interest. Conversely, we might have to borrow money and pay interest in order to finance the project.

A method that takes account of the time value of money is known as discounted cash flow (DCF), which leads to a net present value (NPV) for the project, which means that all of the cash flows in the years after the current one are adjusted to today's value of money. Management accountants work out the discount rate to use in a discounted cash-flow calculation by studying a number of factors, including the likely movement of money-market interest rates in the next few years. The mechanism for doing this is outside the scope of this book, but interested readers are referred to the 'Further reading' section at the end of this chapter. Let us suppose that the management accountants decide we should be using a discount rate of 10 per cent. We can then find the amounts by which we should discount the cash flows in years 2–5 by either using the appropriate formula in a spreadsheet or looking up the factors in an accounting textbook. For a 10 per cent discount rate, the relevant factors are shown in Table 12.2.

TABLE 12.2 *Net present value calculation*

Year	Net cash flow	Discount factor	Present value
1	−260,000	1.000	−260,000
2	90,000	0.909	81,810
3	90,000	0.826	74,340
4	90,000	0.751	67,590
5	90,000	0.683	61,470
Net present value of project			25,210

Table 12.2 represents the same project that was analysed in Table 12.1. With the cash flows from years 2–5 adjusted to today's values, we can see that the project is not such an attractive investment as the payback calculation suggested. It does pay for itself, but now only in year 5 and not by as great a margin as before.

We can perform a sensitivity analysis on these results to see how much they would be affected by changes in interest rates. If we had used a discount rate of 5 per cent, we would have got an NPV of £59,140, while a rate of 15 per cent would have produced an NPV of –£2960.

One final measure that some organizations like to use is the internal rate of return (IRR). This is a calculation that assesses what sort of return on investment is represented by the project in terms of a single percentage figure. This can then be used to compare projects with each other to see which are the best investment opportunities, and to compare projects with what the same money could earn if it was simply left in the bank. So, for example, if the IRR of a project is calculated at 3 per cent and current bank interest rates are 5 per cent, then on financial grounds alone it would be better not to spend the money.

IRR is worked out by standing the DCF/NPV calculations on their head. We are trying to calculate what discount rate we would have to use in order to get an NPV of zero after five years (or whatever period the organization mandates should be used for the calculation). In other words, at what point would financial costs and benefits balance each other precisely? The problem is that this cannot be worked out by a formula. One has to set up a spreadsheet and try different discount rates until an NPV of zero is produced – Microsoft Excel has an automated function to do this. In the case of our example project, the result is around 14.42 per cent. If this were being compared with another project offering 5 per cent, then our project would be the more attractive option. However, IRR does not take account of the overall size of the project, so the project with the smaller IRR may produce more pounds, or euros, or dollars in the end. For this reason, most accounting textbooks agree that DCF/NPV is the best method of assessing the value of an investment, while acknowledging that many managers like the simplicity of the single-figure IRR.

PRESENTATION OF A BUSINESS CASE

There are two basic ways in which a business case can be presented, and often there is a need for both: as a written document and as a face-to-face presentation. In both cases, the way the business case is presented can have a major impact on whether it is accepted. There are some simple rules that apply to both approaches:

- **Think about the audience:** readers of reports and attendees at presentations have different interests and attitudes. Some like to have 'chapter and verse', others prefer the 'big picture'. As far as possible, try to address the concerns of each of the decision-makers in the report or presentation (see Chapter 6 for more on this).

- **Keep it short:** you may be stuck with a preset format or template for your report, in which case the actual sections may force you into creating a long document. However, try as far as possible to keep the business case concise.

- **Consider the structure:** we have provided here a good basic structure for a written business case. For a presentation, the old rule still holds good:
  – Tell 'em what you're going to tell 'em.
  – Tell 'em.
  – Tell 'em what you've told 'em.
  You need to build to a logical conclusion that starts with the current situation and leads to the decision that needs to be made.

- **Think about appearances:** again, you may be constrained by a template here, but if not, remember you have to induce the decision-makers to read your business case. Use lots of white space, pictures and diagrams instead of tables and colour. For a presentation, avoid dozens of bullet-point slides, which tend to simply repeat what is in the report; instead, use pictures, diagrams and colour to show the decision-makers what you're talking about.

BENEFITS REALIZATION

In recent years, organizations have become increasingly interested in benefits realization, which can be summarized as managing projects such that they are able to deliver the predicted benefits and, after the project has been implemented, checking progress on the achievement of these benefits and taking any actions required to support their delivery. This basic approach is shown in Figure 12.8.

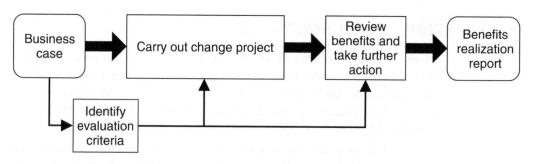

FIGURE 12.8 *Benefits realization approach*

When a business case is being constructed, some thought should be given to how the claimed benefits will be measured. For some tangible benefits this may not be too difficult, for example either we make the expected cost savings or we do not. However, even then there are some problems, such as how do we disaggregate the effects of this project from those of other projects that may be happening at the same time? Or how do we adjust for changes in the external environment, for instance a general upturn or downturn in sales? For intangible benefits, the obstacles are even greater – for instance, how can we measure a change in staff morale? It may be possible to measure reduced staff attrition, but what if there is no other work locally and attrition drops anyway? Whatever the difficulties, however, some thought needs to be given to measurement, and this may involve surveying the situation before the change takes place, so that the situation afterwards can be compared with it.

Figure 12.8 shows an arrow from the evaluation criteria leading back into the change project itself. This highlights the need to try to manage the project in such a way as to maximize the hoped-for benefits. For example, allowing a lot of changes may drive up the costs of the project and therefore extend the period that it will take to pay for itself or wipe out any gains altogether.

The business case is reviewed during the project in order to check whether the predicted benefits are still able to be achieved and to identify any changes required in order to enable the benefits to be delivered. The main evaluation, however, takes place after the project has finished. Consideration should be given to the timescale required for the expected benefits to have appeared. Depending on the type and scale of the project, this could happen months or even years after the project ends. The evaluation will also focus on the progress towards achieving the benefits and will consider whether any further action needs to be taken in order to enable the benefits to be achieved.

Ultimately, a benefits realization report should be produced that assesses frankly whether the hoped-for benefits have been gained. This report has two important uses:

- to reassure the decision-makers and the wider organization that the time, effort and cost of the project have been justified;

- to provide input to future business cases and future projects in order to help make them more successful.

SUMMARY

A coherent and well-researched business case should be an important guiding document for any change project. Developing a business case starts by identifying the possible options and then assessing their feasibility. The business case itself follows a fairly clearly defined format, leading to clear recommendations to the decision-makers. There are several approaches to investment appraisal, which assesses the financial costs and benefits of a proposed change project. After the project has been completed, there should be a review to determine whether the expected benefits have been realized in practice and to identify any actions required to support the delivery of those benefits.

FURTHER READING

Boardman, A.E., Greenberg, D.H., Vining, A.R. and Weimer, D.L. (2001) *Cost–Benefit Analysis: Concepts and Practice*, 2nd edn. Prentice Hall, Upper Saddle River, NJ.

Davenport, T.H. *et al.* (1999) *Harvard Business Review on the Business Value of IT*. Harvard Business School Press, Harvard, MA.

Lucey, T. (2003) *Management Accounting*, 5th edn. Thomson Learning, London.

Remenyi, D., Money, A., Sherwood-Smith, M. and Irani, Z. (2000) *The Effective Measurement and Management of IT Costs and Benefits*, 2nd edn. Butterworth Heinemann, Oxford.

Schmidt, M.J. (2002) *The Business Case Guide*, 2nd edn. Solution Matrix, Boston, MA.

13 Managing business change

KEITH HINDLE

INTRODUCTION

It is important to appreciate that the business analyst's role is vital if organizations are to benefit fully from IT-enabled business change. Earlier chapters have explored many aspects of business analysis work and have covered a range of techniques that will help analysts to identify and specify the changes required to improve the operation of their organizations. In this chapter, we look at the factors that need to be considered when implementing change. We examine the general characteristics of change, the stages of change and the different levels within an individual organization that can be affected by change. We also discuss a four-part change process that includes:

- understanding the impact of the changes;
- planning what needs to take place in order for the changes to be successful;
- carrying out the planned change;
- making sure that the change becomes embedded in the organization.

INTRODUCING A NEW SYSTEM

Introducing a new IT system can have many consequent effects, some obvious and easy to handle but others not so straightforward. The new system may require new skills on the part of the users, or staff members may find that their existing jobs disappear and they have to take on new roles, possibly at different locations. The change of role may also result in changes to the social group or the department to which staff members currently belong. Some staff members may be made redundant, while new people with different skills and aptitudes may be hired. The new or changed roles that they are required to undertake may call for a different approach compared with their old roles. They may, for instance, have more responsibilities or a wider range of tasks to complete or they may be asked to make decisions that previously were left to others. Any change can be unsettling if it is not managed well. It is usual for those in changing circumstances to feel anxious about the change, their ability to adapt to it and its long-term effects on their career prospects. Such anxiety will affect job performance as their morale drops. In more extreme cases, it can lead to overt resistance to the change. Those who have the opportunity – usually the more able and adaptable staff members – may leave for jobs elsewhere that they regard as safer or more predictable.

Change has different components. Many change projects include the implementation of IT systems and the other processes and procedures that support this work. The smooth introduction of these elements will help the change process but will not guarantee success, and yet so often this is the main area on which many projects concentrate. The other, often neglected, area concentrates on how the people concerned react when they are expected to change what is sometimes described as the 'hearts-and-minds aspects'. This involves understanding how people respond to change, the ways in which their initial negative reactions can be reduced, and how their acceptance of the new system and procedures can be achieved quickly and smoothly.

EMOTIONS AND THE CHANGE PROCESS

Most of us react to change in a similar way, as illustrated in Figure 13.1. This change model illustrates how change takes time and that, during this time, individuals feel a range of emotions and discomfort. Initially, we may feel positive to the idea of the change before we realize quite how much it will affect us. As that realization sinks in and the difficulties become clearer, the frustration and resistance build up. At this point, the success of the change may look very doubtful and we feel like giving up the whole thing. With perseverance, however, we can turn the corner and start to see the positive aspects of the change. There are aspects of the new ways of working that will be better than the old. As we get more used to the new processes, they will start to feel more natural and our confidence will grow. As well as changes to our behaviour, our feelings change. Eventually, we will be able to look back on the old ways of working with some disbelief – why did we ever operate in that way? By then, we are committed firmly to the new processes. Hindsight, of course, is wonderful, and sometimes when we look back we forget the discomfort we experienced in the middle of the change. If we know about the stages of Figure 13.1 in advance, then we can understand why we are feeling frustrated and realize that this is to be expected. The curve also indicates that the negative feelings are a necessary step towards the positive upswing.

A popular approach to change mirrors the curve of Figure 13.1 by highlighting the three phases of the change journey: the unfreeze, change and refreeze phases.

The unfreeze phase

Instead of emphasizing the destination, the change journey considers first what we have to move away from – the unfreezing phase. People often

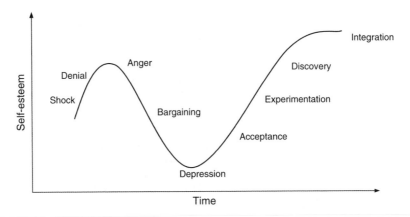

FIGURE 13.1 *Emotions and the change process*

want to stick with the known, familiar ways of working, especially if that is comfortable. The unknown is perceived as a threat. During this initial phase, we have to persuade those affected that the present situation cannot continue. This may involve pointing out the negative aspects of doing nothing, comparing our poor performance with that of our competitors. This can be contrasted with the clear vision that will result from the change. What we are doing is to increase the sense of dissatisfaction with the present in order to provide an incentive for change. The role of the change leader in emphasizing the vision will be important. At the same time, people may also be worried that they will find the process of change too difficult to handle. Training and support and the involvement of staff members in the change planning will give them confidence that the change is feasible and will be handled in a professional manner.

This unfreezing phase is effectively a time to grieve for the loss of the old ways. It will take time, but this can be minimized if it is handled appropriately. It will require significant communication from an early stage so that everyone understands what is happening. This early concern for the unfreezing process is important and is in direct contrast with some change projects that leave it too late and wait until the new system is being rolled out.

The change phase

Once staff members have agreed that change is both necessary and achievable, they can move on to the second phase – the actual change. People will feel uncomfortable as they enter the no-man's land between the known past and the promised land of the new system. This is a time of intense learning, both formal and informal. Inevitably this will mean mistakes – that is the way we learn. It is important that staff members do not feel that they will be penalized for making mistakes, as this will hinder

217

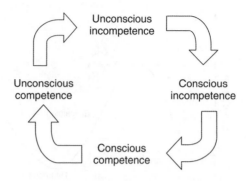

FIGURE 13.2 *Learning cycle*

the learning process. Gradually, people start to feel more confident in their ability to operate the new system. The learning cycle in Figure 13.2 represents how people feel as they learn to work in new ways and use different skills.

At the outset, they are in a state of unconscious incompetence, where they do not realize what they do not know about the system and procedures. As they begin learning about the system, they realize what skills and competences they need in order to carry out their new roles – they become consciously incompetent. Once they have acquired the knowledge and skills required, and with support, they then move on to conscious competence. At this stage, they know what to do but still have to think about it. The processes and procedures are still new. They have not yet become as deeply embedded as in the old ways. After a while, the new methods of working become second nature. People do not have to think 'What should I do now?' – they just do it.

The refreeze phase

As the new system beds in, the new social groups and relationships also develop. This is the refreeze phase, when the changes become permanent. Management can support this through the introduction of appropriate motivation and reward mechanisms. Although these may include financial rewards, the motivational research done by Herzberg (1968) recorded pay a 'hygiene factor': insufficient pay will demotivate people, but more pay will not necessarily motivate them. Herzberg's motivators include achievement, recognition, responsibility, advancement and learning.

With the success of the change, everyone feels more confident and more committed to the new system and productivity rises. We are now at the top of the right-hand curve in Figure 13.1. Looking back towards the unfreeze and change phases, people wonder what the fuss was all about. It is obvious from here that the new system is much better, but it is only by going through the earlier phases that we have been able to reach this successful conclusion. We can now see that organizational change occurs

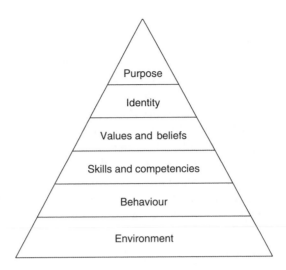

FIGURE 13.3 *Logical levels model*

only when the individuals within that organization change. If we can understand how individuals change, then we will have a better chance of achieving organizational change. The Institute of Human Development in its logical levels model, shown in Figure 13.3, says that change affects us on many levels. Changes to the business environment mean that we have to behave differently, and new behaviour often involves the development of new skills through training and coaching. New behaviour patterns may also be accompanied by changes to our values and feelings.

- **Environment:** the context in which our actions take place. This identifies where and when we do things.
- **Behaviour:** what we do.
- **Skills/competencies:** what we are capable of doing.
- **Values and beliefs:** what is important to us and why we do things.
- **Identity:** our sense of self or role; how we see ourselves.
- **Purpose:** why we are here and what we ultimately want to achieve.

For example, a new customer relationship management system may require people to behave in a completely different way towards the customer. Our identity is often linked to the position we hold within the organization. If the organization structure changes and our job is eliminated or altered significantly, then we get anxious about our identity. The purpose may be described as a vision of where we want to be. It explains what we are doing now as a steppingstone to some future state that may not appeal to everyone. These levels form a hierarchy. If we change a lower level, then this may not have any impact on the higher levels. If we change a higher level, however, this will have some, possibly major, effects on those levels below. Thus, changing one's identity from 'capitalist go-getter' to 'caring, sharing, relationship person' could have enormous consequences in terms of skills and behaviours.

Interestingly, many change programmes concentrate on staff changes at lower levels. Training and coaching are aimed at providing new competences to support new behaviour. Although this is necessary, it may not be sufficient to ensure successful change. If the person with the new abilities still has an identity and purpose that are at odds with those of the new system, then they will not wholeheartedly accept the new job they have been given. Part of the change manager's role is to ensure as far as possible that there are no conflicts between the staff and the proposed changes at any of the levels.

THE NEED FOR CHANGE MANAGEMENT

There has often been a lack of emphasis on change management during the implementation of new IT systems, largely because the change is viewed simply as an IT project rather than a business change programme or project. However, IT development projects exist to enable business change and operational improvement. If IT is regarded as the main driver of the change, then the project will take on more of a technical flavour than if it was driven by the business. For IT staff, the project is all about delivering a computer system that works. A successful system is one that satisfies the requirements in the specification and is developed within the time and budget constraints. This is the focus of the IT staff – they do not have the responsibility or the skills for managing the people changes that usually accompany the introduction of a new system. So long as the system does what it should, the IT staff cannot be held responsible for how the business uses or misuses the system after it has been delivered. Nowadays, however, many organizations are tackling this situation more holistically, and business analysts have a role to play in this newer approach. Business units are now taking over responsibility for change programmes, even where this includes an IT component. Increasingly, the desired outcome is a total business system change, where the IT system, the people, the processes and the organizational structure are changed. Hence, the IT system is only one of several enablers of change that must come together in order to guarantee success.

THE CHANGE PROCESS

The change process consists of four phases:

(i)   **Understand:** analyse the impact of the change.

(ii) **Plan:** decide how the change is to be achieved.

(iii) **Execute:** carry out the plan.

(iv) **Sustain:** ensure that the change is sustained after implementation and that further improvements are achieved.

Change management phase (i): understand the impact

Managing change is concerned largely with helping people to change. Before we can work out how to manage the change, we need to investigate and understand who will be affected by it. The affected individuals and groups are referred to as stakeholders. As we saw in Chapter 6, different stakeholder groups are managed differently. During this initial phase we can check that all the preliminary work necessary to implement the change successfully has been completed. We should be able to see:

- a clear vision of where the change will take us;
- a well-defined scope of change showing how the changed process relates to other parts of the business;
- an outline of the business drivers that make the change necessary;
- a description of the overall business strategy of which the change is a part;
- clearly stated business objectives to be met by the changed business;
- a high level of trust between those leading the change and those affected by it.

Any missing elements bring a risk to the success of the change. Where this is the case, management should be warned and asked to take corrective action.

The main steps within this first phase address the stakeholders and their needs and how they will be affected by the change. Much of this has been covered earlier, but there are special characteristics that are of interest from a change management perspective, including:

- how they will be affected by the change;
- the extent to which they will be affected by the change;
- the relationships they have with other stakeholders;
- the power of the stakeholder and the resources available to them;
- the knowledge of the business and the change;
- how supportive of the change they are at present;
- the level of support that will be required of them in order for the change to be successful.

Dealing with these issues brings two benefits. First, we want to assess the significance of each stakeholder group. There may be many stakeholders that we could involve. It makes sense to target those who will provide the best return for our efforts. Once we have prioritized the stakeholders, we need to identify how much attention we should give them. Chapter 6 explored an approach to analysing and managing stakeholders using the power/interest grid. An alternative use of this grid is to consider the power of stakeholders against the impact that the changes will have upon them, as this may provide additional insights into their concerns and attitudes. The grid used is very similar to that used in Chapter 6 and is shown in Figure 13.4.

Knowing the attitudes of the stakeholders at present, and the attitudes that the stakeholders need to adopt if the change is to be successful, allows us to rate the stakeholders using a simple three-point scale – 'support', 'neutral' or 'oppose'. Force-field analysis can then help us to decide how to obtain the required shift in position. This technique, illustrated in Figure 13.5, shows both the driving and resisting forces to the change. If it is possible to estimate the relative sizes of the forces, then different sized-arrows can be used. A large left-pointing arrow, for example, would indicate that the stakeholder strongly opposes the change. Later, when we consider what actions to take, we will be interested in supplementing the driving forces and reducing the resisting forces.

Change management phase (ii): plan the change

Planning the human dimension of change is necessary if we are to succeed. It is worthwhile remembering, however, that the transition from the old to the new way of working is not a mechanical activity, the pace of which can be accurately predicted in advance. Different people will make the transition at different rates. There will be unanticipated problems that seem to threaten the progress of the whole project. Unless the change is relatively straightforward, we might think of the transition as an

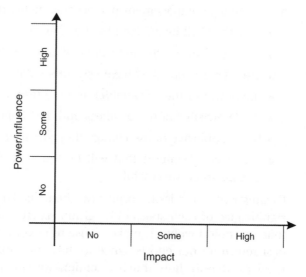

FIGURE 13.4 *The power/impact grid*

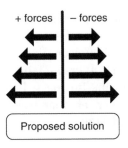

+ forces | − forces

Proposed solution

FIGURE 13.5 *Force-field analysis*

experiment in which people find their own ways of adapting to the new circumstances. As a result, the plan cannot be set in concrete – it must be flexible enough to handle the problems that occur.

Developing trust

Change requires trust between the instigators and those affected by the change. Regardless of whether that trust already exists, we need to develop it and ensure that it remains. At the beginning of the project, it is helpful to develop and communicate a set of ground rules that outline how the project is to be conducted. These are high-level statements that need the active support of senior management. They may be described as principles and cover aspects such as business values, customer focus, the project itself, the impact of the project on staff, and management behaviour.

By reiterating our main business values, we are assuring the staff that the organization is fundamentally the same, even if the detailed activities are changing. This provides continuity and guards against any accusations about loss of integrity. The project principles will assure staff of the professionalism and fairness of the proposed changes. Examples might state that staff members will be involved in the decisions that affect their jobs and that existing processes will be analysed in order to decide which elements can continue unchanged. The staff impact principles will address the fears that individuals often have when changes are announced concerning redundancy, relocation or change of organizational structure. Examples might include that staff members will be trained and coached when they take on new jobs and there will be no compulsory redundancy.

The management principles address people's concerns over management's intentions. They will help to undermine the rumours and suspicions that inevitably surface. They could include statements to the effect that management will be available for formal and informal discussions about the change, that management will be open in those discussions, and that two-way dialogues will be encouraged.

The purpose of publishing these principles is to build up greater trust; consequently, everyone must act according to these principles. Trust will make the change process much easier. Because the principles are so far reaching, they must be agreed with senior management. Ideally, those managers should present them to the staff. The project members can then develop the trust created by these principles as they work with the individuals in the business. If the principles, once announced, are later abandoned, then all that trust can disappear and damage the change process significantly.

Plan the change activities

The change plan is designed to help individuals to move from the comfort of their existing jobs, through the discomfort of the changeover period, and on to the comfort of the new system. There are two main aspects to this journey:

- The stages of the journey, particularly:
  - the ending of the old ways;
  - the neutral zone;
  - the beginning of the new ways.
- The impact of information about the change on the individual.

All these stages need to be managed if they are to be completed successfully. Communication is key to managing these stages. The following checklists can be used in preparing for this communication activity:

Communication checklist for managing the end stage.

☐ Increase understanding of current problems and why change is necessary.

☐ Expect an emotional reaction and handle sympathetically.

☐ Define what is over but also what will continue and improve.

☐ Be respectful to the past.

☐ Use the 'What's in it for me?' approach.

☐ Communicate repeatedly, using varied channels.

Communications checklist for the neutral zone.

☐ Involve people and get them to try things out.

☐ Provide prototypes and mock-ups.

☐ Encourage the plan–do–study–act cycle in order to gain insights.

☐ Collect ideas and thank people for their contributions.

☐ Feed back what has happened as a result of the suggestions.

☐ Communicate repeatedly, using varied channels.

Communications checklist for the new beginning.

☐ Inform people clearly about their part in the new system.

☐ Ensure that all communications, from high-level policy statements to detailed procedures, are consistent.

☐ Celebrate/publicize success and give credit.

☐ Communicate repeatedly, using varied channels.

Care needs to be taken so that people do not become overloaded with information. It is often better to present the information in chunks that can be digested more easily. One framework that we have found deals with the:

- **Purpose:** why are we doing this?
- **Picture:** what will it look like when we get there?
- **Plan:** how will we get there?
- **Part:** what will be my role, both in getting there and when we arrive?

This approach helps to structure the information and increases understanding. An extended version of this framework, known as the concerns-based adoption model, is shown in Figure 13.6. It outlines the stages that people will go through in order to accept fully the change. Each stage lists the major concerns that people have. The model operates on the premise that none of the stages may be bypassed. For example, until someone knows what the change is, it is pointless discussing how he or she will be affected. At any one point in time, different people will be at different stages and will have different concerns. How and what we communicate will depend on where they are on the model.

Develop the communications plan

The communications plan should outline:

- who the target of the communication is, i.e. the recipient;
- what is to be communicated, i.e. the message;
- who sends the message, i.e. the messenger;
- how the message is transmitted, i.e. the medium;
- when the message is to be transmitted, i.e. the schedule;
- why the message is important, i.e. the purpose or concern addressed.

The recipients are the stakeholder groups, which should have been segmented so that all the members of any one group will have similar information needs. The message to be communicated will depend on the target audience and the stage we are at in the project. The frameworks outlined in Figure 13.6 indicate the topics that should be included and will help us to identify the audience's current concerns. We then have to

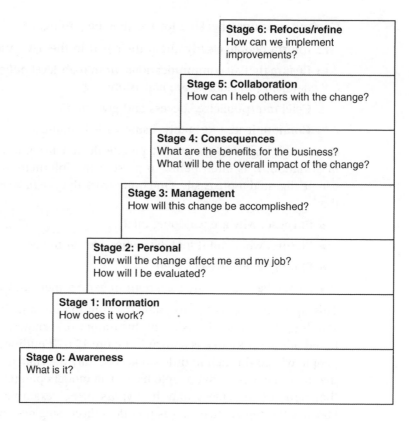

FIGURE 13.6 *Concerns-based adoption model – stages of concern*

decide the purpose of the message – what difference we want to make with respect to a particular concern.

The messenger should be chosen carefully, bearing in mind the need to develop people's confidence and trust. The higher the level of the message, the higher the level of the messenger needs to be. Thus, senior management should present the main business and management principles.

The medium is the mechanism by which the message is distributed. There is a variety of possible mechanisms, including:

- presentations supported by handouts for people to take away, discuss and study at their leisure;

- information posted on a dedicated website that also has news of the latest developments;

- newsletters that are produced periodically.

For more interactive approaches, we might arrange discussion groups or one-to-one meetings. We may also give demonstrations or show prototypes of the new system and provide opportunities for stakeholders to comment and suggest improvements.

Change management phase (iii): execute the plan

In this phase we need to consider the need for professionalism in the delivery of the plan, i.e. how key staff members can help to cascade the message and the sequence of activities as they are rolled out. Learning and adapting the plan as the roll-out takes place out will be important, as will training and coaching and dealing with practical issues as they arise.

Professionalism

Professional delivery of the message is essential on two counts. First, we are trying to build up people's confidence and trust. Sloppy presentations, inconsistent content and the inability to handle objections will undermine that confidence. Second, communication is a two-way process that requires quick thinking and the ability to adapt to varying needs and circumstances. On the first count, we could call upon skilled staff to prepare brochures, newsletters and websites. Accomplished speakers can not only get a message across but also generate enthusiasm for the changes – the goal is for the change team members to show that they are well organized, know what they are doing and are capable of leading the change project. On the second count, as well as the typical presentation and writing skills, more developed communication skills such as facilitation, negotiation, conflict resolution and problem-solving will be important. Successful communication requires the development of a rapport with the audience. This will help to create an open discussion and engage the audience and enable them to contribute comments and ideas.

Key staff

In any organization, there are key staff members – often called change agents or change champions – who influence what happens. They are not necessarily part of the management structure but, because of their experience, knowledge, personality and contacts, others go to them for help and advice. If we can identify these key individuals, then we may be able to speed up the acceptance of the changes. People trust these individuals already, so if the key players endorse the change others will accept the change more easily. Getting the buy-in of the key staff is not necessarily easy, as they may have concerns themselves about the change. In order to develop these staff members as 'early adopters', it is important to identify their current attitudes to the change and their current concerns, identify with them how those concerns could be addressed, and assess their potential to influence others. If their influence is significant, then we can work with them closely so that they can act as change agents. In this role, they will take others through the same steps and will help to cascade the change through the organization.

Sequencing the roll-out

The use of key staff to cascade the change reflects the way that the communication plan is rolled out a bit at a time, beginning at a high level with management to develop the set of change principles and set up the change team, which then develops an initial version of the communications plan. As management announces the change, those affected will be taken through the first two levels of the stages of concern model. In the second phase of the roll-out, we concentrate on the key staff and identify the stakeholders and their concerns. The final phase is a wider version of phase (ii), targeting all the other stakeholders.

Learning and adapting

Throughout the whole roll-out, we are collecting feedback from all the stakeholders and adapting the programme to take this feedback into account. It is not uncommon, for example, for stakeholders to lose enthusiasm and to slip back to earlier stages of the change journey, and so the plan will evolve in response to the reactions of the people involved.

Very often there is little time to reflect on how well a particular piece of work has been done and some important lessons are not learned. Taking time to learn and share the lessons of change from each project will help the organization to learn and develop its ability to handle change. The change methods would improve and people would be more aware of the need for change. The beliefs and culture of the organization would be more conducive to change. This different approach is increasingly significant as the pace of change intensifies.

Training and coaching

Training is important in improving people's skills and competences and often takes place away from the workplace. The training units are standard modules designed to meet the needs of the average member of staff. The timing of the training sessions may not coincide directly with the scheduled roll-out of the new system. Consequently, much of the training effort may be wasted. Coaching can overcome these problems. It is tailored to suit the individual's needs, takes place as required and relates directly to the job in hand. Change leaders, business analysts and managers can develop their coaching skills so that they can support their staff.

Managing objections

The roll-out will always hit problems, and it is worthwhile thinking through what objections are likely to arise so that better-quality responses to problems can be given. Through anticipating likely issues, it becomes possible to ensure that adequate time and resources are made available and that qualified appropriate support is on hand. Anticipating objections and taking appropriate action to overcome them will ensure that there is a planned response rather than a reactive short-term fix.

Change management phase (iv): improve continuously

Once the change has been implemented, we need to monitor performance to ensure that the change is actually achieving the desired effects. The U-curve of Figure 13.1 shows that we cannot obtain meaningful measures until the change has had an opportunity to bed in. This can take some time, so it is common for post-implementation reviews to take place three to six months after the changeover date. At this point in the change cycle, change management and benefits management are related closely. If there are any significant shortfalls in the actual performance or benefits, then we need to identify the underlying cause of the shortfall and remove any blockages. This may, for example, be the result of inadequate training or support for the new system users. Arranging further training or coaching may sort out the problem, leading to improved performance.

Sustaining the change

Sustaining the change is about ensuring that the change persists. Sometimes bad practices creep in, and it is not unknown for staff to abandon the use of new IT systems or processes and revert to the old ways. Sustainability cannot be managed simply by directing people to use the new system or process; this can lead to opposition or even subversive resistance. Instead, sustainability has to be facilitated; that is, we should create the right conditions that will lead to continued and evolving use of the new system. In addition, it is useful to encourage the spread of the changes to other parts of the organization.

There are many reasons why change is not sustained. A common cause is that something was missed or handled inadequately during the change process; the lack of training referred to above is an example. The change may have been regarded as an isolated project. As soon as the project has ended, resources are withdrawn, the spotlight is turned off the change area and the users drift back quietly into their old habits. Sometimes some of the stakeholders have not been involved properly, resulting in a lack of commitment to the change; this can undermine the project and cause the initial improvements to diminish. In other cases, the change area may have been defined too narrowly, resulting in problems with interactions between the changed and the unchanged areas. Earlier we highlighted the significance of values and beliefs; if the change is not aligned with the stakeholders' values and sense of purpose, then any behavioural changes are likely to be short-lived.

Before we consider how we can sustain change most effectively, it may be worthwhile considering the following points. First, not all changes are worth sustaining. Change has an element of exploration: we cannot always predict exactly what we will find. If the results we achieve from the change are disappointing, then we may not wish to continue. Second, we can suffer from too much sustainability: resistance to the change may arise because the old way of working is too sustainable. What we are seeking is the appropriate level of sustainability. We need enough to consolidate the gains but not so much that further change is blocked. Generally we want to sustain the specific improvement in the process or system, the measured outcome from the change, the basic concept underpinning the change and the changes to culture, values and relationships that accompany the change.

If we are trying to sustain the outcome, then we are accepting that the process or system may have to change further as conditions vary. Sustaining the concepts, culture or values implies that the outward forms of the present change may be altered significantly so long as the more fundamental aspects are maintained. The choice of alternatives from the list above will influence the actions required. Bear in mind the following estimate – up to 80 per cent of change failures can be put down to social factors.

There are several actions that we can take in order to increase the sustainability of a change:

- Establish clear benefits for all the stakeholders:
  - ensuring win–win situations;
  - with different stakeholders seeking different benefits.

- Provide appropriate support:
  - give sufficient suitable training to build up staff confidence in their ability to handle the change;
  - develop the coaching skills of selected staff members so that they can help others.

- Build change into the whole organization:
  - policies and strategy are brought in line with other changes;
  - remove all aspects of the old processes and systems.

- Report performance measurements:
  - build these into the reporting mechanisms;
  - make it obvious that the change is actually working.

- Celebrate success:
  - reward people for a job well done;
  - recognize that sustainability is about emotional commitment to the changed environment.

Spreading the change

Spread is the second aspect of ensuring that the change sticks. Spread occurs when the change goes beyond the boundary of the original project and is adopted by others. It often occurs when others outside the original change see how they can make similar or related changes themselves. The attributes that make a change more attractive and, hence, more likely to be adopted include:

- clear, measurable benefits to a range of stakeholders;
- compatibility with existing systems, values and beliefs;
- simplicity of the change itself;
- ease of testing the change before making a wholesale commitment.

Approaches that encourage the wider adoption of change include:

- emphasizing the basic concept underpinning the change;
- understanding the people who may want to adopt the change;
- organizing events so that others can find out about the change.

The details of the current change initiative are specific to the environment and the circumstances in which the change is being made. Others will be operating under different conditions and are unlikely to be able to change in exactly the same way. Underpinning concepts, however, can be reinterpreted to fit into different situations. If you can identify the key change agents and understand their problems and needs, then you can start to see how to reinterpret the concept as required. Publicity and information events are a way of raising people's curiosity without them having to make too much of a commitment.

SUMMARY

'Human change isn't something we do, it's everything we do.' This quote appears in Roger Burlton's book *Business Process Management*. All process improvement and many system development projects aim to change the way in which people do their jobs. Change management is not something that can be tacked on to the end of a project. Instead, it should affect all aspects of the project, right from the start to the end.

Just as we cannot relegate change management to a particular phase of a project, neither can we think of it as a particular person's responsibility. Increasingly, projects include change managers whose job it is to plan and coordinate the change effort. In certain respects, change managers are like project managers, because they work through others. For example, change managers will ensure that stakeholders are involved and can influence the change process. But who will be working directly with the stakeholders to accommodate their needs? The business analyst acts as a bridge between the business and the IT providers and, hence, plays a crucial role in ensuring that change is successful. If the business analyst has a wider understanding of the change process, why change needs to be managed, and what has to happen for change to be successful, then not only will the analyst be better at their job but also they will find that job more interesting and rewarding.

The successful business analyst will be seen as a natural change agent. To help develop this aspect of your role, try to:

- keep aware of the rate of change within your organization;
- collect evidence of the benefits of that change and regard change as a positive force;
- identify how you can influence what changes occur;
- keep track of the unfreeze–change–refreeze phases in order to help yourself and others through the change process.

REFERENCES

Herzberg, F. (1968) One more time: how do you motivate employees? *Harvard Business Review,* January/February.

FURTHER READING

Burlton, R. (2001) *Business Process Management: Profiting from Process.* Sams Publishing, Indianapolis, IN.

Cameron, E. and Green, M. (2004) *Making Sense of Change Management.* Kogan Page, London.

Senge, P.M. (1999) *The Dance of Change: The Challenges to Sustaining Momentum in a Learning Organization.* Nicholas Brealey, London.

Index

BCS products and services

Other products and services from the British Computer Society that might be of interest to you include:

Publishing

BCS publications, including books, magazine and peer-reviewed journals, provide readers with informed content on business, management, legal and emerging technological issues, supporting the professional, academic and practical needs of the IT community. Subjects covered include business process management, IT law for managers and transition management. www.bcs.org/publications

BCS professional products and services

The BCS promotes the use of the SFIA*plus* IT skills framework, which forms the basis of a range of professional development products and services for both individual practitioners and employers. This includes BCS Skills*Manager* and BCS Career*Developer*. www.bcs.org/products

Qualifications

Information Systems Examination Board (ISEB) qualifications are the industry standard both in the UK and abroad. With over 100,000 practitioners now qualified, it is proof of the popularity of the qualifications. These qualifications ensure that IT professionals develop the skills, knowledge and confidence to perform to their full potential. There is a huge range on offer, covering all major areas of IT. In essence, ISEB qualifications are for forward-looking individuals and companies who want to stay ahead and who are serious about driving business forward. www.iseb.org.uk

BCS professional examinations are examined to the academic level of a UK honours degree and are the essential qualifications for a career in computing and IT. Whether you seek greater job recognition, promotion or a new career direction, you will find that BCS professional examinations are internationally recognized, flexible and suited to the needs of the IT industry. www.bcs.org/exams

The European Certification of IT Professionals (EUCIP) is aimed at IT professionals and practitioners wishing to gain professional certification and competency development. www.bcs.org/eucip

European Computer Driving Licence (ECDL) is the internationally recognized computer skills qualification that enables people to demonstrate their competence in computer skills. ECDL is managed in the UK by the BCS. ECDL Advanced has been introduced to take computer skills certification to the next level and teaches extensive knowledge of particular computing tools. www.ecdl.co.uk

Networking and events

BCS's specialist groups and branches provide excellent professional networking opportunities by keeping members abreast of latest developments, discussing topical issues and making useful contacts. www.bcs.org/bcs/groups

The society's programme of social events, lectures, awards schemes and competitions provides more opportunities to network. www.bcs.org/events

Further information

This information was correct at the time of publication but could change in the future. For the latest information, please contact:

The British Computer Society
First Floor, Block D
North Star House
North Star Avenue
Swindon SN2 1FA

Telephone: 0845 300 4417 (UK only) or +44 1793 417424 (overseas)
Email: customerservice@hq.bcs.org.uk
Web: www.bcs.org